What is to be Done?

What is to be Done?

Burning Questions of Our Movement

Vladimir I. Lenin

Introduction by Prakash Karat

LeftWord

First published in January 2024.

LeftWord Books
2254/2A, Shadi Khampur
New Ranjit Nagar
New Delhi 110008
INDIA

LeftWord Books and Vaam Prakashan are imprints of
Naya Rasta Publishers Pvt. Ltd.

leftword.com

ISBN 978-93-92018-89-3 (paperback)

Digital print edition, July 2024

Contents

Note on the Text

Lenin's text — *What is to be Done? Burning Questions of Our Movement* — was written in 1901 and published in March 1902 by J. H. W. Dietz Verlag in Stuttgart. The book was republished in 1907 with some changes made by Lenin and with the addition of some footnotes. We are using the text translated in the USSR for a pamphlet in 1952 and subsequently published in 1961 by Foreign Languages Publishing House in Lenin's *Collected Works*, vol. 5, pp. 347-530. The text has been annotated to provide some biographical details of people not widely known and with some background on the publications and groups mentioned by Lenin.

Prakash Karat

Introduction

V. I. Lenin (1870-1924) took forward Marxist theory and practice in critical areas. His thesis on imperialism (*Imperialism, the Highest Stage of Capitalism*, 1916) had the most far-reaching impact and opened the strategic path for the revolutions of the twentieth century. Lenin's concept of the state (*The State and Revolution*, 1917) as an instrument of class power was a seminal contribution; it explained the necessity for the seizure of state power by the proletariat and for the replacement of the old state by a new state apparatus dominated by the proletariat.

Lenin pioneered the new strategic perspective of dovetailing the bourgeois-democratic revolution with the socialist revolution under the leadership of the working class. This would be possible in relatively underdeveloped capitalist countries if a worker-peasant alliance was forged (*Two Tactics of Social Democracy in the Democratic Revolution*, 1905).

An equally important and crucial contribution by Lenin was his theory of organisation. This vital component of Leninism has been the subject of relentless criticism and controversy not only amongst anti-Communist circles but also within sections of the Left.

Organisation, for Lenin, was not a technical question or a tactical issue. Organisation was integral to revolutionary theory. 'Without a revolutionary theory, there can be no revolutionary movement', asserted Lenin in his thick pamphlet *What is to be Done?* The booklet goes on to elaborate on how an appropriate organisation alone can translate revolutionary theory into a revolutionary movement.

Georgi Lukács, the Hungarian Marxist philosopher, was the first to discern this role accorded to the Leninist concept of the organisation:

> Organisation is the form of mediation between theory and practice. And, as in every dialectical relationship, the terms of the relation only acquire concreteness and reality in and by virtue of this mediation. The ability of organisation to mediate between theory and practice is seen most clearly by the way in which it manifests a much greater, finer and more confident sensitivity towards divergent trends than any other sector of political thought and action. On the level of pure theory, the most disparate views and tendencies are able to co-exist peacefully, antagonisms are only expressed in the form of discussions which can be contained within the framework of one and the same organisation without disrupting it. But no sooner are these same questions given organisational form than they turn out to be sharply opposed and even incompatible.[1]

What is to be Done? has to be set in the context of this struggle for building a revolutionary organisation, which can translate theory into practice. The text was written in late 1901 and published in 1902, when Lenin was the editor of *Iskra* (1900-1905), a journal being published from various centres in Europe by those Russian revolutionaries living in exile from czarist Russia. The Editorial Board of *Iskra* included prominent leaders of Russian social democracy at that time, including Georgi Plekhanov, Julius Martov, Aleksandr Potresov, Pavel Axelrod, Dmitri Ilyich Ulyanov, and Vera Zasulich. *Iskra* became the platform from which the struggle to create an All-Russian Social Democratic Labour Party

[1] Georgi Lukács, 'Towards a Methodology for the Problem of Organisation', *History and Class Consciousness*, London: Merlin Press, 1971, p. 299.

was waged.[2] *Iskra* was founded at a time when, in Russia, the social democratic movement was represented by various study circles, groups and trade unions, which were fragmented and worked locally.

Lenin's booklet is directed against the Economists, who represented a trend within and outside Russian social democracy. The Economists maintained that the economic struggle of the workers was primary and that this struggle should be the basis for building the political movement and organisation.

The polemics in *What is to be Done?* are directed against the authors of the writings in two journals — *Rabocheye Dyelo* (Workers' Cause) and *Rabachaya Mysl* (Workers' Thought) — and leaders who represent the views of the Economists. As such, these polemics sound obscure and obtuse to a reader today. The text would make a difficult read even for a person with some acquaintance with Marxist theory and the history of the working-class movement. But if one perseveres, the outline of the Leninist concept of a revolutionary party can be mined from *What is to be Done?*

SPONTANEITY AND CONSCIOUSNESS

The first attack Lenin launches is the reliance on spontaneity in the working-class struggles, which marks out the terrain of Economism. The economic struggle (which is the trade union struggle) emanates from the workers' elementary response to oppression and working conditions. Such spontaneous struggles can only develop trade union consciousness. Lenin says, this is

[2] The Russian Social Democratic Labour Party or RSDLP, was formed in Minsk (today's Belarus) in 1898 to unite all the sections of the Russian left. In 1903, the RSDLP split into two factions, the Mensheviks (*menshinstvo* or minority) and the Bolsheviks (*bolshinstvo* or majority). Lenin led the Bolshevik faction, while many of the editorial board of the RSDLP became Mensheviks (Axelrod, Martov, and Potresov).

the universal experience as 'The history of all countries shows that the working class exclusively by its own effort is able to develop only trade union consciousness' (p. 57 of the present volume), and further, 'The spontaneous element in essence represents nothing more nor less than consciousness in an embryonic form' (p. 56).

Lenin underlines the fact that the spontaneous trade union movement would come under the influence of the bourgeoisie since it is dominant in society, and it is necessary to 'divert the working-class movement from this spontaneous, trade unionist striving to come under the wing of the bourgeoisie and to bring it under the wing of the revolutionary Social Democracy' (p. 68).

Lenin was not denigrating spontaneous struggles but pointing to the limitations of such spontaneous actions being able to create a socialist consciousness. 'The spontaneous struggle of the proletariat will not become its genuine "class struggle" until the struggle is led by a strong organisation of the revolutionaries', he wrote (p. 171).

On the issue of consciousness, Lenin proceeds to make another point by arguing that socialist consciousness or class consciousness develops only 'from without'.

> Class political consciousness can be brought to the workers *only from without*, that is, only from outside the economic struggle, from outside the sphere of relations between workers and employers. The sphere from which alone it is possible to obtain this knowledge is the sphere of relationships of all classes and strata to the state and the government, the sphere of the interrelations between *all classes*. (p. 111)

Lenin's position that class consciousness can be brought only 'from without' has been criticised on the grounds that it goes against Marx's conception of the self-emancipation of the working-class.[3] But Lenin's understanding of how consciousness emerges and develops among the working-class is based on a deep understanding of the nature of the working-class and the stratifications within it. His assessment does not contradict the Marxist vision of self-emancipation.

Different strata, levels of production and income variations — all have a bearing on how workers develop consciousness through trade union struggles. Moreover, as Lenin pointed out, class political consciousness can be brought to the workers 'only from outside the sphere of relations between workers and employees'. Here is where the role of an organisation with an advanced theory comes into play.

In the early stages of the revolutionary movement, the revolutionary theory was imparted through intellectuals who had joined the movement. Subsequently, a party organised on the basis of Marxist theory would be the agency 'from without', which would be able to inculcate class consciousness amongst the workers.

CENTRALISATION

What is to be Done? deals with the 'primitiveness' of organisation in Russia, where there existed only social democratic study circles and groups operating in conditions of clandestinity. The trade unions were also working locally with no links to other unions. So, the main plank of *Iskra* and Lenin, was to create a centralised All-Russia party that would unite these groups and unions. The idea that it should be a centralised party was also accepted by the editors of *Isrka* and by the leaders of the All-Russian Social Democratic Labour Party at that time. A centralised party was not envisaged by Lenin merely to meet the conditions of underground

[3] In 1864, Marx wrote that 'the emancipation of the working classes must be conquered by the working classes themselves'. 'Provisional Rules of the Association', Karl Marx and Friedrich Engels, *Collected Works*, vol. 20, p. 14.

work and police repression. It was mainly to provide a politically unified party under a centralised political leadership. It would be an error to dismiss Lenin's understanding of organisation as being merely about building unity in a time of autocracy; his insights into the process of building an organisation of workers can be extended out of the exact context of *What is to be Done?*

It is to accomplish the political-organisational centralisation of socialist activity that Lenin stressed the need for an all-Russian newspaper as against local newspapers. Lenin outlined many of the ideas that appear in *What is to be Done?* in an article that was published in *Iskra* in May 1901 called 'Where to Begin'. Responses to that article allow Lenin to further develop many of his ideas in *What is to be Done?* It was in 'Where to Being' that Lenin wrote, 'A newspaper is not only a collective propagandist and a collective agitator, it is also a collective organiser'. That is the precise formulation he repeats in *What is to be Done?* after he dismisses the criticisms of that idea that came from many of the Economists. At the Second Congress of the Russian Social Democratic Labour Party (1903), *Iskra* was designed as its official, all-Russia newspaper.

Underpinning the goal of centralism was the absolute requirement to take on the might of the state with all the Party's centralised resources. It was the centralism principle advocated in What that was attacked by various social democratic leaders, both Russian and European. One of the most trenchant critics of the idea of democratic centralism was the Polish-German Marxist Rosa Luxemburg. Luxemburg denounced the 'pitiless centralism' advocated by Lenin, where 'the Central Committee would be the only thinking element in the party. All other groupings would be its executive limbs'. Luxemburg criticised the idea of centralism for advocating the 'absolute and blind submission of the party sections to the will of the centre'.[4] Luxemburg's criticism was off the

4 Rosa Luxemburg, 'Organisational Questions of Russian Social Democracy', *The Rosa Luxemburg Reader*, eds. Peter Hudis and Kevin B. Anderson, New

mark. Centralism in the Leninist scheme was not divorced from democracy. Centralisation was not meant to provide the centre with concentration of all powers, but it was an organisational policy to ensure a central political strategy and a unified political line.

The *form* of centralism set out in *What is to be Done?* was determined by the specific conditions in Russia at that time, namely the situation of illegality and repression of all political activities. This *form* could vary in changed conditions. The content, in essence, however, was political — how to build a party from top to bottom with a unified political leadership. If Lenin stressed the centralised principle more in *What is to be Done?*, it was because of the impossibility of practising inner-party democracy and having committees constituted by elections at all levels.

This would change after the 1905 revolutionary upheaval.

VANGUARD

For Lenin, the Social Democratic Party, being the party of the working class, could not be an organisation open to all, irrespective of their level of consciousness and commitment. He set out the concept of a 'vanguard', a party consisting of an advanced detachment of the working class. This idea of the vanguard implies a selection of the most conscious and militant workers as members of the party who will then work among the workers and masses in general through a network of organisations.

Lenin called for an organisation of professional revolutionaries: 'The organisation of the revolutionaries must consist first and foremost of people who make revolutionary activity their profession' (p. 146).

Lenin's demand that the vanguard be made up of professional revolutionaries was dictated by the exigencies of the situation.

York: Monthly Review Press, 2004, pp. 248-265.

As soon as the 1905 revolutionary upsurge occurred, Lenin saw the immense possibilities of recruiting thousands of militant and conscious workers. Lenin observed that the revolutionary struggle had produced workers with a Social-Democratic consciousness. The Bolshevik party, which developed henceforth, had a core of professional revolutionaries at various levels, along with a rising number of proletarian members who were not full-time workers of the party.

The concept of a vanguard meant that an advanced detachment of workers should constitute the party. But Lenin made it clear that 'the role of vanguard fighter can be fulfilled only by a party that is guided by the most advanced theory' (pp. 50–51).

The *Communist Manifesto* had defined the role of Communists as 'The most advanced and resolute section of the working-class parties of every country and that theoretically, they have over the great mass of the proletariat the advantage of clearly understanding the line of march, the conditions, and the ultimate general results of the proletarian movement'.[5]

Lenin's concept of the vanguard party is a realisation of this exposition of Marx and Engels in the *Manifesto*. The vanguard contains a dialectical approach: the organisation consists of the selected imbued with working-class political consciousness, and, in turn, it is this vanguard which champions and acts and supports of not just the working-class, but all sections of society who are oppressed.

It is only such a vanguard that can unite the various sections of the working class who were stratified into various segments and impart them with working-class consciousness. Not only that, but the vanguard party is necessary to rally other supporting classes and sections into the revolutionary movement and to further draw in their advanced sections into the vanguard party.

[5] See *A World To Win: Essays on The Communist Manifesto*, edited by Prakash Karat, LeftWord, New Delhi, 2017, p. 102.

In Lenin's theory, there is a dialectic between consciousness and organisations. Political consciousness requires that 'the workers are trained to respond to all cases of tyranny, oppression, violence and abuse, no matter what class is affected' (p. 101); it is this level of consciousness achieved by the vanguard which enables it to take up the fight against oppression and exploitation of the peasantry and all other sections of the working people. This vanguard is connected to the mass of workers and peasants through a network of organisations, trade unions and societies.

MEMBERSHIP RULES

Lenin had to wage a determined struggle to get the basic organisational concept set out in *What is to be Done?* accepted within the Russian Social Democratic Labour Party (RSDLP). Though it was the *Iskra* group which waged the struggle for an All-Russian centralised party, at the Second Congress of the RSDLP in 1903, different approaches to organisation emerged between Lenin and the others in the Editorial Board, who later became the Mensheviks.

The difference came to the fore when the rules for membership in the party were debated. There were two drafts for the paragraph on the rules of membership. Lenin's draft stated: 'a party member is one who accepts the party's programme and supports the party both financially and by personal participation in one of its organisations'. Martov's draft stated: 'a member of the Russian Social-Democratic Labour Party is one who, accepting its programme, works actively to accomplish its aims under the control and direction of the organs of the party'.[6]

The difference in the criteria for membership apparently seems minor, and only a question of nomenclature, but the debate

[6] V. I. Lenin, 'One Step Forward, Two Steps Back' (1904), *Collected Works*, vol. 7, pp. 239-247.

in the Congress on the rules revealed a deeper schism on the idea of who should be a party member. Lenin's criteria for membership required 'participation in a party organisation' while in Martov's definition, a party member only has to be under the control of the party. Lenin argued that such a definition would lead to a free-floating membership upon whom discipline cannot be enforced. Only if a party member works in an organisation will he or she come under discipline.

Martov's draft of paragraph one was accepted by a majority vote (28 to 22 votes). Though the split which developed between the Bolsheviks and the Mensheviks was not due to this division, but due to other factors, Lenin did not give up the struggle to mould the RSDLP into a revolutionary organisation.

Lenin wrote another substantial booklet, *One Step Forward, Two Steps Back,* in 1904 in which he spelt out the difference in outlook between the Bolsheviks and the Mensheviks. Finally, this struggle resulted in Lenin's membership rule being accepted at the Unity Congress held in 1906. It was in this Congress that the principle of democratic centralism was adopted through the Party Rules. The resolution moved by Lenin stated that: 'The principle of democratic centralism in the party is now universally recognised'.[7]

DEMOCRATIC CENTRALISM

The importance of *What is to be Done?* is that it came at a time when the struggle to form a revolutionary social democratic party was at a crucial juncture. From the polemics waged by Lenin in this booklet emerged the theoretical basis for an organisation equipped to lead the revolutionary movement and the contours of such an organisation.

In November 1907, a collection of Lenin's writings of the previous years was published, which was called *Twelve Years*. In the

[7] V. I. Lenin, 'A Tactical Platform for the Unity Congress of the RSDLP' (1906), *Collected Works*, vol. 10, p. 163.

preface to the *Twelve Years*, Lenin made some observations about *What is to be Done?* He said, 'The basic mistake made by those who now criticise *What is to be Done?* is to treat the pamphlet apart from its connection with the concrete historical situation of a definite, and now long past, period of development of our Party'.[8]

What Lenin meant by this was that some of the methods of organisation suggested were determined by the concrete conditions at that time (1901-02). For instance, the form of centralism was designed to meet the onslaught and repression of the Tsarist autocracy. The form of centralism changed after the revolution of 1905. While earlier, the Central Committee had to wield all powers *vis-à-vis* the lower party committees, in the post-1905 period, Lenin emphasised the elective principle for all committees. The powers of the Central Committee were pruned, and the lower committees gained greater autonomy.

Democratic centralism is a distillation of the Leninist theory of organisation. It is the framework in which the fusion of centralism and democracy is to be worked out in the concrete conditions in which a revolutionary party is working.

At the heart of the issue of democratic centralism is not just the organisational structure of the party, but the basic role of a communist party. For social democratic parties, whose perspective is to work within the capitalist system itself, the need for a revolutionary organisation does not arise. Hence, democratic centralism is anathema to them. For a communist party which works to overthrow capitalism and the ruling class order and replace it eventually with socialism, the party organisation has to be one which is equipped to wage the political, ideological, and organisational struggle against the powerful State and the dominant ruling classes. Such a Party organisation cannot be only geared to fight elections in a parliamentary democratic system, however stable and long-lasting it is, or to be engaged only in exercising and

[8] V. I. Lenin, 'Preface to the Collection Twelve Years' (1908), *Collected Works*, vol. 13, p. 101.

utilising the democratic rights and institutions available within the framework of the hegemony of a bourgeois state. The key issue would be whether the party is equipped to organise and lead the working class and the revolutionary mass movement?

Lenin's conception of the party was to build an organisation which could prepare and develop such a revolutionary mass movement. For this, he stressed the importance of recruiting the advanced sections of the working class into the Party who can be made politically conscious and hence constitute the vanguard. Such an organisation is steeled through class struggle and mass movements and is able to function in all conditions — of legality, semi-legality and illegality. The exigencies of class politics require an organisation which is able to change the forms of struggle according to the prevailing situation. This requires a centralised party. Democratic centralism is best suited as the organisational principle for a party based on Marxism and class struggle. Class struggle is a collective act. Democratic centralism promotes collective decision-making and collective activity; it allows for freedom of thought and unity in action.

Many communist parties have operated in a non-revolutionary situation in the second half of the twentieth century. The situation has become more so in the first two decades of the twenty-first century. But many of these parties have survived because they adhered to democratic centralism. Whatever the ideological-political shortcomings or mistakes, democratic centralism has kept them alive with their potential as a revolutionary party intact. Whereas those parties which abandoned democratic centralism either ceased to be Communist parties or disintegrated. The classic example is the Italian Communist Party, the biggest party outside the socialist countries till the early eighties. But much before the collapse of the Soviet Union, it began the journey to liquidation by first giving up democratic centralism, a process that culminated in the abandonment of Marxism.

The historical experience of revolutions in the twentieth

century affirms the validity of Lenin's theory of organisation and the practice of democratic centralism in the making of revolutions.

PARTY AND STATE

However, the experience of democratic centralism in the post-revolutionary State is a chequered one. The experience of the Soviet Union shows both degeneration in theory and bureaucratic centralism in the party, the CPSU. One of the problems that can be identified is that democratic centralism was made into an organising principle of the State structure.[9] This equated the party with the class, merged the identity of the State with the party and imposed a degree of centralism on the State bodies, which stifled democracy. This transfer of the party principle of democratic centralism into the State structure is one of the continuing problems in socialist countries.

Lenin, in his last days, was grappling with the nature of the party's relations with the State and seeking to expand democracy in the State structure after the period of the civil war and War Communism. Lenin's endeavours in this regard were cut short by his premature death. How does democratic centralism works when a party is running the government? How are relations between the party and the State to be mediated? Can democratic centralism be the principle of State functioning? These were all questions which remained to be addressed. In that sense, Lenin's theory of organisation in relation to the party and the Socialist State and its institutions remained an unfinished project.

<<>>

[9] Article 3 of the *Constitution* (Fundamental Law) of the USSR (1977) states, 'The Soviet state is organised and functions on the principle of democratic centralism'. Samuel Edward Finer (ed.), *Five Constitutions*, Harmondsworth: Penguin, 1979, p. 149.

The significance of *What is to be Done?* is that it began the journey of the evolution of the idea and practice of democratic centralism, which became the bedrock of the Leninist party organisation.

Lenin had asserted in the thick of the revolutionary movement that: 'In its struggle for power, the proletariat has no other weapon but organisation.'[10] *What is to be Done?* was a brilliant salvo in the struggle to build such an organisation. That is its abiding relevance for all revolutionaries in the world.

[10] V. I. Lenin, 'One Step Forward, Two Steps Back', p. 412.

What is to be Done?

'...Party struggles lend a party strength and vitality; the greatest proof of a party's weakness is its diffuseness and the blurring of clear demarcations; a party becomes stronger by purging itself....'
Ferdinand Lassalle to Karl Marx, 24 June 1852

Preface

According to the author's original plan, the present pamphlet was to have been devoted to a detailed development of the ideas expressed in the article 'Where To Begin'.[1] We must first apologize to the reader for the delay in fulfilling the promise made in that article (and repeated in response to many private inquiries and letters). One of the reasons for this delay was the attempt, undertaken in June of the past year (1901), to unite all the Social-Democratic organizations abroad. It was natural to wait for the results of this attempt, for, had the effort proved successful, it would perhaps have been necessary to expound *Iskra*'s conceptions of organization from a somewhat different approach; in any case, such a success promised to put an end very quickly to the existence of the two trends in the Russian Social-Democratic movement. As the reader knows, the attempt failed and, as we propose to show,

[1] Lenin, 'Where to Begin', *Iskra*, no. 4, May 1901. *Collected Works*, vol. 5, pp. 13-24.

Iskra (*The Spark*) was first published in December 1900 by the Russian Marxists in Leipzig (Germany) due to the conditions of proscription in Tsarist Russia (it was later published in Munich, then London, and then Geneva). Lenin began the process to bring out this paper while he was in exile in Siberia. The editorial board brought together the main leaders of the Russian Social Democratic Labour Party — Lenin, G. V. Plekhanov (1856–1918), L. Martov (1873–1923), P. B. Axelrod (1850–1928), A. N. Potresov (1869–1934), and Vera I. Zasulich (1849–1919), with I. G. Smidovich-Leman and then N. Krupskaya (1869-1939) as secretaries for the paper. *Iskra* ceased publication in 1905.

was bound to fail after the new swing, of *Rabocheye Dyelo*, in its issue No. 10, towards Economism.[2] It was found to be absolutely essential to begin a determined struggle against this trend, diffuse and ill-defined, but for that reason the more persistent, the more capable of reasserting itself in diverse forms. Accordingly, the original plan of the pamphlet was altered and considerably enlarged.

Its main theme was to have been the three questions raised in the article 'Where To Begin' — the character and main content of our political agitation; our organizational tasks; and the plan for building, simultaneously and from various sides, a militant, all-Russia organization. These questions have long engaged the mind of the author, who tried to raise them in *Rabochaya Gazeta* during one of the unsuccessful attempts to revive that paper (see Chapter Five.).[3] But the original plan to confine the pamphlet to an analysis of only these three questions and to set forth our views as far as possible in a positive form, without, or almost without, entering into polemics, proved wholly impracticabl, for two reasons. On the one hand, Economism proved to be much more tenacious than we had supposed (we employ the term Economism in the broad sense, as explained in *Iskra*, No. 12 (December 1901), in the article entitled 'A Talk With Defenders of Economism', which was a synopsis, so to speak, of the present pamphlet[4]). It became clear beyond doubt

[2] *Robocheye Dyelo* (Workers' Cause) was a magazine that was published in Geneva (Switzerland), irregularly from April 1899 to February 1902. The chief editor was A. S. Martynov (1865–1935), who argued that the tempo of revolutionary struggle must be defined by workers in their unions ('the economic struggle is the most widely applicable means of drawing the masses into active political struggle'). This is why *Martynov* and *Robocheye Dyelo* were called the Economists.

[3] *Robochaya Gazeta (Workers' Gazette)* was the paper of the Kiev Social Democratic group. Only two issues of the paper were published in August and December 1897. The first congress of the Russian Social Democratic Labour Party in 1898 adopted it as party's official paper. However, police repression of the press and the arrest of the party's central committee resulted in the closure of the paper.

[4] Lenin, 'A Talk with Defenders of Economism', *Iskra*, issue no. 12, December

that the differences regarding the solution of the three questions mentioned were explainable to a far greater degree by the basic antithesis between the two trends in the Russian Social-Democratic movement than by differences over details. On the other hand, the perplexity of the Economists over the practical application of our views in *Iskra* clearly revealed that we often speak literally in different tongues and therefore *cannot* arrive at an understanding without beginning *ab ovo* (from the very beginning), and that an attempt must be made, in the simplest possible style, illustrated by numerous and concrete examples, *systematically to 'clarify' all* our basic points of difference with *all* the Economists. I resolved to make such an attempt at 'clarification', fully realizing that it would greatly increase the size of the pamphlet and delay its publication; I saw *no other way* of meeting my pledge I had made in the article 'Where To Begin'. Thus, to the apologies for the delay, I must add others for the serious literary shortcomings of the pamphlet. I had to work *in great haste,* with frequent interruptions by a variety of other tasks.

The examination of the above three questions still constitutes the main theme of this pamphlet, but I found it necessary to begin with two questions of a more general nature — why such an 'innocent' and 'natural' slogan as 'freedom of criticism' should be for us a veritable war-cry, and why we cannot come to an understanding even on the fundamental question of the role of Social-Democrats in relation to the spontaneous mass movement. Further, the exposition of our views on the character and substance of political agitation developed into an explanation of the difference between trade-unionist politics and Social-Democratic politics, while the exposition of our views on organizational tasks developed into an explanation of the difference between the amateurish methods which satisfy the Economists, and the organization of revolutionaries which we hold to be indispensable.

1901, *Collected Works*, vol. 5, pp. 313–20.

Further, I advance the 'plan' for an all-Russia political newspaper with all the more insistence because the objections raised against it are untenable, and because no real answer has been given to the question I raised in the article 'Where To Begin' as to how we can set to work from all sides simultaneously to create the organization we need. Finally, in the concluding part, I hope to show that we did all we could to prevent a decisive break with the Economists, a break which nevertheless proved inevitable; that *Rabocheye Dyelo* acquired a special significance, a 'historical' significance, if you will, because it expressed fully and strikingly, not consistent Economism, but the confusion and vacillation which constitute the distinguishing feature of *an entire period* in the history of Russian Social-Democracy; and that therefore, the polemic with *Rabocheye Dyelo,* which may upon first view seem excessively detailed, also acquires significance, for we can make no progress until we have completely put an end to this period.

N. Lenin
February 1902

Chapter 1

Dogmatism and 'Freedom of Criticism'

1.1. WHAT DOES 'FREEDOM OF CRITICISM' MEAN?

'Freedom of criticism' is undoubtedly the most fashionable slogan at the present time, and the one most frequently employed in the controversies between socialists and democrats in all countries. At first sight, nothing would appear to be more strange than the solemn appeals to freedom of criticism made by one of the parties to the dispute. Have voices been raised in the advanced parties against the constitutional law of the majority of European countries which guarantees freedom to science and scientific investigation? 'Something must be wrong here', will be the comment of the onlooker who has heard this fashionable slogan repeated at every turn but has not yet penetrated the essence of the disagreement among the disputants; evidently this slogan is one of the conventional phrases which, like nicknames, become legitimized by use, and become almost generic terms'.

In fact, it is no secret for anyone that two trends have taken form in present-day international Social-Democracy.[1] The

[1] Lenin — [Incidentally, in the history of modern socialism this is a phenomenon, perhaps unique and in its way very consoling, namely, that the strife of the various trends within the socialist movement has from national become international. Formerly, the disputes between Lassalleans and Eisenachers, between Guesdists and Possibilists, between Fabians and Social-Democrats, and between *Narodnaya Volya* adherents and Social-Democrats, remained confined within purely national frameworks, reflecting purely national features, and proceeding, as it were, on different planes. At the present time (as is now evident), the English Fabians, the French Ministerialists, the German Bernsteinians, and the Russian Critics —all belong to the same family, all extol each other, learn from each other,

conflict between these trends now flares up in a bright flame and now dies down and smoulders under the ashes of imposing 'truce resolutions'. The essence of the 'new' trend, which adopts a 'critical' attitude towards 'obsolete dogmatic' Marxism, has been clearly enough *presented* by Bernstein and *demonstrated* by Millerand.[2]

Social-Democracy must change from a party of social revolution into a democratic party of social reforms. Bernstein has surrounded this political demand with a whole battery of well-attuned 'new' arguments and reasonings. Denied was the possibility of putting socialism on a scientific basis and of demonstrating its necessity and inevitability from the point of view of the materialist conception of history. Denied was the fact of growing impoverishment, the process of proletarization, and the intensification of capitalist contradictions; the very concept, '*ultimate aim*', was declared to be unsound, and the idea of the dictatorship of the proletariat was completely rejected. Denied was the antithesis in principle between liberalism and socialism. Denied was *the theory of the class struggle,* on the alleged grounds

---

and together take up arms against 'dogmatic' Marxism. In this first real international battle with socialist opportunism, international revolutionary Social-Democracy will perhaps become sufficiently strengthened to put an end to the political reaction that has long reigned in Europe?]

Narodnaya Volya (*People's Will*) was a clandestine society of the Narodniks (a group of intellectuals mainly driven by the slogan, *khozhdeniye v narod* ('going to the people'), which made them commit to various forms of agrarian socialism. The organization was founded in June 1879 and was disbanded in March 1887. In the dying days of *Narodnaya Volya,* Lenin's brother — Aleksandr Ulyanov (1866–1887) — was one of its members and then later participated in the assassination plot against Tsar Alexander III, for which he was executed.

2 Eduard Bernstein (1850–1932) was a leader of the Social Democratic Party of Germany and a member of the Reichstag. He was the author of *Evolutionary Socialism* (1899), which argued for the gradual adoption of socialism rather than for a revolutionary rupture with capitalism.

Alexandre Millerand (1859–1943) was a leader of the Republican-Socialist Party in France and ascended both to the post of prime minister and president. His political career began in the heart of the socialist movement, but it began to be defined by his consistent drift to the right.

that it could not be applied to a strictly democratic society governed according to the will of the majority, etc.

Thus, the demand for a decisive turn from revolutionary Social-Democracy to bourgeois social-reformism was accompanied by a no less decisive turn towards bourgeois criticism of all the fundamental ideas of Marxism. In view of the fact that this criticism of Marxism has long been directed from the political platform, from university chairs, in numerous pamphlets and in a series of learned treatises, in view of the fact that the entire younger generation of the educated classes has been systematically reared for decades on this criticism, it is not surprising that the 'new critical' trend in Social-Democracy should spring up, all complete, like Minerva from the head of Jove. The content of this new trend did not have to grow and take shape, it was transferred bodily from bourgeois to socialist literature.

To proceed. If Bernstein's theoretical criticism and political yearnings were still unclear to anyone, the French took the trouble strikingly to demonstrate the 'new method'. In this instance, too, France has justified its old reputation of being 'the land where, more than anywhere else, the historical class struggles were each time fought out to a decision…' (Engels, Introduction to Marx's *Der 18 Brumaire*). The French socialists have begun not to theorize, but to act. The democratically more highly developed political conditions in France have permitted them to put 'Bernsteinism into practice' immediately, with all its consequences. Millerand has furnished an excellent example of practical Bernsteinism; not without reason did Bernstein and Vollmar rush so zealously to defend and laud him.[3] Indeed, if Social-Democracy, in essence, is merely a party of reform and must be bold enough to admit this openly, then

[3] Georg von Vollmar (1850–1922) was a member of the German Social Democratic Party, an editor of the *Social Demokrat*, and a member of parliament. He rejected the idea of the revolutionary rupture, making the case (in 'On State Socialism', *Die Neue Zeit*, 1892) for an alliance with the bourgeois reformers and for co-existence with private property.

not only has a socialist the right to join a bourgeois cabinet, but he must always strive to do so. If democracy, in essence, means the abolition of class domination, then why should not a socialist minister charm the whole bourgeois world by orations on class collaboration? Why should he not remain in the cabinet even after the shooting-down of workers by gendarmes has exposed, for the hundredth and thousandth time, the real nature of the democratic collaboration of classes? Why should he not personally take part in greeting the tsar, for whom the French socialists now have no other name than the hero of the gallows, knout, and exile (*knouteur, pendeur et deportateur*)? And the reward for this utter humiliation and self-degradation of socialism in the face of the whole world, for the corruption of the socialist consciousness of the working masses — the only basis that can guarantee our victory — the reward for this is pompous *projects* for miserable reforms, so miserable in fact that much more has been obtained from bourgeois governments!

He who does not deliberately close his eyes cannot fail to see that the new 'critical' trend in socialism is nothing more nor less than a new variety of *opportunism*. And if we judge people, not by the glittering uniforms they don or by the high-sounding appellations they give themselves, but by their actions and by what they actually advocate, it will be clear that 'freedom of criticism' means freedom for an opportunist trend in Social-Democracy, freedom to convert Social-Democracy into a democratic party of reform, freedom to introduce bourgeois ideas and bourgeois elements into socialism.

'Freedom' is a grand word, but under the banner of freedom for industry, the most predatory wars were waged, under the banner of freedom of labour, the working people were robbed. The modern use of the term 'freedom of criticism' contains the same inherent falsehood. Those who are really convinced that they have made progress in science would not demand freedom for the new views to continue side by side with the old, but the substitution of the new views for the old. The cry heard today , 'Long live freedom of criticism', is too strongly reminiscent of the fable of the empty barrel.

We are marching in a compact group along a precipitous and difficult path, firmly holding each other by the hand. We are surrounded on all sides by enemies, and we have to advance almost constantly under their fire. We have combined, by a freely adopted decision, for the purpose of fighting the enemy, and not of retreating into the neighbouring marsh, the inhabitants of which, from the very outset, have reproached us with having separated ourselves into an exclusive group and with having chosen the path of struggle instead of the path of conciliation. And now, some among us begin to cry out: Let us go into the marsh! And when we begin to shame them, they retort: What backward people you are! Are you not ashamed to deny us the liberty to invite you to take a better road! Oh, yes, gentlemen! You are free not only to invite us, but to go yourselves wherever you will, even into the marsh. In fact, we think that the marsh is your proper place, and we are prepared to render you every assistance to get there. Only let go of our hands, don't clutch at us and don't besmirch the grand word freedom, for we too are 'free' to go where we please, free to fight not only against the marsh, but also against those who are turning towards the marsh!

1.2. THE NEW ADVOCATES OF 'FREEDOM OF CRITICISM'.

Now, this slogan ('freedom of criticism') has in recent times been solemnly advanced by *Rabocheye Dyelo* (No. 10), organ of the Union of Russian Social-Democrats Abroad, not as a theoretical postulate, but as a political demand, as a reply to the question, 'Is it possible to unite the Social-Democratic organizations operating abroad?': 'For a durable unity, there must be freedom of criticism' (p. 36).[4]

[4] The Union of Russian Social-Democrats Abroad was founded in Geneva in 1894 by the Emancipation of Labour Group, led by Plekhanov. Within a few

From this statement, two definite conclusions follow: (1) that *Rabocheye Dyelo* has taken under its wing the opportunist trend in international Social-Democracy in general, and (2) that *Rabocheye Dyelo* demands freedom for opportunism in Russian Social-Democracy. Let us examine these conclusions.

Rabocheye Dyelo is 'particularly' displeased with the 'inclination of *Iskra* and *Zarya* to predict a rupture between the *Mountain* and the *Gironde* in international Social-Democracy'.[5]

'Generally speaking,' writes B. Krichevsky, editor of *Rabocheye Dyelo*, 'this talk of the *Mountain* and the *Gironde* heard in the ranks of Social-Democracy represents a shallow historical analogy, a strange thing to come from the pen of a Marxist. The Mountain and the Gironde did not represent different temperaments, or intellectual trends, as the historians of social thought may think, but different classes or strata — the middle bourgeoisie, on the one hand, and the petty bourgeoisie and the proletariat on the other. In the modern socialist movement, however, there is no conflict of class interests; the socialist movement in its entirety, in *all* of its diverse forms [Krichevsky's italics], including the most pronounced Bernsteinians, stands on the basis of the class interests of the proletariat and its class struggle for political and economic emancipation (pp. 32–33).'

A bold assertion! Has not Krichevsky heard of the fact, long ago noted, that it is precisely the extensive participation of an

years, it became clear that the Union had been taken over by the Economists. At its first congress in 1898, the Emancipation of Labour Group began to break with the Union, which would eventually occur at the second congress in April 1900.

5 Lenin's note to the 1907 edition: [A comparison of the two trends within the revolutionary proletariat (the revolutionary and the opportunist), and the two trends within the revolutionary bourgeoisie in the eighteenth century (the Jacobin, known as the Mountain, and the Girondist) was made in the leading article in No. 2 of *Iskra* (February 1901). The article was written by Plekhanov. The Cadets, the Bezzaglavtsi, and the Mensheviks, to this day, love to refer to Jacobinism in Russian Social-Democracy. But how Plekhanov came to apply this concept for the first time against the Right wing of Social-Democracy — about this, they prefer to keep silent or to forget.]

'academic' *stratum* in the socialist movement in recent years that has promoted such a rapid spread of Bernsteinism? And what is most important — on what does our author found his opinion that even 'the most pronounced Bernsteinians' stand on the basis of the class struggle for the political and economic emancipation of the proletariat? No one knows. This determined defence of the most pronounced Bernsteinians is not supported by any argument or reasoning whatsoever. Apparently, the author believes that if he repeats what the most pronounced Bernsteinians say about themselves, his assertion requires no proof. But can anything more 'shallow' be imagined than this judgement of an entire trend based on nothing more than what the representatives of that trend say about themselves? Can anything more shallow be imagined than the subsequent 'homily' on the two different and even diametrically opposite types, or paths, of party development? (*Rabocheye Dyelo*, pp. 34–35.) The German Social-Democrats, in other words, recognize complete freedom of criticism, but the French do not, and it is precisely their example that demonstrates the 'bane of intolerance'.

To this, we can only say that the very example B. Krichevsky affords us attests to the fact that the name Marxists is at times assumed by people who conceive history literally in the 'Ilovaisky manner'.[6] To explain the unity of the German Socialist Party and the disunity of the French Socialist Party, there is no need whatever to go into the special features in the history of these countries, to contrast the conditions of military semi-absolutism in the one with republican parliamentarism in the other, to analyze the effects of the Paris Commune and the effects of the 'Exceptional Law Against the Socialists', to compare the economic life and economic development of the two countries, or to recall that 'the unexampled growth of German Social-Democracy' was accompanied by a strenuous struggle, unique in the history

6 Dmirtry Ilovaysky (1832–1920) was a Russian historian who wrote empirical histories of Russia in the manner of Leopold von Ranke (1795–1886).

of socialism, not only against erroneous theories (Mu¨hlberger, Du¨hring,[7] the *Katheder*-Socialists), but also against erroneous tactics (Lassalle), etc., etc. All that is superfluous! The French quarrel among themselves because they are intolerant; the Germans are united because they are good boys.

And observe, this piece of matchless profundity is designed to 'refute' the fact that puts to rout the defence of the Bernsteinians. The question whether or not the Bernsteinians *stand* on the basis of the class struggle of the proletariat is one that can be completely and irrevocably answered only by historical experience. Consequently, the example of France holds the greatest significance in this respect, because France is the only country in which the Bernsteinians attempted *to stand* independently, on their own feet, with the warm approval of their German colleagues (and partly also of the Russian opportunists; cf. *Rabocheye Dyelo*, No. 2–3, pp. 83–84). The reference to the 'intolerance' of the French, apart from its 'historical' significance (in the Nozdryov sense), turns out to be merely an attempt to hush up very unpleasant facts with angry invectives.[8]

Nor are we inclined to make a present of the Germans to Krichevsky and the numerous other champions of 'freedom of

[7] Lenin — [At the time Engels dealt his blows at Dühring, many representatives of German Social-Democracy inclined towards the latter's views and accusations of acerbity, intolerance, uncomradely polemics, etc., were hurled at Engels even publicly at a Party Congress. At the Congress of 1877, Most, and his supporters, introduced a resolution to prohibit the publication of Engels's articles in *Vorwarts* because 'they do not interest the overwhelming majority of the readers', and Vahlteich declared that their publication had caused great damage to the Party, that Dühring too had rendered services to Social-Democracy: 'We must utilize everyone in the interests of the Party; let the professors engage in polemics if they care to do so, but *Vorwarts* is not the place in which to conduct them' (*Vorwarts*, no. 65, June 6, 1877). Here we have another example of the defence of 'freedom of criticism', and our legal critics and illegal opportunists, who love so much to cite the example of the Germans, would do well to ponder it!]

[8] Nozdryov is a landowner and swindler in Nikolai Gogol's novel *Dead Souls* (1842). Lenin referred to characters from this very popular novel throughout his writings.

criticism'. If the 'most pronounced Bernsteinians' are still tolerated in the ranks of the German party, it is only to the extent that they *submit* to the Hanover resolution, which emphatically rejected Bernstein's 'amendments', and to the Lubeck resolution, which (notwithstanding the diplomatic terms in which it is couched) contains a direct warning to Bernstein. It is debatable, from the standpoint of the interests of the German party, whether diplomacy was appropriate and whether, in this case, a bad peace is better than a good quarrel; in short, opinions may differ as to the expediency of any one of the *methods* employed to reject Bernsteinism, but that the German party *did reject* Bernsteinism on two occasions, is a fact no one can fail to see. Therefore, to think that the German example confirms the thesis that 'the most pronounced Bernsteinians stand on the basis of the class struggle of the proletariat, for political and economic emancipation', means to fail completely to understand what is going on under our very eyes.[9]

Nor is that all. As we have seen, *Rabocheye Dyelo* demands 'freedom of criticism' and defends Bernsteinism before *Russian* Social-Democracy. Apparently, it convinced itself that we were unfair to our 'Critics' and Bernsteinians. But to which ones?

[9] Lenin — [It should be observed that *Rabocheye Dyelo* has always confined itself to a bare statement of facts concerning Bernsteinism in the German party and completely 'refrained' from expressing its own opinion. See, for instance, the reports of the Stuttgart Congress in No. 2–3 (p. 66), in which all the disagreements are reduced to 'tactics' and the statement is merely made that the overwhelming majority remain true to the previous revolutionary tactics. Or, No. 4-5 (p. 25, *et. seq.*), in which we have nothing but a paraphrasing of the speeches delivered at the Hanover Congress, with a reprint of Bebel's resolution. An exposition and a criticism of Bernstein's views are again put off (as was the case in No. 2-8) to be dealt with in a 'special article'. Curiously enough, in No. 4–5 (p. 33), we read the following: 'The views expounded by Bebel have the support of the vast majority of the Congress', and a few lines thereafter: 'David defended Bernstein's views. . . . First of all, he tried to show that . . . Bernstein and his friends, after all is said and done (sic!), stand on the basis of the class struggle'. This was written in December 1899, and in September 1901 *Rabocheye Dyelo*, apparently no longer believing that Bebel was right, repeats David's views as, its own!]

Who? Where? When? What did the unfairness represent? About this, not a word. *Rabocheye Dyelo* does not name a single Russian Critic or Bernsteinian! We are left with but one of two possible suppositions. *Either* the unfairly treated party is none other than *Rabocheye Dyelo* itself (this is confirmed by the fact that in the two articles in No. 10 reference is made only to the wrongs suffered by *Rabocheye Dyelo* at the hands of *Zarya* and *Iskra*). If that is the case, how is the strange fact to be explained that *Rabocheye Dyelo*, which always vehemently dissociated itself from all solidarity with Bernsteinism, could not defend itself without putting in a word in defence of the 'most pronounced Bernsteinians' and of freedom of criticism? Or some third persons have been treated unfairly. if this is the case, then what reasons may there be for not naming them?

We see, therefore, that *Rabocheye Dyelo* is continuing to play the game of hide-and-seek it has played (as we shall show below) ever since its founding. And let us note further this *first* practical application of the vaunted 'freedom of criticism'. In actual fact, not only was it forthwith reduced to abstention from all criticism, but also to abstention from expressing independent views altogether. The very *Rabocheye Dyelo*, which avoids mentioning Russian Bernsteinism as if it were a shameful disease (to use Starover's apt expression), proposes, for the treatment of this disease, to copy word for word the latest German prescription for the German variety of the malady![10] Instead of freedom of criticism, slavish (worse: apish) imitation! The very same social and political content of modern international opportunism reveals itself in a variety of ways according to national peculiarities. In one country, the opportunists have long ago come out under a separate flag; in another, they have ignored theory and in fact, pursued the policy of the Radicals-Socialists; in a third, some members of the

[10] Starover was the pen name of Alexander Potresov (1869–1934), one of the original editors of *Iskra* and later a leader of the Menshevik faction of the Russian Social Democratic Labour Party, later becoming alienated from his colleagues for his view that the USSR was run by an oligarchy.

revolutionary party have deserted to the camp of opportunism and strive to achieve their aims, not in open struggle for principles and for new tactics, but by gradual, imperceptible, and, if one may so put it, unpunishable corruption of their party; in a fourth country, similar deserters employ the same methods in the gloom of political slavery, and with a completely original combination of 'legal' and 'illegal' activity, etc. To talk of freedom of criticism and Bernsteinism as a condition for uniting the *Russian* Social-Democrats and not to explain how *Russian* Bernsteinism has manifested itself and what particular fruits it has borne, amounts to talking with the aim of saying nothing.

Let us ourselves try if only in a few words, to say what *Rabocheye Dyelo* did not want to say (or which was, perhaps, beyond its comprehension).

1.3. CRITICISM IN RUSSIA

The chief distinguishing feature of Russia in regard to the point we are examining is that *the very beginning* of the spontaneous working-class movement, on the one hand, and of the turn of progressive public opinion towards Marxism, on the other, was marked by the combination of manifestly heterogeneous elements under a common flag to fight the common enemy (the obsolete social and political world outlook). We refer to the heyday of 'legal Marxism'. Speaking generally, this was an altogether curious phenomenon that no one in the eighties or the beginning of the nineties would have believed possible. In a country ruled by an autocracy, with a completely enslaved press, in a period of desperate political reaction in which even the tiniest outgrowth of political discontent and protest is persecuted, the theory of revolutionary Marxism suddenly forces its way into the *censored* literature and, though expounded in Aesopian language, is understood by all the 'interested'. The government had accustomed itself to regarding only the theory of the (revolutionary) *Narodnaya Volya* as dangerous, without, as is usual, observing its internal evolution, and rejoicing at any criticism levelled against it. Quite a considerable time elapsed (by our Russian standards) before the government realized what had happened and the unwieldy army of censors and gendarmes discovered the new enemy and flung itself upon him. Meanwhile, Marxist books were published one after another, Marxist journals and newspapers were founded, nearly everyone became a Marxist, Marxists were flattered, Marxists were courted, and the book publishers rejoiced at the extraordinary, ready sale of Marxist literature. It was quite natural, therefore, that among the Marxian neophytes, who were caught up in this atmosphere, there should be more than one 'author who got a swelled head'.[11]

We can now speak calmly of this period as an event of the past. It is no secret that the brief period in which Marxism blossomed on the surface of our literature was called forth by an alliance between people of extreme and very moderate views. In point of fact, the latter were bourgeois democrats; this conclusion (so markedly confirmed by their subsequent 'critical' development) suggested itself to some even when the 'alliance' was still intact.[12]

That being the case, are not the revolutionary Social-Democrats who entered into the alliance with the future 'Critics' mainly responsible for the subsequent 'confusion'? This question, together with a reply in the affirmative, is sometimes heard from people with too rigid a view. But such people are entirely in the wrong. Only those who are not sure of themselves can fear to enter into temporary alliances even with unreliable people; not a single political party could exist without such alliances. The combination with the legal Marxists was, in its way, the first really political alliance entered into by Russian Social-Democrats. Thanks to this alliance,

[11] This is a reference to one of Maxim Gorky's stories, 'The Author Who Got a Swelled Head'.

[12] Lenin's note to the 1907 edition — [The reference is to an article by K. Tulin directed against Struve. (See *Collected Works*, vol. 1, pp. 333–507). The article was based on an essay entitled 'The Reflection of Marxism in Bourgeois Literature'.]

an astonishingly rapid victory was obtained over Narodism, and Marxist ideas (even though in a vulgarized form) became very widespread. Moreover, the alliance was not concluded altogether without 'conditions'. Evidence of this is the burning by the censor, in 1895, of the Marxist collection *Material on the Question of the Economic Development of Russia.*[13] If the literary agreement with the legal Marxists can be compared with a political alliance, then that book can be compared with a political treaty.

The rupture, of course, did not occur because the 'allies' proved to be bourgeois democrats. On the contrary, the representatives of the latter trend are natural and desirable allies of Social-Democracy in so far as its democratic tasks, brought to the fore by the prevailing situation in Russia, are concerned. But an essential condition for such an alliance must be the full opportunity for the socialists to reveal to the working class that its interests are diametrically opposed to the interests of the bourgeoisie. However, the Bernsteinian and 'critical' trend, to which the majority of the legal Marxists turned, deprived the socialists of this opportunity and demoralized the socialist consciousness by vulgarizing Marxism, by advocating the theory of the blunting of social contradictions, by declaring the idea of the social revolution and of the dictatorship of the proletariat to be absurd, by reducing the working-class movement and the class struggle to narrow trade-unionism and to a 'realistic' struggle for petty, gradual reforms. This was synonymous with bourgeois democracy's denial of socialism's right to independence and, consequently, of its right to existence; in practice, it meant a striving to convert the nascent working-class movement into an appendage of the liberals.

Naturally, under such circumstances, the rupture was necessary. But the 'peculiar' feature of Russia manifested itself

[13] This collection was published in April 1895. It contained Lenin's article, 'The Economic Content of Nardoism and the Criticism of it in Mr. Stuve's Book (*The Reflection of Marxism in Bourgeois Literature*)', which was a polemic against the 'legal Marxists'. *Collected Works*, volume 1, pp. 333-508.

in the fact that this rupture simply meant the elimination of the Social-Democrats from the most accessible and widespread 'legal' literature. The 'ex-Marxists', who took up the flag of 'criticism' and who obtained almost a monopoly to 'demolish' Marxism, entrenched themselves in this literature. Catchwords like 'Against orthodoxy' and 'Long live freedom of criticism' (now repeated by *Rabocheye Dyelo*) forthwith became the vogue, and the fact that neither the censor nor the gendarmes could resist this vogue is apparent from the publication of *three* Russian editions of the work of the celebrated Bernstein (celebrated in the Herostratean sense) and from the fact that the works of Bernstein, Mr Prokopovich, and others were recommended by Zubatov (*Iskra*, No. 10).[14] A task now devolved upon the Social Democrats that was difficult in itself and was made incredibly more difficult by purely external obstacles — the task of combating the new trend. This trend did not confine itself to the sphere of literature. The turn towards 'criticism' was accompanied by an infatuation for Economism among Social-Democratic practical workers.

The manner in which the connection between, and interdependence of, legal criticism and illegal Economism arose and grew is in itself an interesting subject, one that could serve as the theme of a special article. We need only note here that this connection undoubtedly existed. The notoriety deservedly acquired by the *Credo* was due precisely to the frankness with which it formulated this connection and blurted out the fundamental political tendency of Economism — let the workers carry on

[14] Herostratean refers to Herostratus, the Greek who destroyed the Temple of Artemis at Ephesus simply to become famous. The term is used to describe people who do criminal things to attain fame.

Sergei Nikolaevich Prokopovich (1871–1955) was a Russian economist and leader of the Russian Social Democratic Labour Party, which he left in 1899 to try and shape a liberal movement in Russia with his wife, Yekaterina Dmitriyevna Kuskova (1869–1958). Both Prokopovich and Kuskova opposed the October Revolution and went into exile.

Sergei Zubatov (1864–1917) was a police administrator who advocated for 'police socialism', namely for legal, police-controlled trade unions.

the economic struggle (it would be more correct to say the trade unionist struggle because the latter also embraces specifically working- class politics) and let the Marxist intelligentsia merge with the liberals for the political 'struggle'. Thus, trade-unionist work 'among the people' meant fulfilling the first part of this task, while legal criticism meant fulfilling the second. This statement was such an excellent weapon against Economism that, had there been no *Credo*, it would have been worth inventing one.

The *Credo* was not invented, but it was published without the consent and perhaps even against the will of its authors. At all events, the present writer, who took part in dragging this new 'programme' into the light of day, has heard complaints and reproaches to the effect that copies of the resume of the speakers' views were distributed, dubbed the *Credo*, and even published in the press together with the protest![15] We refer to this episode because it reveals a very peculiar feature of our Economism — fear of publicity. This is a feature of Economism generally, and not of the authors of the *Credo* alone. It was revealed by that most outspoken and honest advocate of Economism, *Rabochaya Mysl*, and by *Rabocheye Dyelo* (which was indignant over the publication of 'Economist' documents in the *Vademecum*), as well as by the Kiev Committee, which two years ago refused to permit the publication of its *profession de foi*, together with a repudiation of

[15] Lenin's note to the 1907 edition — [The reference is to the *Protest of the Seventeen against the Credo*. The present writer took part in drawing up this protest (the end of 1899). The *Protest* and the *Credo* were published abroad in the spring of 1900. (See 'A Protest of Russian Social-Democrats', *Collected Works*, vol. 4, pp. 167–82) It is now known from the article written by Madame Kuskova (I think in *Byloye*) that she was the author of the *Credo* and that Mr. Prokopovich was very prominent among the Economists abroad at the time.] The *Credo* was given to Lenin by his sister Ana Ulyanova Yelizarova (1864–1935), a revolutionary who participated actively in the October Revolution and in building the USSR. Lenin reacted to the *Credo* by writing the Protest with advice from other exiled Russians. It was published by Plekhanov in his *Vademecum for the Editors of Rabocheye Dyelo* (Geneva, 1900).

it,[16] and by many other individual representatives of Economism.[17]

This fear of criticism displayed by the advocates of freedom of criticism cannot be attributed solely to craftiness (although, on occasion, no doubt craftiness is brought into play: it would be improvident to expose the young and as yet frail shoots of the new trend to attacks by opponents). No, the majority of the Economists look with sincere resentment (as by the very nature of Economism they must) upon all theoretical controversies, factional disagreements, broad political questions, plans for organising revolutionaries, etc. 'Leave all that to the people abroad', said a fairly consistent Economist to me one day, thereby expressing a very widespread (and again purely trade-unionist) view; our concern is the working-class movement, the workers, organizations here, in our localities; all the rest is merely the invention of doctrinaires, 'the overrating of ideology', as the authors of the letter, published in *Iskra*, No. 12, expressed it, in unison with *Rabocheye Dyelo*, No. 10.

The question now arises: such being the peculiar features of Russian 'criticism' and Russian Bernsteinism, what should have been the task of those who sought to oppose opportunism in deeds and not merely in words? First, they should have made efforts to resume the theoretical work that had barely begun in the period of legal Marxism and that fell anew on the shoulders of the comrades working underground. Without such work, the successful growth of the movement was impossible. Secondly, they should have

[16] Lenin — [As far as our information goes, the composition of the Kiev Committee has changed since then.]

[17] *Rabochaya Mysl* (*Workers' Thought*) was an Economist magazine, 16 issues of which were published between October 1897 and December 1902. Started by workers in St. Petersburg, it was edited by Konstantin Tachtarev (1871–1925). Later, Jakov Andreev, one of the founding workers, wrote of their effort, 'Our life was disordered, our ideas were confused; all this was reflected in our articles' (Jakov Andreev, 'Glianni 1897 e 1898 a Kolpino', *Proletarskaja Revoljucija*, no. 2, 1923, p. 83.).

Profession de foi (*Profession of Faith*) is an 1899 leaflet put out by the Kiev Committee that resembled the Economists' *Credo*. Lenin criticized it in his article, 'Apropos of the *Profession de foi*', 1899, *Collected Works*, vol. 4, pp. 286–296.

actively combated the legal 'criticism' that was perverting people's minds on a considerable scale. Thirdly, they should have actively opposed confusion and vacillation in the practical movement, exposing and repudiating every conscious or unconscious attempt to degrade our programme and our tactics.

That *Rabocheye Dyelo* did none of these things is well known; we shall have occasion below to deal with this well-known fact in detail and from various aspects. At the moment, however, we desire merely to show the glaring contradiction that exists between the demand for 'freedom of criticism' and the specific features of our native criticism and Russian Economism. It suffices but to glance at the text of the resolution in which the Union of Russian Social Democrats Abroad endorsed the point of view of *Rabocheye Dyelo*.

> 'In the interests of the further ideological development of Social-Democracy, we recognize the freedom of criticism of Social-Democratic theory in Party literature to be absolutely necessary insofar as the criticism does not run counter to the class and revolutionary character of this theory' (*Two Conferences*, p. 10).

And the motivation? The resolution 'in its first part coincides with the resolution of the Lubeck Party Congress on Bernstein'. In the simplicity of their souls, the 'Unionists' failed to observe what a *testimonium paupertatis* (attestation of poverty) they betray with this copying. 'But . . . in its second part, it restricts freedom of criticism much more than did the Lubeck Party Congress'.

The resolution of the Union Abroad, then, is directed against the Russian Bernsteinians? If it is not, then the reference to Lubeck would be utterly absurd. But it is not true to say that it 'restricts freedom of criticism'. In adopting their Hanover resolution, the Germans, point by point, rejected *precisely* the amendments proposed by Bernstein, while in their Lubeck resolution they cautioned *Bernstein personally*, by naming him.

Our 'free' imitators, however, make *not a single allusion* to a *single* manifestation of specifically Russian 'criticism' and Russian Economism. In view of this omission, the bare reference to the class and revolutionary character of the theory leaves far wider scope for misinterpretation, particularly when the Union Abroad refuses to identify 'so-called Economism' with opportunism (*Two Conferences*, p. 8, Paragraph 1). But all this, in passing. The main thing to note is that the positions of the opportunists in relation to the revolutionary Social-Democrats in Russia are diametrically opposed to those in Germany. In that country, as we know, the revolutionary Social-Democrats are in favour of preserving that which exists — the old programme and the tactics, which are universally known and have been elucidated in all their details by many decades of experience. But the 'Critics' desire to introduce changes, and since these Critics represent an insignificant minority, and since they are very timid in their revisionist efforts, one can understand the motives of the majority in confining themselves to the dry rejection of 'innovations'. In Russia, however, it is the Critics and the Economists who are in favour of preserving that which exists: the 'Critics' want us to go on regarding them as Marxists and to guarantee them the 'freedom of criticism' they enjoyed to the full (for, in fact, they never recognized any kind of *party* ties,[18]

[18] Lenin — [The fact alone of the absence of public party ties and party traditions, representing as it does a cardinal difference between Russia and Germany, should have warned all sensible socialists against blind imitation. But, here is an instance of the lengths to which 'freedom of criticism' goes in Russia. Mr. Bulgakov, the Russian Critic, utters the following reprimand to the Austrian Critic, Hertz: 'Notwithstanding the independence of his conclusions, Hertz on this point on the question of co-operative societies) apparently remains excessively bound by the opinions of his party, and although he disagrees with it in details, he dare not reject the common principle' (*Capitalism and Agriculture*, Vol. II, p. 287). The subject of a politically enslaved state, in which nine hundred and ninety-nine out of a thousand of the population are corrupted to the marrow by political subservience and completely lack the conception of party honour and party ties, superciliously reproves a citizen of a constitutional state for being excessively 'bound by the opinions of his party'! Our illegal organizations

and, moreover, we never had a generally recognized party body that could 'restrict' freedom of criticism, if only by counsel); the Economists want the revolutionaries to recognize the sovereign character of the present movement' (*Rabocheye Dyelo*, No. 10, p. 25), i.e., to recognize the 'legitimacy' of that which exists; they want the 'ideologists' not to try to 'divert' the movement from the path that 'is determined by the interaction of material. elements and material environment' ('Letter' in *Iskra*, No. 12); they want to have that struggle recognized as desirable 'which it is possible for the workers to wage under the present conditions', and as the only possible struggle, that 'which they are actually waging at the present time' ('*Separate Supplement*' to *Rabochaya Mysl*, p. 14). We revolutionary Social-Democrats, on the contrary, are dissatisfied with this worship of spontaneity, i.e., of that which exists 'at the present moment'. We demand that the tactics that have prevailed in recent years be changed; we declare that 'before we can unite, and in order that we may unite, we must first of all draw firm and definite lines of demarcation' (see announcement of the publication of *Iskra*).[19] In a word, the Germans stand for that which exists and reject changes; we demand a change of that which exists, and reject subservience thereto and reconciliation to it.

This 'slight' difference our 'free' copyists of German resolutions failed to notice.

1.4. ENGELS ON THE IMPORTANCE OF THE THEORETICAL STRUGGLE.

'Dogmatism, doctrinairism', 'ossification of the party — the inevitable retribution that follows the violent strait-lacing of thought' — these are the enemies against which the knightly

have nothing else to do, of course, but draw up resolutions on freedom of criticism. . . .].

19 'Declaration of the Editorial Board of *Iskra*', 1900, *Collected Works*, Vol. 4, p. 354.

champions of 'freedom of criticism' in *Rabocheye Dyelo* rise up in arms. We are very glad that this question has been placed on the order of the day and we would only propose to add to it one other:

And who are the judges?

We have before us two publishers' announcements. One, 'The Programme of the Periodical Organ of the Union of Russian Social Democrats Abroad — *Rabocheye Dyelo*' (reprint from No. 1 of *Rabocheye Dyelo*), and the other, the 'Announcement of the Resumption of the Publications of the Emancipation of Labour Group'. Both are dated 1899, when the 'crisis of Marxism' had long been under discussion. And what do we find? We would seek in vain in the first announcement for any reference to this phenomenon, or a definite statement of the position the new organ intends to adopt on this question. Not a word is said about theoretical work and the urgent tasks that now confront it, either in this programme or in the supplements to it that were adopted by the Third Congress of the Union Abroad in 1901 (Two Conferences, pp. 15-18). During this entire time, the Editorial Board of *Rabocheye Dyelo* ignored theoretical questions, in spite of the fact that these were questions that disturbed the minds of all Social-Democrats the world over.

The other announcement, on the contrary, points first of all to the declining interest in theory in recent years, imperatively demands 'vigilant attention to the theoretical aspect of the revolutionary movement of the proletariat', and calls for 'ruthless criticism of the Bernsteinian and other anti-revolutionary tendencies' in our movement. The issues of Zarya to date show how this programme has been carried out.

Thus, we see those high-sounding phrases against the ossification of thought, etc., conceal unconcern and helplessness with regard to the development of theoretical thought. The case of the Russian Social-Democrats manifestly illustrates the general European phenomenon (long ago noted also by the German Marxists) that the much-vaunted freedom of criticism does not imply substitution of one theory for another, but freedom from all integral and well-considered theory; it implies eclecticism and lack of principle. Those who have the slightest acquaintance with the actual state of our movement cannot but see that the widespread of Marxism was accompanied by a certain lowering of the theoretical level. Quite a number of people with very little, and even a total lack of theoretical training joined the movement because of its practical significance and its practical successes. We can judge from that how tactless *Rabocheye Dyelo* is when, with an air of triumph, it quotes Marx's statement: 'Every step of real movement is more important than a dozen programmes'. To repeat these words in a period of theoretical disorder is like wishing mourners at a funeral many happy returns of the day. Moreover, these words of Marx are taken from his letter on the Gotha Programme, in which he sharply condemns eclecticism in the formulation of principles.[20] If you must unite, Marx wrote to the party leaders, then enter into agreements to satisfy the practical aims of the movement, but do not allow any bargaining over principles, do not make theoretical 'concessions'. This was Marx's idea, and yet there are people among us who seek in his name to belittle the significance of theory!

Without revolutionary theory, there can be no revolutionary movement. This idea cannot be insisted upon too strongly at a time when the fashionable preaching of opportunism goes hand in hand with an infatuation for the narrowest forms of practical activity. Yet, for Russian Social-Democrats, the importance of theory is enhanced by three other circumstances, which are often forgotten: first, by the fact that our Party is only in process of formation, its features are only just becoming defined, and it has as yet far from settled accounts with the other trends of revolutionary thought that threaten to divert the movement from the correct path. On the contrary, precisely the very recent past was marked by a revival of non-Social-Democratic revolutionary trends (an eventuality

20 Marx to Wilhelm Bracke, 5 May 1875, Marx and Engels, *Collected Works*, vol. 45, p. 70.

regarding which Axelrod long ago warned the Economists).[21] Under these circumstances, what at first sight appears to be an 'unimportant' error may lead to most deplorable consequences, and only short-sighted people can consider factional disputes and a strict differentiation between shades of opinion inopportune or superfluous. The fate of Russian Social-Democracy for very many years to come may depend on the strengthening of one or the other 'shade'.

Secondly, the Social-Democratic movement is in its very essence an international movement. This means, not only that we must combat national chauvinism, but that an incipient movement in a young country can be successful only if it makes use of the experiences of other countries. In order to make use of these experiences, it is not enough merely to be acquainted with them or simply to copy out the latest resolutions. What is required is the ability to treat these experiences critically and to test them independently. He who realizes how enormously the modern working-class movement has grown and branched out will understand what a reserve of theoretical forces and political (as well as revolutionary) experience is required to carry out this task.

Thirdly, the national tasks of Russian Social-Democracy are such as have never confronted any other socialist party in the world. We shall have occasion further on to deal with the political and organizational duties which the task of emancipating the whole people from the yoke of autocracy imposes upon us. At this point, we wish to state only that the *role of vanguard fighter can be fulfilled only by a party that is guided by the most advanced*

[21] Pavel Axelrod (1850–1928) was an early Marxist in Russia, who — with Plekhanov, Vera Zasulich and others — formed the Emancipation of Labour Group. After the 1903, the second Congress of the Russian Social Democratic Labour Party, Axelrod defined himself as part of the Menshevik (minority) faction. Lenin refers to — Pavel Axelrod, *Concerning the Present Tasks and Tactics of the Russian Social-Democrats*, Union of Russian Social Democrats, Geneva, 1898.

theory. To have a concrete understanding of what this means, let the reader recall such predecessors of Russian Social Democracy as Herzen, Belinsky, Chernyshevsky, and the brilliant galaxy of revolutionaries of the seventies; let the reader ponder over the world significance which Russian literature is now acquiring; let the reader . . . but be that enough!

Let us quote what Engels said in 1874 concerning the significance of theory in the Social-Democratic movement. Engels recognizes, *not two* forms of the great struggle of Social Democracy (political and economic), as is the fashion among us, *but three, placing the theoretical struggle on a par with the first two*. His recommendations to the German working-class movement, which had become strong, practically and politically, are so instructive from the standpoint of present-day problems and controversies, that we hope the reader will not be vexed with us for quoting a long passage from his prefatory note to *Der deutsche Bauernkrieg*,[22] which has long become a great bibliographical rarity:

> 'The German workers have two important advantages over those of the rest of Europe. First, they belong to the most theoretical people of Europe; and they have retained that sense of theory which the so-called 'educated' classes of Germany have almost completely lost. Without German philosophy, which preceded it, particularly that of Hegel, German scientific socialism — the only scientific socialism that has ever existed — would never have come into being. Without a sense of theory among the workers, this scientific socialism would never have entered their flesh and blood as much as is the case. What an immeasurable advantage this is may be seen, on the one hand, from the indifference towards all theory,

[22] Friedrich Engels, *The Peasant War in Germany* (1850), Marx and Engels, *Collected Works*, vol. 10. Lenin used the third edition in German published in 1875 by Leipzig's Verlag der Genossenschaftsbuchdruckerei (Cooperative Publishers).

which is one of the main reasons why the English working-class movement crawls along so slowly in spite of the splendid organization of the individual unions; on the other hand, from the mischief and confusion wrought by Proudhonism, in its original form, among the French and Belgians, and, in the form further caricatured by Bakunin, among the Spaniards and Italians.

The second advantage is that, chronologically speaking, the Germans were about the last to come into the workers' movement. Just as German theoretical socialism will never forget that it rests on the shoulders of Saint-Simon, Fourier, and Owen — three men who, in spite of all their fantastic notions and all their utopianism, have their place among the most eminent thinkers of all times, and whose genius anticipated innumerable things, the correctness of which is now being scientifically proved by us — so the practical workers' movement in Germany ought never to forget that it has developed on the shoulders of the English and French movements, that it was able simply to utilize their dearly bought experience, and could now avoid their mistakes, which in their time were mostly unavoidable. Without the precedent of the English trade unions and French workers' political struggles, without the gigantic impulse given especially by the Paris Commune, where would we be now?

It must be said to the credit of the German workers that they have exploited the advantages of their situation with rare understanding. For the first time since a workers' movement has existed, the struggle is being conducted pursuant to its three sides — the theoretical, the political, and the practical-economic (resistance to the capitalists) — in harmony and in its interconnections, and in a systematic way. It is precisely in this, as it were, concentric attack, that the strength and invincibility of the German movement lies.

Due to this advantageous situation, on the one hand, and

> to the insular peculiarities of the English and the forcible suppression of the French movement, on the other, the German workers have, for the moment, been placed in the vanguard of the proletarian struggle. How long events will allow them to occupy this post of honour cannot be foretold. But let us hope that as long as they occupy it, they will fill it fittingly. This demands redoubled efforts in every field of struggle and agitation. In particular, it will be the duty of the leaders to gain an ever-clearer insight into all theoretical questions, to free themselves more and more from the influence of traditional phrases inherited from the old world outlook, and constantly to keep in mind that socialism, since it has become a science, demands that it be pursued as a science, i.e., that it be studied. The task will be to spread with increased zeal among the masses of the workers the ever more clarified understanding thus acquired, to knit together ever more firmly the organization both of the party and of the trade unions. . . .
>
> If the German workers progress in this way, they will not. be marching exactly at the head of the movement — it is not at all in the interest of this movement that the workers of any particular country should march at its head — but they will occupy an honourable place in the battle line; and they will stand armed for battle when either unexpectedly grave trials or momentous events demand of them increased courage, increased determination and energy.'

Engels's words proved prophetic. Within a few years, the German workers were subjected to unexpectedly grave trials in the form of the Exceptional Law Against the Socialists. And they met those trials armed for battle and succeeded in emerging from them victorious.

The Russian proletariat will have to undergo trials immeasurably graver; it will have to fight a monster compared with which an antisocialist law in a constitutional country seems but a goblin. History has now confronted us with an immediate task which is the *most revolutionary* of all the *immediate* tasks confronting the proletariat of any country. The fulfilment of this task, the destruction of the most powerful bulwark, not only of European, but (it may now be said) of Asiatic reaction, would make the Russian proletariat the vanguard of the international revolutionary proletariat. And we have the right to count upon acquiring this honourable title, already earned by our predecessors, the revolutionaries of the seventies, if we succeed in inspiring our movement, which is a thousand times broader and deeper, with the same devoted determination and vigour.

Chapter 2

The Spontaneity of the Masses and the Consciousness of the Social-Democrats

We have said that our movement, much more extensive and deep than the movement of the seventies, must be inspired with the same devoted determination and energy that inspired the movement at that time. Indeed, no one, we think, has until now doubted that the strength of the present-day movement lies in the awakening of the masses (principally, the industrial proletariat) and that its weakness lies in the lack of consciousness and initiative among the revolutionary leaders.

However, of late, a staggering discovery has been made which threatens to disestablish all hitherto prevailing views on this question. This discovery was made by *Rabocheye Dyelo*, which in its polemic with *Iskra* and *Zarya,* did not confine itself to making objections on separate points, but tried to ascribe 'general disagreements' to a more profound cause to the 'different appraisals of the *relative* importance of the spontaneous and consciously "methodical" element'. *Rabocheye Dyelo* formulated its indictment as a *'belittling of the significance of the objective or the spontaneous element of development'.*[1] To this, we say: had the polemics with *Iskra* and *Zarya* resulted in nothing more than causing *Rabocheye Dyelo* to hit upon these 'general disagreements', that alone would give us considerable satisfaction, so significant is this thesis and so clear is the light it sheds on the quintessence of the present-day theoretical and political differences that exist among Russian Social-Democrats.

[1] *Rabocheye Dyelo*, No. 10, September 1901, pp. 17–18. *Rabocheye Dyelo*'s italics.

For this reason, the question of the relation between consciousness and spontaneity is of such enormous general interest, and for this reason, the question must be dealt with in great detail.

2.1. THE BEGINNING OF THE SPONTANEOUS UPSURGE

In the previous chapter, we pointed out how *universally* absorbed the educated youth of Russia was in the theories of Marxism in the middle of the nineties. In the same period, the strikes that followed the famous St. Petersburg industrial war of 1896 assumed a similar general character. Their spread over the whole of Russia clearly showed the depth of the newly awakening popular movement, and if we are to speak of the 'spontaneous element', then, of course, it is this strike movement which, first and foremost, must be regarded as spontaneous. But there is spontaneity and spontaneity. Strikes occurred in Russia in the seventies and sixties (and even in the first half of the nineteenth century), and they were accompanied by the 'spontaneous' destruction of machinery, etc. Compared with these 'revolts', the strikes of the nineties might even be described as 'conscious' to such an extent do they mark the progress which the working-class movement made in that period. This shows that the 'spontaneous element', in essence, represents nothing more nor less than consciousness in an *embryonic form.* Even the primitive revolts expressed the awakening of consciousness to a certain extent. The workers were losing their age-long faith in the permanence of the system which oppressed them and began . . . I shall not say to understand but to sense the necessity for collective resistance, definitely abandoning their slavish submission to the authorities. But this was, nevertheless, more in the nature of outbursts of desperation and vengeance than of *struggle.* The strikes of the nineties revealed far greater flashes of consciousness; definite demands were advanced, the strike was carefully timed, known cases and instances in other places were discussed, etc. The revolts were simply the resistance of the oppressed, whereas the systematic strikes represented the class struggle in embryo, but only in embryo. Taken by themselves, these strikes were simply trade union struggles, not yet Social-Democratic struggles. They marked the awakening antagonisms between workers and employers; but the workers, were not, and could not be, conscious of the irreconcilable antagonism of their interests to the whole of the modern political and social system, i.e., theirs was not yet Social-Democratic consciousness. In this sense, the strikes of the nineties, despite the enormous progress they represented as compared with the 'revolts', remained a purely spontaneous movement.

We have said that t*here could not have been* Social-Democratic consciousness among the workers. It would have to be brought to them from without. The history of all countries shows that the working class, exclusively by its own effort, is able to develop only trade union consciousness, i.e., the conviction that it is necessary to combine in unions, fight the employers, and strive to compel the government to pass necessary labour legislation, etc.[2] The theory of socialism, however, grew out of the philosophic, historical, and economic theories elaborated by educated representatives of the propertied classes, by intellectuals. By their social status, the founders of modern scientific socialism, Marx and Engels, themselves belonged to the bourgeois intelligentsia. In the very same way, in Russia, the theoretical doctrine of Social-Democracy arose altogether independently of the spontaneous growth of the working-class movement; it arose as a natural and inevitable outcome of the development of thought among the revolutionary socialist intelligentsia. In the period under discussion, the middle nineties, this doctrine not only represented the completely formulated programme of the Emancipation of Labour group, but

[2] Trade-unionism does not exclude 'politics' altogether, as some imagine. Trade unions have always conducted some political (but not Social-Democratic) agitation and struggle. We shall deal with the difference between trade union politics and Social-Democratic politics in the next chapter.

had already won over to its side the majority of the revolutionary youth in Russia.

Hence, we had both the spontaneous awakening of the working masses, their awakening to conscious life and conscious struggle, and a revolutionary youth, armed with Social-Democratic theory and straining towards the workers. In this connection, it is particularly important to state the oft-forgotten (and comparatively little-known) fact that, although the *early* Social-Democrats of that period *zealously carried on economic agitation* (being guided in this activity by the truly useful indications contained in the pamphlet *On Agitation*, then still in manuscript), they did not regard this as their sole task.[3] On the contrary, *from the very beginning*, they set for Russian Social-Democracy — the most far-reaching historical tasks, in general, and the task of overthrowing the autocracy, in particular. Thus, towards the end of 1895, the St. Petersburg group of Social-Democrats, which founded the League of Struggle for the Emancipation of the Working Class, prepared the first issue of a newspaper called *Rabocheye Dyelo*. This issue was ready to go to press when it was seized by the gendarmes, on the night of 8 December 1895 in a raid on the house of one of the members of the group, Anatoly Alexeyevich Vaneyey,[4] so that the first edition of *Rabocheye Dyelo* was not destined to see the light of day. The leading article in this issue (which, perhaps thirty years hence, some *Russkaya Starina* will unearth in the archives of the

[3] Arkadi Kremer (1865–1935) was the author of *On Agitation*, edited by Martov and published in Vilno in 1894 (distributed as hectographed copies) and then in Geneva in 1897 with a preface from Axelrod. The pamphlet argued that revolutionaries must move from study circles to mass agitation among workers for their everyday needs. Axelrod warned that the thrust of Kremer's essay was Vilno Economism; Plekhanov wrote about it at length in his *Once More on Socialism and Struggle*.

[4] Lenin — [A. A. Vaneyev died in Eastern Siberia in 1899 from consumption, which he contracted during solitary confinement in prison prior to his banishment. That is why we considered it possible to publish the above information, the authenticity of which we guarantee, for it comes from persons who were closely and directly acquainted with A. A. Vaneyev.]

Department of Police) outlined the historical tasks of the working class in Russia and placed the achievement of political liberty at their head.[5] The issue also contained an article entitled 'What Are Our Ministers Thinking About?' which dealt with the crushing of the elementary education committees by the police.[6] In addition, there was some correspondence from St. Petersburg, and from other parts of Russia (e.g., a letter on the massacre of the workers in Yaroslavl Gubernia). This 'first effort', if we are not mistaken, of the Russian Social-Democrats of the nineties was not a purely local, or less still, 'Economic', newspaper, but one that aimed to unite the strike movement with the revolutionary movement against the autocracy, and to win over to the side of Social-Democracy all who were oppressed by the policy of reactionary obscurantism. No one in the slightest degree acquainted with the state of the movement at that period could doubt that such a paper would have met with a warm response among the workers of the capital and the revolutionary intelligentsia and would have had a wide circulation. The failure of the enterprise merely showed that the Social-Democrats of that period were unable to meet the immediate requirements of the time owing to their lack of revolutionary experience and practical training. This must be said, too, with regard to the *S. Peterburgsky Rabochy Listok* and particularly with regard to *Rabochaya Gazeta* and the *Manifesto* of the Russian Social-Democratic Labour Party, founded in the spring of 1898.[7] Of course, we would not dream of blaming the Social-Democrats of that time for this unpreparedness. But in order to profit from the experience of that movement, and to

[5] *Russkaya Starina* (*Russian Antiquary*) was a monthly history magazine published in St. Petersburg from 1870 to 1918.

[6] Lenin, 'What Are Our Ministers Thinking About?', *Rabocheye Dyelo*, 1895, *Collected Works*, vol. 2, pp. 87–92.

[7] The *St. Peterburgsky Rabochy Listok* or the *Workers' Paper* was published illegally by the St. Petersburg League of Struggle for the Emancipation of the Working Class in two issues — no. 1 (February 1897 within Russia) and no. 2 (September 1897 in Geneva).

draw practical lessons from it, we must thoroughly understand the causes and significance of this or that shortcoming. It is therefore highly important to establish the fact that a part (perhaps even a majority) of the Social-Democrats, active in the period of 1895–98, justly considered it possible even then, at the very beginning of the 'spontaneous' movement, to come forward with a most extensive programme and a militant tactical line.[8] The lack of training of the majority of the revolutionaries, an entirely natural phenomenon, could not have roused any particular fears. Once the tasks were correctly defined, once the energy existed for repeated attempts to fulfil them, temporary failures represented only part of misfortune. Revolutionary experience and organizational skills are things that can be acquired, provided the desire is there to acquire them, provided the shortcomings are recognized, which in revolutionary activity is more than halfway towards their removal.

But what was only part misfortune became full misfortune when this consciousness began to grow dim (it was very much alive among the members of the groups mentioned), when there appeared people — and even Social-Democratic organs — that were prepared to regard shortcomings as virtues, that even tried to invent a *theoretical* basis for their *slavish cringing before spontaneity*. It is time to draw conclusions from this trend, the content of which is incorrectly and too narrowly characterized as Economism.

[8] Lenin — ['In adopting a hostile attitude towards the activities of the Social-Democrats of the late nineties, *Iskra* ignores the absence at that time of conditions for any work other than the struggle for petty demands,' declare the Economists in their 'Letter to Russian Social-Democratic Organs' (*Iskra* No. 12). The facts given above show that the assertion about 'absence of conditions' is *diametrically opposed to the truth*. Not only at the end, but even in the mid-nineties, all the conditions existed for other work, besides the struggle for petty demands — all the conditions except adequate training of leaders. Instead of frankly admitting that we, the ideologists, the leaders, lacked sufficient training — the Economists seek to shift the blame entirely upon the 'absence of conditions', upon the effect of the material environment that determines the road from which no ideologist will be able to divert the movement. What is this but slavish cringing before spontaneity, what but the infatuation of the 'ideologists' with their own shortcomings?]

2.2. BOWING TO SPONTANEITY. RABOCHAYA MYSL.

Before dealing with the literary manifestation of this subservience to spontaneity, we should like to note the following characteristic fact (communicated to us from the above-mentioned source), which throws light on the conditions in which the two future conflicting trends in Russian Social-Democracy arose and grew among the comrades working in St. Petersburg. At the beginning of 1897, just prior to their banishment, A. A. Vaneyev and several of his comrades attended a private meeting at which 'old' and 'young' members of the League of Struggle for the Emancipation of the Working Class gathered.[9] The conversation centred chiefly on the question of organization, particularly about the 'rules for the workers' mutual benefit fund', which, in their final form, were published in *'Listok' Rabotnika,* No. 9-10, p. 46.[10] Sharp differences immediately showed themselves between the 'old' members ('Decembrists', as the St. Petersburg Social Democrats jestingly called them) and several of the 'young' members (who subsequently took an active part in the work of *Rabochaya Mysl*), with a heated discussion ensuing. The 'young' members defended the main principles of the rules in the form in which they were published. The 'old' members contended that the prime necessity was not this, but the consolidation of the League of Struggle into an organization of revolutionaries to which all the various

[9] The meeting was held in St. Petersburg between 14 and 17 February (26 February and 1 March) 1897. Lenin, A. A. Vaneyev, G. M. Krzhizhanovsky, and other members of the St. Petersburg League of Struggle for the Emancipation of the Working Class attended this meeting. This group included the 'old' — leaders just released from prison for three days before being exiled to Siberia — and the 'young' — those who had taken over the League's leadership after Lenin's arrest in December 1895.

[10] *'Listok' Rabotnika* (*Workingman's Paper*) was published in Geneva by the Union of Russian Social Democrats Abroad from 1896 to 1899 over ten issues, with the first eight edited by the Emancipation of Labour Group. When the Union adopted Economism in late 1898, the group split and the last two issues were published by a new editorial board.

workers' mutual benefit funds, students' propaganda circles, etc., should be subordinated. It goes without saying that the disputing sides far from realized at the time that these disagreements were the beginning of a cleavage; on the contrary, they regarded them as something isolated and casual. But this fact shows that in Russia, too, Economism did not arise and spread without a struggle against the 'old' Social-Democrats (which the Economists of today are apt to forget). And if, in the main, this struggle has not left 'documentary' traces behind it, it is *solely* because the membership of the circles then functioning underwent such constant change that no continuity was established and, consequently, differences in point of view were not recorded in any documents.

The founding of *Rabochaya Mysl* brought Economism to the light of day, but not at one stroke. We must picture to ourselves concretely the conditions for activity and the short-lived character of the majority of the Russian study circles (a thing that is possible only for those who have themselves experienced it) in order to understand how much there was of the fortuitous in the successes and failures of the new trend in various towns, and the length of time during which neither the advocates nor the opponents of the 'new' could make up their minds — and literally had no opportunity of so doing — as to whether this really expressed a distinct trend or merely the lack of training of certain individuals. For example, the first mimeographed copies of *Rabochaya Mysl* never reached the great majority of Social-Democrats, and if we are able to refer to the leading article in the first number, it is only because it was reproduced in an article by V. I. Lenin (*'Listok' Rabotnika*, No. 9–10, p. 47, et seq.), who, of course, did not fail to extol with more zeal than reason the new paper, which was so different from the papers and projects for papers mentioned above.[11] It is well worth dwelling on this leading article because

[11] Lenin — [It should be stated in passing that the praise of *Rabochaya Mysl* in November 1898, when Economism had become fully defined, especially abroad, emanated from the self-same V. I, who very soon after became one

it brings out in bold relief *the entire spirit of Rabochaya Mysl* and Economism generally.

After stating that the arm of the 'blue-coats' could never halt the progress of the working-class movement, the leading article goes on to say: '. . .The virility of the working-class movement is due to the fact that the workers themselves are at last taking their fate into their own hands, and out of the hands of the leaders'; this fundamental thesis is then developed in greater detail.[12] Actually, the leaders (i.e., the Social-Democrats, the organizers of the League of Struggle) were, one might say, torn out of the hands of the workers[13] by the police; yet it is made to appear that the workers were fighting against the leaders and liberated themselves from their yoke! Instead of sounding the call to go forward towards the consolidation of the revolutionary organization and the expansion of political activity, the call was issued for a *retreat* to the pure trade union struggle. It was announced that 'the economic basis of the movement is eclipsed by the effort never to forget the political ideal', and that the watchword for the working-class movement was 'Struggle for economic conditions' (!) or, better still, 'The workers for the workers'. It was declared that strike funds 'are more valuable to the movement than a hundred other Organizations' (compare this statement made in October 1897, with the polemic between the 'Decembrists' and the young members at the beginning of 1897), etc. Catchwords like 'We must concentrate, not on the 'cream' of

of the editors of *Rabocheye Dyelo*. And yet, *Rabocheye Dyelo* denied that there were two trends in Russian Social-Democracy, and continues to deny It to this day!] The V.I. in question was V. P. Ivanshin (1869–1904), one of the editors of *Rabocheye Dyelo*.

12 The police of the Tsarist regime wore cornflower bluecoats since the time of Peter the Great (1672–1725).

13 Lenin — [That this simile is a correct one is shown by the following characteristic fact. When, after the arrest of the 'Decembrists', the news spread among the workers of the Schlüsselburg Highway that the discovery and arrest were facilitated by an *agent provocateur*, N. N. Mikhailov, a dentist, who had been in contact with a group associated with the 'Decembrists', the workers were so enraged that they decided to kill him.]

the workers, but on the 'average', mass worker'; 'Politics always obediently follows economics',[14] etc., etc., became the fashion, exercising an irresistible influence upon the masses of the youth who were attracted to the movement but who, in the majority of cases, were acquainted only with such fragments of Marxism as were expounded in legally appearing publications.

Political consciousness was completely overwhelmed by spontaneity — the spontaneity of the 'Social-Democrats' who repeated Mr. V. V.'s 'ideas', the spontaneity of those workers who were carried away by the arguments that a kopek added to a ruble was worth more than any socialism or politics, and that they must 'fight, knowing that they are fighting, not for the sake of some future generation, but for themselves and their children' (leader in *Rabochaya Mysl*, No. 1). Phrases like these have always been a favourite weapon of the West-European bourgeois, who, in their hatred for socialism, strove (like the German *'Sozial-Politiker'* Hirsch) to transplant English trade-unionism to their native soil and to preach to the workers that by engaging in the pure trade union[15] struggle they would be fighting for themselves and for their children, and not for some future generations with some future socialism. And now, the 'V. V.s of Russian Social-Democracy' have

[14] Lenin — [These quotations are taken from the same leading article in the first number of *Rabochaya Mysl*. One can judge from this the degree of theoretical training possessed by these 'V. V.s of Russian Social-Democracy', who kept repeating the crude vulgarization of 'economic materialism' at a time when the Marxists were carrying on a literary war against the real Mr V. V., who had long ago been dubbed as 'a past master of reactionary deeds' for holding similar views on the relations between politics and economics!]. V. V. is a pseudonym of V. P. Vorontsov (1847–1918), a *Narodnik* economist and sociologist who held the line for his views in the debate in the 1880s and 1890s against the Marxists led by Plekhanov. Vorontsov, an early interpreter of Marx in Russia, argued that the country required a long period of capitalism before it could move toward socialism (a view attacked by N. F. Danielson, who had translated Lenin's *Capital* in 1872). The 'V.V.'s of Russian Social-Democracy' are the Economists of his time.

[15] Lenin — [The Germans even have a special expression, *Nur-Gewerkschaftler*, which means an advocate of the 'pure trade union' struggle].

set about repeating these bourgeois phrases. It is important at this point to note three circumstances that will be useful to our further analysis of *contemporary* differences.[16]

In the first place, the overwhelming of political consciousness by spontaneity, to which we referred above, also took place *spontaneously*. This may sound like a pun, but, alas, it is the bitter truth. It did not take place as a result of an open struggle between two diametrically opposed points of view, in which one triumphed over the other; it occurred because of the fact that an increasing number of 'old' revolutionaries were 'torn away' by the gendarmes and increasing numbers of 'young' 'V. V.s of Russian Social Democracy' appeared on the scene. Everyone, who has, I shall not say, participated in, but at least breathed the atmosphere of the *present-day* Russian movement — knows perfectly well that this is precisely the case. And if, nevertheless, we insist strongly that the reader be fully clear on this generally known fact, if we cite, for explicitness, as it were, the facts of the first edition of *Rabocheye Dyelo* and of the polemic between the 'old' and the 'young' at the beginning of 1897, we do this because the people who vaunt their 'democracy' speculate on the ignorance of these facts on the part of the broad public (or of the very young generation). We shall return to this point further on.

Secondly, in the very first literary expression of Economism we observe the exceedingly curious phenomenon — highly characteristic for an understanding of all the differences prevailing among present-day Social Democrats — that the adherents of the 'labour movement pure and simple', worshippers of the closest

[16] Lenin — [We emphasize the word *contemporary* for the benefit of those who may pharisaically shrug their shoulders and say: It is easy enough to attack *Rabochaya Mysl* now, but is not all this ancient history? *Mutato nomine de te fabula narratur* is our answer to such contemporary Pharisees, whose complete subjection to the ideas of *Rabochaya Mysl* will be proved further on]. The full Latin phrase from the Roman poet Horace is '*Quid rides? Mutato nomine de te fabula narratur*' — Why are you laughing? Change the name, and the story could be about you.

'organic' contacts (*Rabocheye Dyelo*'s term) with the proletarian struggle, opponents of any non-worker intelligentsia (even a socialist intelligentsia), are compelled, in order to defend their positions, to resort to the arguments of the *bourgeois* 'pure trade-unionists'. This shows that from the very outset, *Rabochaya Mysl* began — unconsciously — to implement the programme of the *Credo*. This shows (something *Rabocheye Dyelo* cannot grasp) that *all* worship of the spontaneity of the working- class movement, all belittling of the role of 'the conscious element', of the role of Social-Democracy, *means, quite independently of whether he who belittles that role desires it or not, a strengthening of the influence of bourgeois ideology upon the workers.* All those who talk about 'overrating the importance of ideology',[17] about exaggerating the role of the conscious element,[18] etc., imagine that the labour movement pure and simple can elaborate, and will elaborate, an independent ideology for itself, if only the workers 'wrest their fate from the hands of the leaders'. But this is a profound mistake. To supplement what has been said above, we shall quote the following profoundly true and important words of Karl Kautsky on the new draft programme of the Austrian Social-Democratic Party:[19]

> 'Many of our revisionist critics believe that Marx asserted that economic development and the class struggle create, not only the conditions for socialist production, but also, and directly, the *consciousness* [Kautsky's italics] of its necessity. And these critics assert that England, the country most highly developed capitalistically, is more remote than any other from this consciousness. Judging by the draft, one might assume that this allegedly orthodox Marxist view, which is thus refuted, was shared by the committee that drafted the

[17] Lenin — [Letter of the Economists, in *Iskra*, No. 12].

[18] Lenin — [*Rabocheye Dyelo*, No. 10].

[19] Lenin — [*Neue Zeit*, 1901–02, XX, I, No. 3, p. 79. The committee's draft to which Kautsky refers was adopted by the Vienna Congress (at the end of last year) in a slightly amended form].

Austrian programme. In the draft programme, it is stated: 'The more capitalist development increases the numbers of the proletariat, the more the proletariat is compelled and becomes fit to fight against capitalism. The proletariat becomes conscious of the possibility and of the necessity for socialism'. In this connection, socialist consciousness appears to be a necessary and direct result of the proletarian class struggle. But this is absolutely untrue. Of course, socialism, as a doctrine, has its roots in modern economic relationships just as the class struggle of the proletariat has, and like the latter, emerges from the struggle against the capitalist-created poverty and misery of the masses. But socialism and the class struggle arise side by side and not one out of the other; each arises under different conditions. Modern socialist consciousness can arise only on the basis of profound scientific knowledge. Indeed, modern economic science is as much a condition for socialist production as, say, modern technology and the proletariat can create neither the one nor the other, no matter how much it may desire to do so; both arise out of the modern social process. The vehicle of science is not the proletariat, but the *bourgeois intelligentsia* [Kautsky's italics]: it was in the minds of individual members of this stratum that modern socialism originated, and it was they who communicated it to the more intellectually developed proletarians who, in their turn, introduce it into the proletarian class struggle where conditions allow that to be done. Thus, socialist consciousness is something introduced into the proletarian class struggle from without [*von Aussen Hineingetragenes*] and not something that arose within it spontaneously [*urwu¨chsig*]. Accordingly, the old Hainfeld programme quite rightly stated that the task of Social-Democracy is to imbue the proletariat (literally: saturate the proletariat) with the *consciousness* of its position and the consciousness of its task. There would be no need for this if consciousness arose of itself from the class struggle. The new draft copied this proposition from the old programme and attached it to the proposition mentioned above. But this completely broke the line of thought...'

Since there can be no talk of an independent ideology formulated by the working masses themselves in the process of their movement,[20] the only choice is — either bourgeois or socialist ideology. There is no middle course (for mankind has not created a 'third' ideology, and, moreover, in a society torn by class antagonisms there can never be a non-class or an above-class ideology). Hence, to belittle the socialist ideology *in any way, to turn aside from it in the slightest degree* means to strengthen bourgeois ideology. There is much talk of spontaneity. But the *spontaneous* development of the working-class movement leads to its subordination to bourgeois ideology, *to its development along the lines of the Credo programme;* for the spontaneous working-class movement is trade-unionism, is *Nur-Gewerkschaftlerei,* and trade unionism means the ideological enslavement of the workers by the bourgeoisie. Hence, our task, the task of Social-Democracy, is t*o combat spontaneity, to divert* the working-class movement from this spontaneous, trade-unionist striving to come under the wing of the bourgeoisie, and to bring it under the wing

[20] Lenin — [This does not mean, of course, that the workers have no part in creating such an ideology. They take part, however, not as workers, but as socialist theoreticians, as Proudhons and Weitlings; in other words, they take part only when they are able, and to the extent that they are able, more or less, to acquire the knowledge of their age and develop that knowledge. But in order that working men *may succeed in this more often*, every effort must be made to raise the level of the consciousness of the workers in general; it is necessary that the workers do not confine themselves to the artificially restricted limits of '*literature for workers*' but that they learn to an increasing degree to master *general literature.* It would be even truer to say 'are not confined', instead of 'do not confine themselves', because the workers themselves wish to read and do read all that is written for the intelligentsia, and only a few (bad) intellectuals believe that it is enough 'for workers' to be told a few things about factory conditions and to have repeated to them over and over again what has long been known].

of revolutionary Social Democracy. The sentence employed by the authors of the Economist letter published in *Iskra*, No. 12, is that the efforts of the most inspired ideologists fail to divert the working-class movement from the path that is determined by the interaction of the material elements and the material environment is therefore *tantamount to renouncing socialism*. If these authors were capable of fearlessly, consistently, and thoroughly considering what they say, as everyone who enters the arena of literary and public activity should be, there would be nothing left for them but to 'fold their useless arms over their empty breasts' and surrender the field of action to the Struves and Prokopoviches, who are dragging the working-class movement 'along the line of least resistance', i.e., along the line of bourgeois trade-unionism, or to the Zubatovs, who are dragging it along the line of clerical and gendarme 'ideology'.

Let us recall the example of Germany. What was the historic service Lassalle rendered to the German working-class movement? It was that he *diverted* that movement from the path of progressionist trade-unionism and co-operativism towards which it had been spontaneously moving (*with the benign assistance of Schulze-Delitzsch and his like*). To fulfil such a task, it was necessary to do something quite different from talking of underrating the spontaneous element, of tactics-as-process, of the interaction between elements and environment, etc. *A fierce struggle against spontaneity* was necessary, and only after such a struggle, extending over many years, was it possible, for instance, to convert the working population of Berlin from a bulwark of the progressionist party into one of the finest strongholds of Social-Democracy. This struggle is by no means over even today (as might seem to those who learn the history of the German movement from Prokopovich, and its philosophy from Struve). Even now, the German working class is, so to speak, split up among a number of ideologies. A section of the workers is organized in Catholic and monarchist trade unions; another section is organized in the

Hirsch-Duricker unions, founded by the bourgeois worshippers of English trade-unionism; the third is organized in Social-Democratic trade unions.[21] The last-named group is immeasurably more numerous than the rest, but the Social-Democratic ideology was able to achieve this superiority, and will be able to maintain it, only in an unswerving struggle against all other ideologies.

But why, the reader will ask, does the spontaneous movement, the movement along the line of least resistance, lead to the domination of bourgeois ideology? For the simple reason that bourgeois ideology is far older in origin than socialist ideology, that it is more fully developed, and that it has at its disposal *immeasurably* more means of dissemination.[22] And the younger the socialist movement in any given country, the more vigorously it must struggle against all attempts to entrench non-socialist ideology, and the more resolutely the workers must be warned against the bad counsellors who shout against 'overrating the conscious element', etc. The authors of the Economist letter, in unison with *Rabocheye Dyelo*, inveigh against the intolerance that is characteristic of the infancy of the movement. To this we reply:

[21] Two bourgeois liberals — Max Hirsch (1832-1905) and Franz Duncker (1822-1888) — established the Hirsch-Dunckersche Gewerkvereine in 1868 to preach the 'harmony of class interests,' to draw workers away from revolutionary struggle, and to restrict the role of trade unions to that of mutual benefit and educational societies. Duncker ran a publishing house, whose list included Marx's *Contribution to the Critique of Political Economy* (1859) and founded Germany's Progressive Party in 1861. Hirsch, a political economist, wrote two important books on his travels across Northern Africa.

[22] Lenin — [It is often said that the working class *spontaneously* gravitates towards socialism. This is perfectly true in the sense that socialist theory reveals the causes of the misery of the working class more profoundly and more correctly than any other theory, and for that reason, the workers are able to assimilate it so easily, *provided*, however, this theory does not itself yield to spontaneity, *provided* it subordinates spontaneity to itself. Usually, this is taken for granted, but it is precisely this which *Rabocheye Dyelo* forgets or distorts. The working class spontaneously gravitates towards socialism; nevertheless, the most widespread (and continuously and diversely revived) bourgeois ideology spontaneously imposes itself upon the working class to a still greater degree].

Yes, our movement is indeed in its infancy, and in order that it may grow up faster, it must become imbued with intolerance against those who retard its growth by their subservience to spontaneity. Nothing is so ridiculous and harmful as pretending that we are 'old hands' who have long ago experienced all the decisive stages of the struggle.

Thirdly, the first issue of *Rabochaya Mysl* shows that the term 'Economism' (which, of course, we do not propose to abandon, since, in one way or another, this designation has already established itself) does not adequately convey the real character of the new trend. *Rabochaya Mysl* does not altogether repudiate the political struggle; the rules for a workers' mutual benefit fund published in its first issue contain a reference to combating the government. *Rabochaya Mysl* believes, however, that 'politics always obediently follows economics' (*Rabocheye Dyelo* varies this thesis when it asserts in its programme that 'in Russia more than in any other country, the economic struggle is *inseparable* from the political struggle'). *If by politics is meant Social-Democratic politics,* then the theses of *Rabochaya Mysl* and *Rabocheye Dyelo* are utterly incorrect. The economic struggle of the workers is very often connected (although not inseparably) with bourgeois politics, clerical politics, etc., as we have seen. *Rabocheye Dyelo*'s theses are correct, if by politics is meant trade union politics, viz., the common striving of all workers to secure from the government measures for alleviating the distress to which their condition gives rise, but which do not abolish that condition, i.e., which do not remove the subjection of labour to capital. That striving indeed is common to the English trade-unionists, who are hostile to socialism, to the Catholic workers, to the 'Zubatov' workers, etc. There is politics and there is politics. Thus, we see that *Rabochaya Mysl* does not so much deny the political struggle, as it bows to its *spontaneity*, to its unconsciousness. While fully recognizing the political struggle (better: the political desires and demands of the workers), which arises spontaneously from the working-class movement itself, it absolutely refuses *independently to work out* a specifically *Social-Democratic politics* corresponding to the general tasks of socialism and to present-day conditions in Russia. Further on we shall show that *Rabocheye Dyelo* commits the same error.

2.3 THE SELF-EMANCIPATION GROUP AND RABOCHEYE DYELO[23]

We have dealt at such length with the little-known and now almost forgotten leading article in the first issue of *Rabochaya Mysl* because it was the first and most striking expression of that general stream of thought which afterwards emerged into the light of day in innumerable streamlets. V. I. was perfectly right when, in praising the first issue and the leading article of *Rabochaya Mysl*, he said that the article had been written in a 'sharp and fervent' manner (*'Listok' Rabotnika*, No. 9-10, p. 49). Every man with convictions who thinks he has something new to say writes 'fervently' and in such a way as to make his views stand out in bold relief. Only those who are accustomed to sitting between two stools lack 'fervour'; only such people are able to praise the fervour of *Rabochaya Mysl* one day and attack the 'fervent polemics' of its opponents the next.

We shall not dwell on the *'Separate Supplement' to Rabochaya Mysl* (below we shall have occasion, on various points, to refer to this work, which expresses the ideas of the Economists more consistently than any other), but shall briefly mention the 'Appeal of the Self -Emancipation of the Workers Group' (March 1899, reprinted in the London *Nakanune*, No. 7, July 1899). The authors of the 'Appeal' rightly say that 'the workers of Russia are *only just awakening*, are just beginning to look about them, and are *instinctively clutching at the first available means of struggle*'. Yet

[23] *The Self-Emancipation of the Workers Group* was formed in St. Petersburg in 1898 by a small group of Economists, existing for a few months and publishing a short pamphlet that it published in *Nakanune* (*On the Eve*) in London. The journal ran from January 1899 to February 1902, producing 37 issues that provided a venue for the point of view of the various petty-bourgeois Russian parties.

they draw from this the same false conclusion as that drawn by *Rabochaya Mysl*, forgetting that the instinctive is the unconscious (the spontaneous) to the aid of which socialists must come; that the 'first available means of struggle' will always be, in modern society, the trade union means of struggle, and the 'first available' ideology the bourgeois (trade union) ideology. Similarly, these authors do not 'repudiate' politics they merely (merely!) echo Mr. V. V. that politics is the superstructure, and therefore, 'political agitation must be the superstructure to the agitation carried on in favour of the economic struggle; it must arise on the basis of this struggle and follow in its wake'.

As for *Rabocheye Dyelo*, it began its activity with the 'defence' of the Economists. It stated a *downright untruth* in its opening issue (No. 1, pp. 141–42) in claiming that it 'does not know to which young comrades Axelrod referred' when he warned the Economists in his well-known pamphlet.[24] In the polemic that flared up with Axelrod and Plekhanov over this untruth, *Rabocheye Dyelo* had to admit that 'in the form of perplexity, it sought *to defend* all the younger Social-Democrats abroad from this unjust accusation' (the charge of narrowness levelled by Axelrod at the Economists). In reality this accusation was completely justified, and *Rabocheye Dyelo* knew perfectly well that, among others, it applied also to V. I., a member of its Editorial Board. Let me note in passing that in this polemic, Axelrod was entirely right and *Rabocheye Dyelo* entirely wrong in their respective interpretations of my pamphlet, *The Tasks of the Russian Social-Democrats*.[25] The pamphlet was written in 1897, before the appearance of *Rabochaya Mysl*, when I thought, rightly, that the *original tendency* of the St. Petersburg League of Struggle, which I characterised above, was dominant. And this tendency was dominant at least until the middle of 1898.

[24] Lenin — [*Present Tasks and Tactics of the Russian Social-Democracy*, Geneva, 1898. Two letters to *Rabochaya Gazeta*, written in 1897].

[25] See Lenin, 'The Tasks of the Russian Social Democrats' (pamphlet from 1898), *Collected Works*, vol. 2, pp. 323–51.

Consequently, *Rabocheye Dyelo* had no right whatever, in its attempt to deny the existence and danger of Economism, to refer to a pamphlet that expressed views *forced out* by Economist views in St. Petersburg in 1897–98.[26]

But *Rabocheye Dyelo* not only 'defended' the Economists, it itself constantly fell into their fundamental errors. The source of this confusion is to be found in the ambiguity of the interpretation given to the following thesis of the *Rabocheye Dyelo* programme: 'We consider that the most important phenomenon of Russian life, the one that will mainly *determine the tasks* [our italics] and the character of the publication activity of the Union, is the *mass working-class movement* [*Rabocheye Dyelo*'s italics] which has arisen in recent years'. That the mass movement is a most important phenomenon is a fact not to be disputed. But the crux of the matter is, how is one to understand the statement that the mass working-class movement will 'determine the tasks'? It may be interpreted in one of two ways. *Either* it means bowing to the spontaneity of this movement, i.e., reducing the role of Social-Democracy to mere subservience to the working-class movement as such (the interpretation of *Rabochaya Mysl*, the Self-Emancipation Group, and other Economists), or it means that the mass movement places before us new theoretical, political, and organizational tasks, far more complicated than those that might have satisfied us in the period before the rise of the mass

[26] Lenin — [In defending its first untruth ('we do not know to which young comrades Axelrod referred'), *Rabocheye Dyelo* added a second, when it wrote in its *Reply*: 'Since the review of *The Tasks* was published, tendencies have arisen, or become more or less clearly defined, among certain Russian Social-Democrats, towards economic one-sidedness, which represent a step backwards from the state of our movement as described in *The Tasks*' (p. 9). This, in the *Reply*, published *in 1900*. But, the first issue of *Rabocheye Dyelo* (containing the review) appeared in *April 1899*. Did Economism really arise only in 1899? No. The year 1899 saw the first protest of the *Russian* Social-Democrats against Economism (the protest against the *Credo*). Economism arose in 1897, as *Rabocheye Dyelo* very well knows, for already in *November 1898*, V. I. was praising *Rabochaya Mysl* (see *'Listok' Rabotnika*, No. 9-10)].

movement. *Rabocheye Dyelo* inclined and still inclines towards the first interpretation, for it has said nothing definite about any new tasks, but has argued constantly as though the 'mass movement' *relieves* us of the necessity of clearly understanding and fulfilling the tasks it sets before us. We need only point out that *Rabocheye Dyelo* considered that it was impossible to set the overthrow of the autocracy as the *first* task of the mass working-class movement, and that it degraded this task (in the name of the mass movement) to that of a struggle for immediate political demands (*Reply*, p. 25).

We shall pass over the article by B. Krichevsky, editor of *Rabocheye Dyelo*, entitled 'The Economic and the Political Struggle in the Russian Movement', published in No. 7 of that paper, in which these very mistakes[27] are repeated, and proceed directly to *Rabocheye Dyelo*, No. 10. We shall not, of course, enter in detail into the various objections raised by Krichevsky and Martynov

[27] Lenin — [The 'stages theory', or the theory of 'timid zigzags', in the political struggle is expressed, for example, in this article, in the following way, 'Political demands, which in their character are common to the whole of Russia, should, however, at first (this was written in August 1900!) correspond to the experience gained by the given stratum (*sic!*) of workers in the economic struggle. Only [!] on the basis of this experience can and should political agitation be taken up', etc (p. 11). On page 4, the author, protesting against what he regards as the absolutely unfounded charge of Economist heresy, pathetically exclaims, 'What Social-Democrat does not know that according to the theories of Marx and Engels, the economic interests of certain classes play a decisive role in history, and, *consequently*, that particularly the proletariat's struggle for its economic interests must be of paramount importance in its class development and struggle for emancipation?' [our italics]. The word 'consequently' is completely irrelevant. The fact that economic interests play a decisive role *does not in the least imply* that the economic (i.e., trade union) struggle is of prime importance; for the most essential, the 'decisive' interests of classes can be satisfied *only by* radical *political* changes in general. In particular, the fundamental economic interests of the proletariat can be satisfied only by a political revolution that will replace the dictatorship of the bourgeoisie with the dictatorship of the proletariat. Krichevsky repeats the arguments of the 'V. V.s of Russian Social-Democracy' (viz., that politics follows economics, etc.) and of the Bernsteinians of German Social-Democracy (e.g., by similar arguments, Woltmann sought to prove that the workers must first of all acquire 'economic power' before they can think about political revolution)].

against *Zarya* and *Iskra*. We are here interested solely in the basis of principles on which *Rabocheye Dyelo*, in its tenth issue, took its stand. Thus, we shall not examine the strange fact that *Rabocheye Dyelo* saw a 'diametrical contradiction' between the proposition:

> 'Social-Democracy does not tie its hands, it does not restrict its activities to some preconceived plan or method of political struggle; it recognizes all means of struggle as long as they correspond to the forces at the disposal of the Party (*Iskra*, No. 1).'[28]

and the proposition:

> 'Without a strong organization skilled in waging political struggle under all circumstances and at all times, there can be no question of that systematic plan of action, illumined by firm principles and steadfastly carried out, which alone is worthy of the name of tactics (*Iskra*, No. 4).'[29]

To confound recognition, *in principle*, of all means of struggle, of all plans and methods, provided they are expedient, with the demand *at a given political moment* to be guided by a strictly observed plan is tantamount, if we are to talk of tactics, to confounding the recognition by medical science of various methods of treating diseases with the necessity for adopting a certain definite method of treatment for a given disease. The point is, however, that *Rabocheye Dyelo*, itself the victim of a disease which we have called bowing to spontaneity, refuses to recognize any 'method of treatment' for that disease. Hence, it has made the remarkable discovery that 'tactics-as-plan contradicts the

[28] See Lenin, 'The Urgent Task of Our Movement', *Iskra*, no. 1, December 1900, *Collected Works*, vol. 4, pp. 370–71.

[29] See Lenin, 'Where to Begin', *Iskra*, no. 4, May 1901, *Collected Works*, vol. 5, p. 18.

fundamental spirit of Marxism' (No. 10, p. 18), that tactics are '*a process of growth of Party tasks, which grow together with the Party*' [p. 11, *Rabocheye Dyelo*'s italics]. This remark has every chance of becoming a celebrated maxim, a permanent monument to the *Rabocheye Dyelo* 'trend'. To the question, whither? the leading organ replies: Movement is a process of changing the distance between the starting-point and subsequent points of the movement'. This matchless example of profundity is not merely a curiosity (were it that, it would not be worth dealing with at length), but *the programme of a whole trend*, the very programme which R. M. (in the '*Separate Supplement*' to *Rabochaya Mysl*) expressed in the words: That struggle is desirable which is possible, and the struggle which is possible is that which is going on at the given moment. This is precisely the trend of unbounded opportunism, which passively adapts itself to spontaneity.

'Tactics-as-plan contradicts the essence of Marxism!' But this is a slander of Marxism; it means turning Marxism into the caricature held up by the Narodniks in their struggle against us. It means belittling the initiative and energy of class-conscious fighters, whereas Marxism, on the contrary, gives a gigantic impetus to the initiative and energy of the Social-Democrat, opens up for him the widest perspectives, and (if one may so express it) places at his disposal the mighty force of many millions of workers 'spontaneously' rising for the struggle. The entire history of international Social-Democracy teems with plans advanced now by one, now by another political leader, some confirming the far-sightedness and the correct political and organizational views of their authors and others revealing their short-sightedness and their political errors. At the time when Germany was at one of the crucial turning-points in its history — the formation of the Empire, the opening of the Reichstag, and the granting of universal suffrage — Liebknecht had one plan for Social-Democratic politics and work in general, and Schweitzer had another. When the anti-socialist law came down on the heads of the German socialists, Most and

Hasselmann had one plan — they were prepared then and there to call for violence and terror; Hochberg, Schramm, and (partly) Bernstein had another — they began to preach to the Social-Democrats that they themselves had provoked the enactment of the law by being unreasonably bitter and revolutionary, and must now earn forgiveness by their exemplary conduct.[30] There was yet a third plan, proposed by those who prepared and carried out the publication of an illegal organ. It is easy, of course, with hindsight, many years after the struggle over the selection of the path to be followed, and after history has pronounced its verdict as to the expediency of the path selected, to utter profound maxims about the growth of the Party tasks, which grow together with the Party. But at a time of confusion,[31] when the Russian 'Critics' and Economists are degrading Social-Democracy to the level of trade-unionism, and when the terrorists are strongly advocating the adoption of 'tactics-as-plan' that repeats the old mistakes, at such a time, to confine oneself to profundities of this kind, means

[30] Karl Liebknecht (1871–1919) was a founder of the German Social Democratic Party, who — as a member of the Reichstag — voted against World War I and was ejected from the party for that position. Liebknecht, with Rosa Luxemburg (1871–1919), founded the Sparticust Bund and was killed with her during the failed German Revolution. Jean Baptista von Schweitzer (1833–1875) was a leader of the General German Workers Association and then of the German Social Democratic Party (he coined the term 'democratic centralization' to describe the way that the party should be organized). Johann Most (1846–1906) was inspired by Marx to join the German Social Democratic Party, from which he became a member of the Reichstag. Imprisoned for his attacks on religion, Most was exiled to France and then the United States, where he became an adherent of anarchism. Wilhelm Hasselmann (1844–1916) was a member of the General German Workers Association, went to the Reichstag from the Socialist Workers' Party of Germany (later the Social Democratic Party) and then, from 1876, published *Die Rote Fahne*. Karl Hochberg, who financed the party, worked with Carl August Schramm (1830–1905) — along with Bernstein — to push the line that the party needed to be realistic and pragmatic.

[31] Lenin — ['*Ein Jahr der Verwirrung*' ('A Year of Confusion') is the title Mehring gave to the chapter of his *History of German Social-Democracy* in which he describes the hesitancy and lack of determination displayed at first by the socialists in selecting the 'tactics-as- plan' for the new situation].

simply to issue to oneself a 'certificate of poverty'. At a time when many Russian Social-Democrats suffer from a lack of initiative and energy, from an inadequate 'scope of political propaganda, agitation, and organization',[32] from a lack of 'plans' for a broader organization of revolutionary work, at such a time, to declare that 'tactics-as-plan' contradicts the essence of Marxism' means not only to vulgarize Marxism in the realm of theory, but *to drag the Party backwards* in practice.

Rabocheye Dyelo goes on to sermonize:

> 'The task of the revolutionary Social-Democrat is only to accelerate objective development by his conscious work, not to obviate it or substitute his own subjective plans for this development. *Iskra* knows all this in theory, but the enormous importance that Marxism justly attaches to conscious revolutionary work causes it in practice, owing to its doctrinaire view of tactics, *to belittle the significance of the objective or the spontaneous element of development'* (p. 18).

Another example of the extraordinary theoretical confusion worthy of Mr. V. V. and his fraternity. We would ask our philosopher: how may a designer of subjective plans 'belittle' objective development? Obviously by losing sight of the fact that this objective development creates or strengthens, destroys or weakens certain classes, strata, or groups, certain nations or groups of nations, etc., and in this way serves to determine a given international political alignment of forces, or the position adopted by revolutionary parties, etc. If the designer of plans did that, his guilt would not be that he belittled the spontaneous element, but, on the contrary, that he belittled the *conscious* element, for he would then show that he lacked the 'consciousness' properly

[32] Lenin — [Leading article in *Iskra*, No. 1].
Lenin, 'The Urgent Tasks of Our Movement', *Iskra*, no. 1, December 1900, *Collected Works*, vol. 4, p. 369.

to understand objective development. Hence, the very talk of 'estimating the *relative* significance' [*Rabocheye Dyelo*'s italics] of spontaneity and consciousness itself reveals a complete lack of 'consciousness'. If certain 'spontaneous elements of development' can be grasped at all by human understanding, then an incorrect estimation of them will be tantamount to 'belittling the conscious element'. But if they cannot be grasped, then we do not know them, and therefore cannot speak of them. What, then, is Krichevsky discussing? If he thinks that *Iskra*'s 'subjective plans' are erroneous (as he, in fact, declares them to be), he should have shown what objective facts they ignore, and only then charged *Iskra* with *lacking political consciousness* for ignoring them, with 'belittling the conscious element', to use his own words. If, however, displeased with subjective plans, he can bring forward no argument other than that of 'belittling the spontaneous element' (!), he merely shows: (1) that, theoretically, he understands Marxism *a la* Kareev and Mikhailovsky, who have been sufficiently ridiculed by Beltov; and (2) that, practically, he is quite satisfied with the 'spontaneous elements of development' that have drawn our legal Marxists towards Bernsteinism and our Social-Democrats towards Economism, and that he is 'full of wrath' against those who have determined at all costs *to divert* Russian Social-Democracy from the path of 'spontaneous' development.[33]

Further, there follow things that are positively droll. 'Just as human beings will reproduce in the old-fashioned way despite all the discoveries of natural science, so the birth of a new social order will come about, in the future too, *mainly* as a result of elemental outbursts, despite all the discoveries of social science and the increase in the number of conscious fighters' (p. 19). Just as our grandfathers in their old-fashioned wisdom used to say, 'Anyone

[33] Nikolai Kareev (1850–1931) was a historian who was inspired by the social democratic movement. Nikolay Mikhaylovsky (1842–1904) was a literary critic and a theoretician of the Narodnik movement. G. V. Plekhanov published his monumental book, *The Development of the Monist View of History*, in St. Petersburg in 1895, under the pseudonym N. Beltov.

can bring children into the world', so today the 'modern socialists' (*a la* Nartsis Tuporylov) say in their wisdom, 'Anyone can participate in the spontaneous birth of a new social order'.[34] We too hold that anyone can. All that is required for participation of that kind is *to yield* to Economism when Economism reigns and to terrorism when terrorism arises. Thus, in the spring of this year, when it was so important to utter a note of warning against infatuation with terrorism, *Rabocheye Dyelo* stood in amazement, confronted by a problem that was 'new' to it. And now, six months after, when the problem has become less topical, it presents us at one and the same time with the declaration: 'We think that it is not and should not be the task of Social-Democracy to counteract the rise of terroristic sentiments' (*Rabocheye Dyelo*, No. 10, p. 23), and with the Conference resolution: 'The Conference regards systematic and aggressive terror as being inopportune' (*Two Conferences*, p. 18). How beautifully clear and coherent this is! Not to counteract, but to declare inopportune, and to declare it in such a way that the unsystematic and defensive terror does not come within the scope of the 'resolution'. It must be admitted that such a resolution is extremely safe and is fully insured against error, just as a man who talks, but says nothing, insures himself against error. All that is needed to frame such a resolution is an ability to keep *at the tail end* of the movement. When *Iskra* ridiculed *Rabocheye Dyelo* for declaring the question of terror to be new, the latter angrily accused *Iskra* of 'having the incredible effrontery to impose upon the Party organization solutions of tactical questions proposed by a group of emigrant writers more than fifteen years ago' (p. 24).[35] Effrontery, indeed, and what an overestimation of the conscious

[34] Y. O. Martov (1873–1923), the leader of the Menshevik faction of the Russian Social Democratic Labour Party, published his satirical poem 'Hymn of the Contemporary Russian Socialist' in *Zarya* (no. 1, April 1901) under the name *Nartsis Tuporylov* (or Narcissus Blunt-Snout). The poem ridiculed the Economists.

[35] Lenin, 'Where to Begin', *Iskra*, no. 4, May 1901, *Collected Works*, vol. 5, pp. 18–20.

element — first to resolve questions theoretically beforehand, and then to try to convince the organization, the Party, and the masses of the correctness of this solution![36] How much better it would be to repeat the elements and, without 'imposing' anything upon anybody, swing with every 'turn' — whether in the direction of Economism or in the direction of terrorism. *Rabocheye Dyelo* even generalizes this great precept of worldly wisdom and accuses *Iskra* and *Zarya* of 'setting up their programme against the movement, like a spirit hovering over the formless chaos' (p. 29). But what else is the function of Social-Democracy if not to be a 'spirit' that not only hovers over the spontaneous movement, but also *raises* this movement *to the level of 'its programme'*? Surely, it is not its function to drag at the *tail* of the movement. At best, this would be of no service to the movement; at worst, it would be exceedingly harmful. *Rabocheye Dyelo*, however, not only follows this 'tactics-as-process', but elevates it to a principle, so that it would be more correct to describe its tendency not as opportunism, but as *tail-ism* (from the word *tail*). And it must be admitted that those who are determined always to follow behind the movement and be its tail are absolutely and forever guaranteed against 'belittling the spontaneous element of development'.

<<>>

And so, we have become convinced that the fundamental error committed by the 'new trend' in Russian Social-Democracy is its bowing to spontaneity and its failure to understand that the spontaneity of the masses demands a high degree of consciousness from us Social-Democrats. The greater the spontaneous upsurge of the masses and the more widespread the movement, the more rapid, incomparably so, the demand for greater consciousness

[36] Lenin — [Nor must it be forgotten that in solving 'theoretically' the problem of terror, the Emancipation of Labour group *generalized* the experience of the antecedent revolutionary movement].

in the theoretical, political, and organizational work of Social-Democracy.

The spontaneous upsurge of the masses in Russia proceeded (and continues) with such rapidity that the young Social Democrats proved unprepared to meet these gigantic tasks. This unpreparedness is our common misfortune, the misfortune of *all* Russian Social-Democrats. The upsurge of the masses proceeded and spread with uninterrupted continuity; it not only continued in the places where it began, but spread to new localities and to new strata of the population (under the influence of the working-class movement, there was a renewed ferment among the student youth, among the intellectuals generally, and even among the peasantry). Revolutionaries, however, *lagged behind* this upsurge, both in their 'theories' and in their activity; they failed to establish a constant and continuous organization capable of *leading* the whole movement.

In Chapter I, we established that *Rabocheye Dyelo* belittled our theoretical tasks and that it 'spontaneously' repeated the fashionable catchword 'freedom of criticism'; those who repeated this catchword lacked the 'consciousness' to understand that the positions of the opportunist 'Critics' and those of the revolutionaries in Germany and in Russia are diametrically opposed.

In the following chapters, we shall show how this bowing to spontaneity found expression in the sphere of the political tasks and in the organizational work of Social-Democracy.

Chapter 3

Trade-Unionist Politics and Social-Democratic Politics

We shall again begin by praising *Rabocheye Dyelo*. 'Literature of Exposure and the Proletarian Struggle' is the title Martynov gave the article on his differences with *Iskra,* published in *Rabocheye Dyelo*, No. 10.[1] He formulated the substance of the differences as follows: 'We cannot confine ourselves solely to exposing the system that stands in its (the working-class party's) path of development. We must also react to the immediate and current interests of the proletariat. . . . *Iskra* . . .is, in fact, an organ of revolutionary opposition that exposes the state of affairs in our country, particularly the political state of affairs . . . We, however, work and shall continue to work for the cause of the working class in close organic contact with the proletarian struggle' (p. 63). One cannot help being grateful to Martynov for this formula. It is of outstanding general interest, because substantially, it embraces not only our disagreements with *Rabocheye Dyelo* but the general disagreement between ourselves and the Economists on the political struggle. We have shown that the Economists do not altogether repudiate 'politics' but that they are constantly straying from the Social-Democratic to the trade-unionist conception of politics. Martynov strays in precisely this way, and we shall, therefore, take his views as a *model* of Economist error on this question. As we shall endeavour to prove, neither the authors of the '*Separate Supplement*' to *Rabochaya Mysl* nor the authors of the

[1] Alexandr Martynov (1865–1935) was a leader of the Mensheviks, the chief editor of *Rabocheye Dyelo*, and the leader of the Economists in the Russian Social Democratic Labour Party.

manifesto issued by the Self-Emancipation Group, nor the authors of the Economist letter published in *Iskra*, No. 12, will have any right to complain against this choice.

3.1. POLITICAL AGITATION AND ITS RESTRICTIONS BY THE ECONOMISTS

Everyone knows that the economic[2] struggle of the Russian workers underwent widespread development and consolidation simultaneously with the production of 'literature' exposing economic (factory and occupational) conditions. The 'leaflets' were devoted mainly to the exposure of the factory system, and very soon a veritable passion for exposures was roused among the workers. As soon as the workers realized that the Social-Democratic study circles desired to, and could, supply them with a new kind of leaflet that told the whole truth about their miserable existence, about their unbearably hard toil, and their lack of rights, they began to send in, actually flood us with, correspondence from the factories and workshops. This 'exposure literature' created a tremendous sensation, not only in the particular factory exposed in the given leaflet, but in all the factories to which news of the revealed facts spread. And since the poverty and want among the workers in the various enterprises and in the various trades are much the same, the 'truth about the life of the workers' stirred everyone. Even among the most backward workers, a veritable passion arose to 'get into print' — a noble passion for this rudimentary form of war against the whole of the present social system which is based upon robbery and oppression. And, in the overwhelming majority of cases, these 'leaflets' were, in truth, a declaration of war, because

[2] Lenin — [To avoid misunderstanding, we must point out that here, and throughout this pamphlet, by economic struggle, we imply (in keeping with the accepted usage among us) the 'practical economic struggle', which Engels, in the passage quoted above, described as 'resistance to the capitalists', and which in free countries is known as the organized-labour syndical, or trade union struggle].

the exposures served greatly to agitate the workers; they evoked among them common demands for the removal of the most glaring outrages and roused in them a readiness to support the demands with strikes. Finally, the employers themselves were compelled to recognize the significance of these leaflets as a declaration of war, so much so that in a large number of cases, they did not even wait for the outbreak of hostilities. As is always the case, the mere publication of these exposures made them effective, and they acquired the significance of a strong moral influence. On more than one occasion, the mere appearance of a leaflet proved sufficient to secure the satisfaction of all or part of the demands put forward. In a word, economic (factory) exposures were and remain an important lever in the economic struggle. And they will continue to retain this significance as long as there is capitalism, which makes it necessary for the workers to defend themselves. Even in the most advanced countries of Europe, it can still be seen that the exposure of abuses in some backward trade, or in some forgotten branch of domestic industry, serves as a starting point for the awakening of class-consciousness, for the beginning of a trade union struggle, and for the spread of socialism.[3]

The overwhelming majority of Russian Social-Democrats have of late been almost entirely absorbed by this work of organizing

[3] Lenin — [In the present chapter, we deal only with the political struggle, in its broader or narrower meaning. Therefore, we note only in passing, merely as a curiosity, *Rabocheye Dyelo*'s charge that *Iskra* is 'too restrained' in regard to the economic struggle (*Two Conferences*, p. 27, rehashed by Martynov in his pamphlet, *Social-Democracy and the Working Class*). If the accusers computed by the hundredweights or reams (as they are so fond of doing) any given year's discussion of the economic struggle in the industrial section of *Iskra*, in comparison with the corresponding sections of *Rabocheye Dyelo* and *Rabochaya Mysl* combined, they would easily see that the latter lag behind even in this respect. Apparently, the realization of this simple truth compels them to resort to arguments that clearly reveal their confusion. '*Iskra*,' they write, 'willy-nilly [!] is compelled [!] to reckon with the imperative demands of life and to publish at least [!!] correspondence about the working-class movement' (*Two Conferences*, p. 27). Now, this is really a crushing argument!].

the exposure of factory conditions. Suffice it to recall *Rabochaya Mysl* to see the extent to which they have been absorbed by it — so much so, indeed, that they have lost sight of the fact that this, *taken by itself*, is in essence still not Social-Democratic work, but merely trade union work. As a matter of fact, the exposures merely dealt with the relations between the workers *in a given trade* and their employers, and all they achieved was that the sellers of labour power learned to sell their 'commodity' on better terms and to fight the purchasers over a purely commercial deal. These exposures could have served (if properly utilized by an organization of revolutionaries) as a beginning and a component part of Social-Democratic activity; but they could also have led (and, given a worshipful attitude towards spontaneity, were bound to lead) to a 'purely trade union' struggle and to a non-Social-Democratic working-class movement. Social-Democracy leads the struggle of the working class, not only for better terms for the sale of labour power but for the abolition of the social system that compels the property-less to sell themselves to the rich. Social-Democracy represents the working class, not in its relation to a given group of employers alone, but in its relation to all classes of modern society and to the state as an organised political force. Hence, it follows that not only must Social-Democrats not confine themselves exclusively to the economic struggle, but that they must not allow the organization of economic exposures to become the predominant part of their activities. We must take up actively the political education of the working class and the development of its political consciousness. *Now* that *Zarya* and *Iskra* have made the first attack upon Economism, 'all are agreed' on this (although some agree only in words, as we shall soon see).

The question arises, what should political education consist of? Can it be confined to the propaganda of working-class hostility to the autocracy? Of course not. It is not enough *to explain* to the workers that they are politically oppressed (any more than it is *to explain* to them that their interests are antagonistic to the interests of the employers). Agitation must be conducted with regard to every concrete example of *this* oppression (as we have begun to carry on agitation around concrete examples of economic oppression). In as much as this oppression affects the most diverse classes of society, inasmuch as it manifests itself in the most varied spheres of life and activity — vocational, civic, personal, family, religious, scientific, etc., etc. — is it not evident that *we shall not be fulfilling our task* of developing the political consciousness of the workers if we do not *undertake* the organisation of the *political exposure* of the autocracy in *all its aspects*? In order to carry on agitation round concrete instances of oppression, these instances must be exposed (as it is necessary to expose factory abuses in order to carry on economic agitation).

One might think this to be clear enough. It turns out, however, that it is only in words that 'all' are agreed on the need to develop political consciousness, *in all its aspects*. It turns out that *Rabocheye Dyelo*, for example, far from tackling the task of organizing (or making a start in organizing) comprehensive political exposure, is even trying *to drag Iskra*, which has undertaken this task, *away from it*. Listen to the following: 'The political struggle of the working class is merely [it is certainly not 'merely'] the most developed, wide, and effective form of economic struggle' (programme of *Rabocheye Dyelo*, published in issue No. 1, p. 3). 'The Social-Democrats are now confronted with the task of lending the economic struggle itself, as far as possible, a political character' (Martynov, *Rabocheye Dyelo*, No. 10, p. 42). 'The economic struggle is the most widely applicable means of drawing the masses into active political struggle' (resolution adopted by the Conference of the Union Abroad and 'amendments' thereto, *Two Conferences*, pp. 11 and 17). As the reader will observe, all these theses permeate *Rabocheye Dyelo* from its very first number to the latest 'Instructions to the Editors', and all of them evidently express a single view regarding political agitation and struggle. Let us examine this view from the standpoint of the opinion prevailing among all Economists, that political agitation must *follow* economic agitation. Is it true that, in general,[4] the economic struggle 'is the most widely applicable means' of drawing the masses into the political struggle? It is entirely untrue. *Any and every* manifestation of police tyranny and autocratic outrage, not only in connection with the economic struggle, is not one whit less 'widely applicable' as a means of 'drawing in' the masses. The rural superintendents and the flogging of peasants, the corruption of the officials and the police treatment of the 'common people' in the cities, the fight against the famine-stricken and the suppression of the popular striving towards enlightenment and knowledge, the extortion of taxes and the persecution of the religious sects, the humiliating treatment of soldiers and the barrack methods in the treatment of the students and liberal intellectuals — do all these and a thousand other similar manifestations of tyranny, though not directly connected with the 'economic' struggle, represent, in general, *less* 'widely applicable' means and occasions for political agitation and for drawing the masses into the political struggle? The very opposite is true. Of the sum total of cases in which the workers suffer (either on their own account or on account of those closely connected with them) from tyranny, violence, and the lack of rights, undoubtedly only a small minority represent cases of police tyranny in the trade union struggle as such. Why then should we, beforehand, *restrict* the scope of political agitation by declaring only *one* of the means to be 'the most widely applicable',

[4] Lenin — [We say 'in general', because *Rabocheye Dyelo* speaks of general principles and of the general tasks of the Party as a whole. Undoubtedly, cases occur in practice when politics really *must* follow economics, but only Economists can speak of this in a resolution intended to apply to the whole of Russia. Cases do occur when *it is possible* 'right from the beginning' to carry on political agitation 'exclusively on an economic basis'; yet *Rabocheye Dyelo* came in the end to the conclusion that 'there is no need for this whatever' (*Two Conferences*, p. 11). In the following chapter, we shall show that the tactics of the 'politicians' and revolutionaries not only do not ignore the trade union tasks of Social-Democracy, but that, on the contrary, they alone *can secure* their consistent fulfilment].

when Social-Democrats must have, in addition, other, generally speaking, no less 'widely applicable' means?

In the dim and distant past, a full year ago!, *Rabocheye Dyelo* wrote: 'The masses begin to understand immediate political demands after one strike, or at all events, after several', 'as soon as the government sets the police and gendarmerie against them' [August (No. 7) 1900, p. 15]. This opportunist theory of stages has now been rejected by the Union Abroad, which makes a concession to us by declaring: 'There is no need whatever to conduct political agitation right from the beginning, exclusively on an economic basis' (Two Conferences, p. 11). The Union's repudiation of part of its former errors will show the future historian of Russian Social-Democracy better than any number of lengthy arguments the depths to which our Economists have degraded socialism! But the Union Abroad must be very naive indeed to imagine that the abandonment of one form of restricting politics will induce us to agree to another form. Would it not be more logical to say, in this case too, that the economic struggle should be conducted on the widest possible basis, that it should always be utilized for political agitation, but that 'there is no need whatever' to regard the economic struggle as the most widely applicable means of drawing the masses into active political struggle?

The Union Abroad attaches significance to the fact that it has substituted the phrase 'most widely applicable means' for the phrase 'the best means' contained in one of the resolutions of the Fourth Congress of the Jewish Workers' Union (Bund). We confess that we find it difficult to say which of these resolutions is the better one. In our opinion, they are both worse. Both the Union Abroad and the Bund fall into the error (partly, perhaps unconsciously, under the influence of tradition) of giving an Economist, trade-unionist interpretation to politics. Whether this is done by employing the word 'best' or the words 'most widely applicable' makes no essential difference whatever. Had the Union Abroad said that 'political agitation on an economic basis' is the most widely applied (not 'applicable') means, it would have been right in regard to a certain period in the development of our Social-Democratic movement. It would have been right in regard to the Economists and to many (if not the majority) of the practical workers of 1898-1901; for these practical Economists applied political agitation (to the extent that they applied it at all) almost exclusively on an economic basis. Political agitation on such lines was recognized and, as we have seen, even recommended by *Rabochaya Mysl* and the Self-Emancipation Group. *Rabocheye Dyelo* should have strongly condemned the fact that the useful work of economic agitation was accompanied by the harmful restriction of the political struggle; instead, it declares the means most widely applied (by the Economists) to be the most widely applicable! It is not surprising that when we call these people Economists, they can do nothing but pour every manner of abuse upon us; call us 'mystifiers', 'disrupters', 'papal nuncios', and 'slanderers'[5] go complaining to the whole world that we have mortally offended them; and declare almost on oath that 'not a single Social-Democratic organization is now tinged with Economism'.[6] Oh, those evil, slanderous politicians! They must have deliberately invented this Economism out of sheer hatred of mankind in order to mortally offend other people.

What concrete, real meaning attaches to Martynov's words when he sets before Social- Democracy the task of 'lending the economic struggle itself a political character'? The economic struggle is the collective struggle of the workers against their employers for better terms in the sale of their labour-power, for better living and working conditions. This struggle is necessarily a trade union struggle, because working conditions differ greatly in different trades, and, consequently, the struggle to improve them can only be conducted on the basis of trade organizations (in the Western countries, through trade unions; in Russia,

[5] Lenin — [These are the precise expressions used in *Two Conferences*, pp. 31, 32, 28, and 80].

[6] Lenin — [*Two Conferences*, p. 32].

through temporary trade associations and through leaflets, etc.). Lending 'the economic struggle itself a political character' means, therefore, striving to secure satisfaction of these trade demands, the improvement of working conditions in each separate trade by means of 'legislative and administrative measures' (as Martynov puts it on the ensuing page of his article, p. 43). This is precisely what all workers' trade unions do and always have done. Read the works of the soundly scientific (and 'soundly' opportunist) Mr and Mrs Webb and you will see that the British trade unions long ago recognized, and have long been carrying out, the task of 'lending the economic struggle itself a political character'; they have long been fighting for the right to strike, for the removal of all legal hindrances to the cooperative and trade union movements, for laws to protect women and children, for the improvement of labour conditions by means of health and factory legislation, etc.

Thus, the pompous phrase about 'lending the economic struggle itself a political character', which sounds so 'terrifically' profound and revolutionary, serves as a screen to conceal what is, in fact the traditional striving to degrade Social-Democratic politics to the level of trade union politics. Under the guise of rectifying the one-sidedness of *Iskra*, which, it is alleged, places 'the revolutionizing of dogma higher than the revolutionizing of life',[7] we are presented with the struggle for economic reforms as if it were something entirely new. In point of fact, the phrase 'lending the economic struggle itself a political character' means nothing more than the struggle for economic reforms. Martynov himself might have come to this simple conclusion, had he pondered over the significance of his own words. 'Our Party,' he says, training his heaviest guns on *Iskra*, 'could and should have presented concrete

[7] Lenin — [*Rabocheye Dyelo*, No. 10, p. 60. This is the Martynov variation of the application, which we have characterized above, of the thesis 'every step of real movement is more important than a dozen programmes' to the present chaotic state of our movement. In fact, this is merely a translation into Russian of the notorious Bernsteinian sentence: 'The movement is everything, the final aim is nothing'].

demands to the government for legislative and administrative measures against economic exploitation, unemployment, famine, etc.' (*Rabocheye Dyelo*, No. 10, pp. 42–43). Concrete demands for measures — does not this mean demands for social reforms? Again we ask the impartial reader: Are we slandering the *Rabocheye Dyelo*-ites (may I be forgiven for this awkward, currently used designation!) by calling them concealed Bernsteinians when, as their point of disagreement with *Iskra*, they advance their thesis on the necessity of struggling for economic reforms?

Revolutionary Social-Democracy has always included the struggle for reforms as part of its activities. But it utilizes 'economic' agitation for the purpose of presenting to the government, not only demands for all sorts of measures, but also (and primarily) the demand that it cease to be an autocratic government. Moreover, it considers it as its duty to present this demand to the government on the basis, not of the economic struggle alone, but of all manifestations in general of public and political life. In a word, it subordinates the struggle for reforms, as the part to the whole, to the revolutionary struggle for freedom and for socialism. Martynov, however, resuscitates the theory of stages in a new form and strives to prescribe, as it were, an exclusively economic path of development for the political struggle. By advancing at this moment, when the revolutionary movement is on the upgrade, an alleged special 'task' of struggling for reforms, he is dragging the Party backwards and is playing into the hands of both 'Economist' and liberal opportunism.

To proceed. Shamefacedly hiding the struggle for reforms behind the pompous thesis of 'lending the economic struggle itself a political character', Martynov advanced, as if it were a special point, exclusively economic (indeed, exclusively factory) reforms. As to the reason for his doing that, we do not know it. Carelessness, perhaps? Yet, if he had in mind something else besides 'factory' reforms, then the whole of his thesis, which we have cited, loses all sense. Perhaps he did it because he considers it possible and probable that the government will make 'concessions' only in the economic sphere?[8] If so, then it is a strange delusion. Concessions are also possible and are made in the sphere of legislation concerning flogging, passports, land redemption payments, religious sects, the censorship, etc., etc. 'Economic' concessions (or pseudo-concessions) are, of course, the cheapest and most advantageous from the government's point of view, because by these means it hopes to win the confidence of the working masses. For this very reason, we Social-Democrats must not under any circumstances or in any way whatever create grounds for the belief (or the misunderstanding) that we attach greater value to economic reforms, or that we regard them as being particularly important, etc. 'Such demands,' writes Martynov, speaking of the concrete demands for legislative and administrative measures referred to above, 'would not be merely a hollow sound, because, promising certain palpable results, they might be actively supported by the working masses'. We are not Economists, oh no! We only cringe as slavishly before the 'palpableness' of concrete results as do the Bernsteins, the Prokopoviches, the Struves, the R.M.s, and tutti quanti! We only wish to make it understood (together with Nartsis Tuporylov) that all that 'do not promise palpable results' is merely a 'hollow sound'! We are only trying to argue as if the working masses were incapable (and had not already proved their capabilities, notwithstanding those who ascribe their own philistinism to them) of actively supporting every protest against the autocracy, even if it promises absolutely no palpable results whatsoever!

Let us take, for example, the very 'measures' for the relief of unemployment and the famine that Martynov himself advances. *Rabocheye Dyelo* is engaged, judging by what it has promised, in

[8] Lenin — [p. 43. 'Of course, when we advise the workers to present certain economic demands to the government, we do so because in the *economic* sphere the autocratic government is, of necessity, prepared to make certain concessions!'].

drawing up and elaborating a programme of 'concrete [in the form of bills?] demands for legislative and administrative measures', 'promising palpable results', while *Iskra*, which 'constantly places the revolutionizing of dogma higher than the revolutionizing of life', has tried to explain the inseparable connection between unemployment and the whole capitalist system, has given warning that 'famine is coming', has exposed the police 'fight against the famine-stricken', and the outrageous 'provisional penal servitude regulations'; and Zarya has published a special reprint, in the form of an agitational pamphlet, of a section of its 'Review of Home Affairs', dealing with the famine.[9] But good God! How 'one-sided' were these incorrigibly narrow and orthodox doctrinaires, how deaf to the calls of 'life itself'! Their articles contained — oh horror! — not a single, can you imagine it? Not a single 'concrete demand' 'promising palpable results'! Poor doctrinaires! They ought to be sent to Krichevsky and Martynov to be taught that tactics are a process of growth, of that which grows, etc., and that the economic struggle itself should be given a political character![10]

'In addition to its immediate revolutionary significance, the economic struggle of the workers against the employers and the government ['economic struggle against the government'!] has also this significance: it constantly brings home to the workers the fact that they have no political rights' (Martynov, p. 44). We quote this passage, not in order to repeat for the hundredth and thousandth time what has been said above, but in order to express particular thanks to Martynov for this excellent new formula: 'the economic struggle of the workers against the employers and the government'. What a gem! With what inimitable skill and mastery in eliminating all partial disagreements and shades of differences among Economists, this clear and concise proposition expresses the quintessence of Economism, from summoning the workers 'to

[9] Lenin, 'Famine', *Review of Home Affairs*, *Zarya*, December 1901, *Collected Works*, vol 5, pp. 253-74.

[10] Boris Krichevsky (1866–1919) was the editor of *Rabocheye Dyelo*.

the political struggle, which they carry on in the general interest, for the improvement of the conditions of all the workers',[11] continuing through the theory of stages, and ending in the resolution of the Conference on the 'most widely applicable', etc. 'Economic struggle against the government' is precisely trade-unionist politics, which is still very far from being Social-Democratic politics.

3.2 HOW MARTYNOV RENDERED PLEKHANOV MORE PROFOUND

'What a large number of Social-Democratic Lomonosovs have appeared among us lately!', observed a comrade one day, having in mind the astonishing propensity of many who are inclined toward Economism to, arrive, 'necessarily, by their own understanding', at great truths (e.g., that the economic struggle stimulates the workers to ponder over their lack of rights) and in doing so to ignore, with the supreme contempt of born geniuses, all that has been produced by the antecedent development of revolutionary thought and of the revolutionary movement. Lomonosov-Martynov is precisely such a born genius. We need but glance at his article 'Urgent Questions' to see how by 'his own understanding' he *arrives at* what was long ago said by Axelrod (of whom our Lomonosov, naturally, says not a word); how, for instance, he is *beginning* to understand that we cannot ignore the opposition of such or such strata of the bourgeoisie (*Rabocheye Dyelo*, No. 9, pp. 61, 62, 71; compare this with *Rabocheye Dyelo's* Reply to Axelrod, pp. 22, 23-24), etc. But alas, he is only 'arriving' and is only 'beginning', not more than that, for so little has he understood Axelrod's ideas, that he talks about 'the economic struggle against the employers and the government'. For three years (1898–1901) *Rabocheye Dyelo* has tried hard to understand Axelrod, but has so far not understood him! Can one of the reasons be that Social-Democracy, 'like mankind', always sets itself only tasks that can be achieved?

[11] Lenin — [*Rabochaya Mysl*, 'Separate Supplement', p. 14].

But the Lomonosovs are distinguished not only by their ignorance of many things (that would be but half misfortune!), but also by their unawareness of their own ignorance. Now this is a real misfortune, and it is this misfortune that prompts them without further ado to attempt to render Plekhanov 'more profound'.

'Much water', Lomonosov-Martynov says, 'has flowed under the bridge since Plekhanov wrote his book (Tasks of the Socialists in the Fight Against the Famine in Russia). The Social-Democrats who for a decade led the economic struggle of the working class ... have failed as yet to lay down a broad theoretical basis for Party tactics. This question has now come to a head, and if we should wish to lay down such a theoretical basis, we should certainly have to deepen considerably the principles of tactics developed at one time by Plekhanov. ... Our present definition of the distinction between propaganda and agitation would have to be different from Plekhanov's (Martynov has just quoted Plekhanov's words: 'A propagandist presents many ideas to one or a few persons; an agitator presents only one or a few ideas, but he presents them to a mass of people.') By propaganda, we would understand the revolutionary explanation of the present social system, entire or in its partial manifestations, whether that be done in a form intelligible to individuals or to broad masses. By agitation, in the strict sense of the word (sic!), we would understand the call upon the masses to undertake definite, concrete actions and the promotion of the direct revolutionary intervention of the proletariat in social life.'

We congratulate Russian and international-Social-Democracy on having found, thanks to Martynov, a new terminology, more strict and more profound. Hitherto, we thought (with Plekhanov, and with all the leaders of the international working-class movement) that the propagandist, dealing with, say, the question of unemployment, must explain the capitalistic nature of crises, the cause of their inevitability in modern society, the necessity for the transformation of this society into a socialist society, etc. In a word, he must present 'many ideas', so many, indeed, that they will be understood as an integral whole only by a (comparatively) few persons. The agitator, however, speaking on the same subject, will take as an illustration a fact that is most glaring and most widely known to his audience, say, the death of an unemployed worker's family from starvation, the growing impoverishment, etc., and, utilizing this fact, known to all, will direct his efforts to present a single idea to the 'masses', e.g., the senselessness of the contradiction between the increase of wealth and the increase of poverty; he will strive to rouse discontent and indignation among the masses against this crying injustice, leaving a more complete explanation of this contradiction to the propagandist. Consequently, the propagandist operates chiefly by means of the printed word; the agitator by means of the spoken word. The propagandist requires qualities different from those of the agitator. Kautsky and Lafargue, for example, we term propagandists; Bebel and Guesde, we term agitators.[12] To single out a third sphere, or third function, of practical activity and to include in this function 'the call upon the masses to undertake definite concrete actions', is sheer nonsense, because the 'call', as a single act, either naturally and inevitably supplements the theoretical treatise, propagandist pamphlet, and agitational speech, or represents a purely executive function. Let us take, for example, the struggle the German Social-Democrats are now waging against the corn duties. The theoreticians write research works on tariff policy, with the 'call', say, to struggle for commercial treaties and for Free Trade. The propagandist does the same thing in the periodical press, and the agitator in public speeches. At the present time, the 'concrete action' of the masses takes the form of signing petitions to the Reichstag against raising the corn duties. The call for this action

[12] Jules Guesde (1845–1922) was one of the leading French advocates for Marxism through a range of important journals (including *Les Droits de l'Homme* and *Égalité*). Marx accused the Guesdists of 'revolutionary phrase-mongering'. A strong advocate of revolutionary politics, Guesde became reformist at the end of his life, including supporting World War I. Lenin is referring to his and August Bebel's well-known oratory skills.

comes indirectly from the theoreticians, the propagandists, and the agitators, and, directly, from the workers who take the petition lists to the factories and to private homes for the gathering of signatures. According to the 'Martynov terminology', Kautsky and Bebel are both propagandists, while those who solicit the signatures are agitators. Isn't it clear?

The German example recalled to my mind the German word which, literally translated, means 'Ballhorning'. Johann Ballhorn, a Leipzig publisher of the sixteenth century, published a child's reader in which, as was the custom, he introduced a drawing of a cock, but a cock without spurs and with a couple of eggs lying near it. On the cover, he printed the legend, 'Revised edition by Johann Ballhorn'. Ever since then, the Germans describe any 'revision' that is really a worsening as 'ballhorning'. And one cannot help recalling Ballhorn upon seeing how the Martynovs try to render Plekhanov 'more profound'.

Why did our Lomonosov 'invent' this confusion? In order to illustrate how *Iskra* 'devotes attention only to one side of the case, just as Pleklianov did a decade and a half ago' (39). 'With *Iskra*, propagandist tasks force agitational tasks into the background, at least for the present' (52). If we translate this last proposition from the language of Martynov into ordinary human language (because mankind has not yet managed to learn the newly-invented terminology), we shall get the following: with *Iskra*, the tasks of political propaganda and political agitation force into the background the task of 'presenting to the government concrete demands for legislative and administrative measures' that 'promise certain palpable results' (or demands for social reforms, that is, if we are permitted once again to employ the old terminology of the old mankind not yet grown to Martynov's level). We suggest that the reader compare this thesis with the following tirade:

> 'What also astonishes us in these programmes [the programmes advanced by revolutionary Social-Democrats] is

> their constant stress upon the benefits of workers' activity in parliament (non-existent in Russia), though they completely ignore (thanks to their revolutionary nihilism) the importance of workers' participation in the legislative manufacturers' assemblies on factory affairs [which do exist in Russia] . . . or at least the importance of workers' participation in municipal bodies.'

The author of this tirade expresses in a somewhat more forthright and clearer manner the very idea which Lomonosov-Martynov discovered by his own understanding. The author is R. M., in the *'Separate Supplement' to Rabochaya Mysl* (p. 15).

3.3. POLITICAL EXPOSURES AND 'TRAINING IN REVOLUTIONARY ACTIVITY'.

In advancing against *Iskra*, his theory of 'raising the activity of the working masses', Martynov actually betrayed an urge to belittle that activity, for he declared the very economic struggle before which all economists grovel to be the preferable, particularly important, and 'most widely applicable' means of rousing this activity and its broadest field. This error is characteristic, precisely in that it is by no means peculiar to Martynov. In reality, it is possible to 'raise the activity of the working masses' only when this activity is not restricted to 'political agitation on an economic basis'. A basic condition for the necessary expansion of political agitation is the organization of comprehensive political exposure. In no way, except by means of such exposures, can the masses be trained in political consciousness and revolutionary activity. Hence, activity of this kind is one of the most important functions of international Social-Democracy as a whole, for even political freedom does not in any way eliminate exposures; it merely shifts somewhat their sphere of direction. Thus, the German party is especially strengthening its positions and spreading its influence, thanks particularly to the untiring energy with which it is conducting its campaign of political exposure. Working-class consciousness cannot be genuine political consciousness unless the workers are trained to respond to all cases of tyranny, oppression, violence, and abuse, no matter what class is affected — unless they are trained, moreover, to respond from a Social-Democratic point of view and no other. The consciousness of the working masses cannot be genuine class-consciousness, unless the workers learn, from concrete, and above all from topical, political facts and events to observe every other social class in all the manifestations of its intellectual, ethical, and political life; unless they learn to apply in practice the materialist analysis and the materialist estimate of all aspects of the life and activity of all classes, strata, and groups of the population. Those who concentrate the attention, observation, and consciousness of the working class exclusively, or even mainly, upon itself alone are not Social-Democrats; for the self-knowledge of the working class is indissolubly bound up, not solely with a fully clear theoretical understanding —or rather, not so much with the theoretical, as with the practical, understanding — of the relationships between all the various classes of modern society, acquired through the experience of political life. For this reason, the conception of the economic struggle as the most widely applicable means of drawing the masses into the political movement, which our Economists preach, isso extremely harmful and reactionary in its practical significance. In order to become a Social-Democrat, the worker must have a clear picture in his mind of the economic nature and the social and political features of the landlord and the priest, the high state official and the peasant, the student and the vagabond; he must know their strong and weak points; he must grasp the meaning of all the catchwords and sophisms by which each class and each stratum camouflages its selfish strivings and its real 'inner workings'; he must understand what interests are reflected by certain institutions and certain laws and how they are reflected. But this 'clear picture' cannot be obtained from any book. It can be obtained only from living examples and from exposures that follow closely upon what is going on about us at a given moment; upon what is being discussed, in whispers perhaps, by each one in his own way; upon what finds expression in such and such events, in such and such statistics, in such and such court sentences, etc., etc. These comprehensive political exposures are an essential and fundamental condition for training the masses in revolutionary activity.

Why do the Russian workers still manifest little revolutionary activity in response to the brutal treatment of the people by the police, the persecution of religious sects, the flogging of peasants, the outrageous censorship, the torture of soldiers, the persecution of the most innocent cultural undertakings, etc.? Is it because the 'economic struggle' does not 'stimulate' them to this, because such activity does not 'promise palpable results', because it produces little that is 'positive'? To adopt such an opinion, we repeat, is merely to direct the charge where it does not belong, to blame the working masses for one's own philistinism (or Bernsteinism). We must blame ourselves, our lagging behind the mass movement, for still being unable to organize sufficiently wide, striking, and rapid exposures of all the shameful outrages. When we do that (and we must and can do it), the most backward worker will understand *or will feel,* that the students and religious sects, the peasants and the authors are being abused and outraged by those same dark forces that are oppressing and crushing him at every step of his life. Feeling that, he himself will be filled with an irresistible desire to react, and he will know how to hoot the censors one day, on another day to demonstrate outside the house of a governor who has brutally suppressed a peasant uprising, on still another day to teach a lesson to the gendarmes in surplices who are doing the work of the Holy Inquisition, etc. As yet, we have done very little, almost nothing, *to bring* before the working masses prompt exposures on all possible issues. Many of us, as yet do not recognize this as our *bounden duty* but trail spontaneously in the wake of the 'drab everyday struggle', in the narrow confines of factory life. Under such circumstances, to say that '*Iskra* displays a tendency to minimize the significance of the forward march of the drab everyday struggle in comparison with the propaganda of brilliant and complete ideas' (Martynov, op. cit., p. 61), means to drag the Party back, to defend and glorify our unpreparedness and backwardness.

As for calling the masses to action, that will come of itself as soon as energetic political agitation, live and striking exposures come into play. To catch some criminal red-handed and to immediately brand him publicly in all places is of itself far more effective than any number of 'calls'; the effect very often is such as will make it impossible to tell exactly who it was that 'called' upon the masses and who suggested this or that plan of demonstration, etc. Calls for action, not in the general, but in the concrete sense of the term, can be made only at the place of action; only those who themselves go into action, and do so immediately, can sound such calls. Our business as Social-Democratic publicists is to deepen, expand, and intensify political exposure and political agitation.

A word in passing about 'calls to action'. The only newspaper that, prior to the spring events, called upon the workers to intervene actively in a matter that certainly did not promise any palpable results whatever for the workers, i.e., the drafting of the students into the army, was *Iskra*. Immediately after the publication of the order of 11 January, on 'drafting the 183 students into the army', *Iskra* published an article on the matter (in its February issue, No. 2[13]), and, before any demonstration was begun, forthwith called upon 'the workers to go to the aid of the students', called upon the 'people' openly to take up the government's arrogant challenge. We ask: how is the remarkable fact to be explained that although Martynov talks so much about 'calls to action', and even suggests 'calls to action' as a special form of activity, he said not a word about this call? After this, was it not sheer philistinism on Martynov's part

[13] Lenin, 'The Drafting of 183 Students into the Army', *Iskra*, no. 2, February 1901, *Collected Works*, vol. 4, pp. 414–419.

to allege that *Iskra* was one-sided because it did not issue sufficient 'calls' to struggle for demands 'promising palpable results'?

Our Economists, including *Rabocheye Dyelo*, were successful because they adapted themselves to the backward workers. But the Social-Democratic worker, the revolutionary worker (and the number of such workers is growing) will indignantly reject all this talk about the struggle for demands 'promising palpable results', etc., because he will understand that this is only a variation of the old song about adding a kopek to the ruble. Such a worker will say to his counsellors from *Rabochaya Mysl* and *Rabocheye Dyelo*: you are busying yourselves in vain, gentlemen, and shirking your proper duties, by meddling with such excessive zeal in a job that we can very well manage ourselves. There is nothing clever in your assertion that the Social-Democrats' task is to lend the economic struggle itself a political character; that is only the beginning, it is not the main task of the Social-Democrats. For all over the world, including Russia, the police themselves often take the initiative in lending the economic struggle a political character, and the workers themselves learn to understand whom the government supports.[14]

[14] Lenin — [The demand 'to lend the economic struggle itself a political character' most strikingly expresses *subservience to spontaneity* in the sphere of political activity. Very often, the economic struggle *spontaneously* assumes a political character, that is to say, without the intervention of the 'revolutionary bacilli — the intelligentsia', without the intervention of the class-conscious Social-Democrats. The economic struggle of the English workers, for instance, also assumed a political character without any intervention on the part of the socialists. The task of the Social-Democrats, however, is not exhausted by political agitation on an economic basis; their task is *to convert* trade-unionist politics into Social-Democratic political struggle, *to utilize* the sparks of political consciousness which the economic struggle generates among the workers, for the purpose of *raising* the workers to the level of *Social-Democratic* political consciousness. The Martynovs, however, instead of raising and stimulating the spontaneously awakening political consciousness of the workers, *bow to spontaneity* and repeat over and over *ad nauseam* that the economic struggle 'impels' the workers to realize their own lack of political rights. It is unfortunate, gentlemen, that the spontaneously awakening trade-unionist political consciousness does not '*impel*' you to an understanding of your Social-Democratic tasks].

The 'economic struggle of the workers against the employers and the government', about which you make as much fuss as if you had discovered a new America, is being waged in all parts of Russia, even the most remote, by the workers themselves who have heard about strikes, but who have heard almost nothing about socialism. The 'activity' you want to stimulate among us workers, by advancing concrete demands that promise palpable results, we are already displaying and in our everyday limited trade union work, we put forward these concrete demands, very often without any assistance whatever from the intellectuals. But such activity is not enough for us; we are not children to be fed on the thin gruel of 'economic' politics alone; we want to know everything that others know, we want to learn the details of all aspects of political life and to take part actively in every single political event. In order that we may do this, the intellectuals must talk to us less of what we already know and tell us more about what we do not yet know and what we can never learn from our factory and 'economic' experience, namely, political knowledge.[15] You intellectuals can acquire this

[15] Lenin — [To prove that this imaginary speech of a worker to an Economist is based on fact, we shall refer to two witnesses who undoubtedly have direct knowledge of the working-class movement and who are least of all inclined to be partial towards us 'doctrinaires'; for one witness is an Economist (who regards even *Rabocheye Dyelo* as a political organ!), and the other is a terrorist. The first witness is the author of a remarkably truthful and vivid article entitled 'The St. Petersburg Working-Class Movement and the Practical Tasks of Social-Democracy', published in *Rabocheye Dyelo* No. 6. He divides the workers into the following categories: (1) class-conscious revolutionaries; (2) intermediate stratum; and (3) the remaining masses. The intermediate stratum, he says, 'is often more interested in questions of political life than in its own immediate economic interests, the connection between which and the general social conditions it has long understood'. *Rabochaya Mysl* 'is sharply criticized': 'It keeps on repeating the same thing over and over again, things we have long known, read long ago.' 'Again nothing in the political review!' (pp. 30–31). But even the third stratum, 'the younger and more sensitive section of the workers, less corrupted by the tavern and the church, who hardly ever have the opportunity of getting hold of political literature, discuss political events in a rambling way and ponder over the fragmentary news they get about student riots', etc. The terrorist writes as follows: They read over once or twice the petty details of factory

knowledge, and it is your duty to bring it to us in a hundred- and a-thousand-fold greater measure than you have done up to now; and you must bring it to us, not only in the form of discussions, pamphlets, and articles (which very often — pardon our frankness — are rather dull), but precisely in the form of vivid exposures of what our government and our governing classes are doing at this very moment in all spheres of life. Devote more zeal to carrying out this duty and talk less about 'raising the activity of the working masses'. We are far more active than you think, and we are quite able to support, by open street fighting, even demands that do not promise any 'palpable results' whatsoever. It is not for you to 'raise' our activity because activity is precisely the thing you yourselves lack. Bow less in subservience to spontaneity, and think more about raising your own activity, gentlemen!

3.4. WHAT IS THERE IN COMMON BETWEEN ECONOMISM AND TERRORISM?

In the last footnote, we cited the opinion of an Economist and of a non-Social-Democratic terrorist, who showed themselves to be accidentally in agreement. Speaking generally, however, there is not an accidental, but a necessary, inherent connection between the two, of which we shall have need to speak later, and which must be mentioned here in connection with the question of education for revolutionary activity. The Economists and the root, namely, subservience to spontaneity, with which we dealt in the preceding chapter as a general phenomenon and which we shall now examine in relation to its effect upon political activity and the political struggle. At first sight, our assertion may appear

life in other towns, not their own, and then they read no more ... dull, they find it.... To say nothing in a workers' paper about the government ... is to regard the workers as being little children.... The workers are not little children' (*Svoboda*, published by the Revolutionary-Socialist Group, pp. 69-70)].

paradoxical, so great is the difference between those who stress the 'drab everyday struggle' and those who call for the most self-sacrificing struggle of individuals. But this is no paradox. The Economists and the terrorists merely bow to different poles of spontaneity; the Economists bow to the spontaneity of 'the labour movement pure and simple', while the terrorists bow to the spontaneity of the passionate indignation of intellectuals, who lack the ability or opportunity to connect the revolutionary struggle and the working-class movement into an integral whole. It is difficult indeed for those who have lost their belief, or who have never believed, that this is possible, to find some outlet for their indignation and revolutionary energy other than terror. Thus, both forms of subservience to spontaneity we have mentioned are nothing but the beginning of the implementation of the notorious Credo programme: Let the workers wage their 'economic struggle against the employers and the government' (we apologize to the author of the Credo for expressing her views in Martynov's words). We think we have a right to do so since the Credo, too, says that in the economic struggle the workers 'come up against the political regime and let the intellectuals conduct the political struggle by their own efforts — with the aid of terror, of course! This is an absolutely logical and inevitable conclusion which must be insisted on — even though those who are beginning to carry out this programme do not themselves realize that it is inevitable. Political activity has its logic quite apart from the consciousness of those who, with the best intentions, call either for terror or for lending the economic struggle itself a political character. The road to hell is paved with good intentions, and, in this case, good intentions cannot save one from being spontaneously drawn 'along the line of least resistance', along the line of the purely bourgeois Credo programme. Surely, it is no accident either that many Russian liberals — avowed liberals and liberals that wear the mask of Marxism — whole-heartedly sympathize with terror and try to foster the terrorist moods that have surged up in the present time.

The formation of the Revolutionary-Socialist *Svoboda* Group which set itself the aim of helping the working-class movement in every possible way, but which included in its programme terror, and emancipation, so to speak, from Social-Democracy — once again confirmed the remarkable perspicacity of P. B. Axelrod, who literally foretold these results of Social-Democratic waverings as far back as the end of 1897 (Present Tasks and Tactics), when he outlined his famous 'two perspectives'. All the subsequent disputes and disagreements among Russian Social-Democrats are contained, like a plant in the seed, in these two perspectives.[16]

From this point of view, it also becomes clear why *Rabocheye Dyelo*, unable to withstand the spontaneity of Economism, has likewise been unable to withstand the spontaneity of terrorism. It is highly interesting to note here the specific arguments that *Svoboda* has advanced in defence of terrorism. It 'completely denies' the deterrent role of terrorism (The Regeneration of Revolutionism, p. 64), but instead, stresses its 'excitative significance'. This is characteristic, first, as representing one of the stages of the breakup and decline of the traditional (pre-Social-Democratic) cycle of ideas which insisted upon terrorism. The admission that

[16] Lenin — [Martynov 'conceives of another, more realistic [?] dilemma' (*Social-Democracy and the Working Class*, p. 19): 'Either Social-Democracy takes over the direct leadership of the economic struggle of the proletariat and by that [!] transforms it into a revolutionary class struggle'. 'By that', i.e., apparently by the direct leadership of the economic struggle. Can Martynov cite an instance in which leading the trade-union struggle alone has succeeded in transforming a trade unionist movement into a revolutionary class movement? Can he not understand that in order to bring about this 'transformation', we must actively take up the 'direct leadership' of all-sided political agitation? 'Or the other perspective: Social-Democracy refrains from assuming the leadership of the economic struggle of the workers and so . . . clips its own wings'. In *Rabocheye Dyelo*'s opinion, quoted above, it is *Iskra* that 'refrains'. We have seen, however, that the latter *does far more than Rabocheye Dyelo* to lead the economic struggle, but that, moreover, it does not confine itself thereto and *does not narrow down* its political tasks for its sake].

the government cannot now be 'terrified' and hence disrupted, by terror, is tantamount to a complete condemnation of terror as a system of struggle, as a sphere of activity sanctioned by the programme. Secondly, it is still more characteristic as an example of the failure to understand our immediate tasks in regard to 'education for revolutionary activity'. *Svoboda* advocates terror as a means of 'exciting' the working-class movement and of giving it a 'strong impetus'. It is difficult to imagine an argument that more thoroughly disproves itself. Are there not enough outrages committed in Russian life without special 'excitants' having to be invented? On the other hand, is it not obvious that those who are not, and cannot be, roused to excitement even by Russian tyranny will stand by 'twiddling their thumbs' and watch a handful of terrorists engaged in single combat with the government? The fact is that the working masses are roused to a high pitch of excitement by the social evils in Russian life, but we are unable to gather, if one may so put it, and concentrate all these drops and streamlets of popular resentment that are brought forth to a far larger extent than we imagine by the conditions of Russian life, and that must be combined into a single gigantic torrent. That this can be accomplished is irrefutably proved by the enormous growth of the working-class movement and the eagerness, noted above, with which the workers clamour for political literature. On the other hand, calls for terror and calls to lend the economic struggle itself a political character are merely two different forms of evading the most pressing duty now resting upon Russian revolutionaries, namely, the organisation of comprehensive political agitation. *Svoboda* desires to substitute terror for agitation, openly admitting that 'as soon as intensified and strenuous agitation is begun among the masses, the excitative function of terror will be ended' (The Regeneration of Revolutionism, p. 68). This proves precisely that both the terrorists and the Economists underestimate the revolutionary activity of the masses, despite the striking evidence of the events that took place in the spring,[17] and whereas the one group goes out in search of artificial 'excitants', the other talks about 'concrete demands'. But both fail to devote sufficient attention to the development of their own activity in political agitation and in the organization of political exposures. And no other work can serve as a substitute for this task either at the present time or at any other.

3.5. THE WORKING CLASS AS VANGUARD FIGHTER FOR DEMOCRACY

We have seen that the conduct of the broadest political agitation and, consequently, of all-sided political exposures is an absolutely necessary and a *paramount* task of our activity, if this activity is to be truly Social-Democratic. However, we arrived at this conclusion solely on the grounds of the pressing needs of the working class for political knowledge and political training. But such a presentation of the question is too narrow, for it ignores the general democratic tasks of Social-Democracy, in particular of present-day Russian Social-Democracy. In order to explain the point more concretely, we shall approach the subject from an aspect that is 'nearest' to the Economist, namely, from the practical aspect. 'Everyone agrees' that it is necessary to develop the political consciousness of the working class. The question is, *how* that is to be done and what is required to do it. The economic struggle merely 'impels' the workers to realize the government's attitude towards the working class. Consequently, *however much we may try* to 'lend the economic, struggle itself a political character', *we shall never be able* to develop the political consciousness of the workers (to the level of Social-Democratic political consciousness) by keeping within the framework of the economic struggle, for *that framework is too narrow.* The Martynov formula has some value

[17] Lenin's note to the 1907 edition — [The big street demonstrations which began in the spring of 1901].

for us, not because it illustrates Martynov's aptitude for confusing things, but because it pointedly expresses the basic error that all the Economists commit, namely, their conviction that it is possible to develop the class political consciousness of the workers *from within*, so to speak, from their economic struggle, i.e., by making this struggle the exclusive (or, at least, the main) starting-point, by making it the exclusive (or, at least, the main) basis. Such a view is radically wrong. Piqued by our polemics against them, the Economists refuse to ponder deeply over the origins of these disagreements, with the result that we simply cannot understand one another. It is as if we spoke in different tongues.

Class political consciousness can be brought to the workers *only from without*, that is, only from outside the economic struggle, from outside the sphere of relations between workers and employers. The sphere from which alone it is possible to obtain this knowledge is the sphere of relationships of *all* classes and strata to the state and the government, the sphere of the interrelations between *all* classes. For that reason, the reply to the question as to what must be done to bring political knowledge to the workers cannot be merely the answer with which, in the majority of cases, the practical workers, especially those inclined towards Economism, mostly content themselves, namely: 'To go among the workers'. To bring political knowledge to the *workers*, the Social Democrats must *go among all classes of the population*; they must dispatch units of their army *in all directions*.

We deliberately select this blunt formula, we deliberately express ourselves in this sharply simplified manner, not because we desire to indulge in paradoxes, but in order to 'impel' the Economists to a realization of their tasks which they unpardonably ignore, to suggest to them strongly the difference between trade-unionist and Social-Democratic politics, which they refuse to understand. We, therefore, beg the reader not to get wrought up, but to hear us patiently to the end.

Let us take the type of Social-Democratic study circle that has become most widespread in the past few years and examine its work. It has 'contacts with the workers' and rests content with this, issuing leaflets in which abuses in the factories, the government's partiality towards the capitalists, and the tyranny of the police are strongly condemned. At workers' meetings, the discussions never, or rarely ever, go beyond the limits of these subjects. Extremely rare are the lectures and discussions held on the history of the revolutionary movement, on questions of the government's home and foreign policy, on questions of the economic evolution of Russia and of Europe, on the position of the various classes in modern society, etc. As to systematically acquiring and extending contact with other classes of society, no one even dreams of that. In fact, the ideal leader, as the majority of the members of such circles picture him, is something far more in the nature of a trade union secretary than a socialist political leader. For the secretary of any, say English, trade union always helps the workers to carry on the economic struggle; he helps them to expose factory abuses, explains the injustice of the laws and of measures that hamper the freedom to strike and to picket (i.e., to warn all and sundry that a strike is proceeding at a certain factory), explains the partiality of arbitration court judges who belong to the bourgeois classes, etc., etc. In a word, every trade union secretary conducts and helps to conduct 'the economic struggle against the employers and the government'. It cannot be too strongly maintained that this is still not Social-Democracy, that the Social-Democrat's ideal should not be the trade union secretary, but the tribune of the people, who is able to react to every manifestation of tyranny and oppression, no matter where it appears, no matter what stratum or class of the people it affects; who is able to generalize all these manifestations and produce a single picture of police violence and capitalist exploitation; who is able to take advantage of every event, however small, in order to set forth before all his socialist convictions and his democratic demands, in order to clarify for all and everyone the world-historic significance of the struggle for the emancipation of the proletariat. Compare, for example, a leader like Robert Knight (the well-known secretary and leader of the Boiler-Makers' Society, one of the most powerful trade unions in England) with Wilhelm Liebknecht and try to apply to them the contrasts that Martynov draws in his controversy with *Iskra*. You will see — I am running through Martynov's article — that Robert Knight engaged more in 'calling the masses to certain concrete actions' (Martynov, op. cit., p. 39), while Willielin Liebknecht engaged more in 'the revolutionary elucidation of the whole of the present system or partial manifestations of it' (38-39); that Robert Knight 'formulated the immediate demands of the proletariat and indicated the means by which they can be achieved' (41), whereas Wilhelm Liebknecht, while doing this, did not hold back from 'simultaneously guiding the activities of various opposition strata', 'dictating a positive programme of action for them' (41)[18]; that Robert Knight strove 'as far as possible to lend the economic struggle itself a political character' (42) and was excellently able 'to submit to the government's concrete demands promising certain palpable results' (43), whereas Liebknecht engaged to a much greater degree in 'one-sided exposures' (40); that Robert Knight attached more significance to the 'forward march of the drab everyday struggle' (61), whereas Liebknecht attached more significance to the 'propaganda of brilliant and completed ideas' (61); that Liebknecht converted the paper he was directing into 'an organ of revolutionary opposition that exposed the state of affairs in our country, particularly the political state of affairs, insofar as it affected the interests of the most varied strata of the population' (63), whereas Robert Knight 'worked for the cause of the working class in close organic connection with the proletarian struggle' (63) — if by 'close and organic connection' is meant the subservience to spontaneity which we examined above, by taking the examples

[18] Lenin — [For example, during the Franco-Prussian War, Liebknecht dictated a programme of action *for the whole of democracy*; to an even greater extent, Marx and Engels did this in 1848].

of Krichevsky and Martynov — and 'restricted the sphere of his influence', convinced, of course, as is Martynov, that 'by doing so he deepened that influence' (63). In a word, you will see that de facto Martynov reduces Social-Democracy to the level of trade-unionism, though he does so, of course, not because he does not desire the good of Social-Democracy, but simply because he is a little too much in a hurry to render Plekhanov more profound, instead of taking the trouble to understand him.

Let us return, however, to our theses. We said that a Social Democrat, if he really believes it necessary to develop comprehensively the political consciousness of the proletariat, must 'go among all classes of the population'. This gives rise to the questions: how is this to be done? Have we enough forces to do this? Is there a basis for such work among all the other classes? Will this not mean a retreat, or lead to a retreat, from the class point of view? Let us deal with these questions.

We must 'go among all classes of the population' as theoreticians, as propagandists, as agitators, and as organizers. No one doubts that the theoretical work of Social-Democrats should aim at studying all the specific features of the social and political condition of the various classes. But, extremely little is done in this direction as compared with the work that is done in studying the specific features of factory life. In the committees and study circles, one can meet people who are immersed in the study even of some special branch of the metal industry; but one can hardly ever find members of organizations (obliged, as often happens, for some reason or other to give up practical work) who are especially engaged in gathering material on some pressing question of social and political life in our country which could serve as a means for conducting Social-Democratic work among other strata of the population. In dwelling upon the fact that the majority of the present-day leaders of the working-class movement lack training, we cannot refrain from mentioning training in this respect also, for it too is bound up with the Economist conception of 'close organic connection with the proletarian struggle'. The principal thing, of course, is propaganda and agitation among all strata of the people. The work of the West European Social-Democrat is, in this respect, facilitated by the public meetings and rallies, which all are free to attend, and by the fact that in parliament, he addresses the representatives of all classes. We have neither a parliament nor freedom of assembly; nevertheless, we are able to arrange meetings of workers who desire to listen to a Social-Democrat. We must also find ways and means of calling meetings of representatives of all social classes that desire to listen to a democrat; for he is no Social-Democrat who forgets in practice that 'the Communists support every revolutionary movement', that we are obliged for that reason to expound and emphasise general democratic tasks before the whole people, without for a moment concealing our socialist convictions. He is no Social-Democrat who forgets in practice his obligation to be ahead of all in raising, accentuating, and solving every general democratic question.

'But everyone agrees with this!', the impatient reader will exclaim, and the new instructions adopted by the last conference of the Union Abroad for the Editorial Board of *Rabocheye Dyelo* definitely says: 'All events of social and political life that affect the proletariat either directly as a special class or as the vanguard of all the revolutionary forces in the struggle for freedom should serve as subjects for political propaganda and agitation' (*Two Conferences*, p. 17, our italics). Yes, these are very true and very good words, and we would be fully satisfied if *Rabocheye Dyelo* understood them and if it refrained from saying in the next breath things that contradict them. For it is not enough to call ourselves the 'vanguard', the advanced contingent; we must act in such a way that all the other contingents recognize and are obliged to admit that we are marching in the vanguard. And we ask the reader: are the representatives of the other 'contingents' such fools as to take our word for it when we say that we are the 'vanguard'? just picture to yourselves the following: a Social-Democrat comes to the 'contingent' of Russian educated radicals, or liberal constitutionalists, and says, 'We are the vanguard'; 'the task confronting us now is, as far as possible, to lend the economic struggle itself a political character'. The radical, or constitutionalist, if he is at all intelligent (and there are many intelligent men among Russian radicals and constitutionalists), would only smile at such a speech and would say (to himself, of course, for in the majority of cases he is an experienced diplomat): 'Your 'vanguard' must be made up of simpletons. They do not even understand that it is our task, the task of the progressive representatives of bourgeois democracy to lend the workers' economic struggle itself a political character. Why, we too, like the West-European bourgeois, want to draw the workers into politics, but only into trade-unionist, not into Social-Democratic politics. Trade-unionist politics of the working class is precisely bourgeois politics of the working class, and this 'vanguard's' formulation of its task is the formulation of trade-unionist politics! Let them call themselves Social-Democrats to their heart's content, I am not a child to get excited over a label. But they must not fall under the influence of those pernicious orthodox doctrinaires, let them allow 'freedom of criticism' to those who unconsciously are driving Social-Democracy into trade-unionist channels'.

And the faint smile of our constitutionalist will turn into Homeric laughter when he learns that the Social-Democrats who talk of Social-Democracy as the vanguard, today, when spontaneity almost completely dominates our movement, fear nothing so much as 'belittling the spontaneous element', as 'underestimating the significance of the forward movement of the drab everyday struggle, as compared with the propaganda of brilliant and completed ideas', etc., etc.! A 'vanguard' that fears that consciousness will outstrip spontaneity, which fears to put forward a bold 'plan' that would compel general recognition even among those who differ with us. Are they not confusing 'vanguard' with 'rearguard'?

Indeed, let us examine the following piece of reasoning by Martynov. On page 40, he says that *Iskra* is one-sided in its tactics of exposing abuses, that 'however much we may spread distrust and hatred of the government, we shall not achieve our aim until we have succeeded in developing sufficient active social energy for its overthrow'. This, it may be said parenthetically, is the familiar solicitude for the activation of the masses, with a simultaneous striving to restrict one's own activity. But that is not the main point at the moment. Martynov speaks here, accordingly, of revolutionary energy ('for overthrowing'). And what conclusion does he arrive at? Since in ordinary times, various social strata inevitably march separately, 'it is therefore, clear that we Social-Democrats cannot simultaneously guide the activities of various opposition strata, we cannot dictate to them a positive programme of action, we cannot point out to them in what manner they should wage day-to-day struggles for their interests. . . .The liberal strata will themselves take care of the active struggle for their immediate interests, the struggle that will bring them face to face with our political regime' (p. 41). Thus, having begun with talk about revolutionary energy, about the active struggle for the overthrow of the autocracy, Martynov immediately turns toward trade union energy and the active struggle for immediate interests! It goes without saying that we cannot guide the struggle of the students, liberals, etc., for their 'immediate interests'; but this was not the point at issue, most worthy Economist! The point we were discussing was the possible and necessary participation of various social strata in the overthrow of the autocracy; and not only are we able, but it is our bounden duty, to guide these 'activities of the various opposition strata', if we desire to be the 'vanguard'. Not only will our students and liberals, etc., themselves take care of 'the struggle that brings them face to face with our political regime'; the police and the officials of the autocratic government will see to this first and foremost. But if 'we' desire to be front-rank democrats, we must make it our concern to direct the thoughts of those who are dissatisfied only with conditions at the university, or in the Zemstvo, etc., to the idea that the entire political system is worthless.[19] We must take upon ourselves the task of organizing an all-round political struggle under the leadership of our Party in such a manner as to make it possible for all oppositional strata to render their fullest support to the struggle and to our Party. We must train our Social-Democratic practical workers to become political leaders, able to guide all the manifestations of this all-round struggle, able at the right time to 'dictate a positive programme of action' for the aroused students, the discontented Zemstvo people, the incensed religious sects, the offended elementary schoolteachers, etc., etc. For that reason, Martynov's assertion that 'with regard to these, we can function merely in the negative role of exposers of abuses . . . we can only dissipate their hopes in various government commissions' is completely false [our italics]. By saying this, Martynov shows that he absolutely fails to understand the role that the revolutionary 'vanguard' must really play. If the reader bears this in mind, he will be clear as to the real meaning of Martynov's concluding remarks: '*Iskra* is the organ of the revolutionary opposition which exposes the state of affairs in our country, particularly the political state of affairs, insofar as it affects the interests of the most varied strata of the population. We, however, work and will continue to work for the cause of the working class in close organic contact with the proletarian struggle. By restricting the sphere of our active influence, we deepen that influence' (63). The true sense of this conclusion is as follows: *Iskra* desires to elevate the trade-unionist politics of the working class (to which, through misconception, through lack of training, or through conviction, our practical workers frequently confine themselves) to the level of Social-Democratic politics. *Rabocheye Dyelo*, however, desires to degrade

[19] Zemstro is an elected provincial or district council set in place during the 1864 reforms by Tsar Alexander II.

Social-Democratic politics to trade-unionist politics. Moreover, it assures the world that the two positions are 'entirely compatible within the common cause' (63). 0, sancta simplicitas![20]

To proceed . . . Have we sufficient forces to direct our propaganda and agitation among all social classes? Most certainly. Our Economists, who are frequently inclined to deny this, lose sight of the gigantic progress our movement has made from (approximately) 1894 to 1901. Like real 'tail-enders', they often go on living in the bygone stages of the movement's inception. In the earlier period, indeed, we had astonishingly few forces, and it was perfectly natural and legitimate then to devote ourselves exclusively to activities among the workers and to condemn severely any deviation from this course. The entire task then was to consolidate our position in the working class. At the present time, however, gigantic forces have been attracted to the movement. The best representatives of the younger generation of the educated classes are coming over to us. Everywhere in the provinces there are people, resident there by dint of circumstance, who have taken part in the movement in the past or who desire to do so now and, who are gravitating towards Social-Democracy (whereas in 1894, one could count the Social-Democrats on the fingers of one's hand). A basic political and organizational shortcoming of our movement is our inability to utilize all these forces and give them appropriate work (we shall deal with this more fully in the next chapter). The overwhelming majority of these forces entirely lack the opportunity of 'going among the workers', so that there are no grounds for fearing that we shall divert forces from our main work. In order to be able to provide the workers with real, comprehensive, and live political knowledge, we must have 'our own people', Social-Democrats, everywhere, among all social

[20] This Latin phrase is attributed to the Czech Christian reformer Jan Hus (1369–1415), meaning 'O, holy simplicity!', uttered after the Catholic executioner could not get the fire started, but when an old woman threw brushwood to get the fire going that burnt him at the stake.

strata, and in all positions from which we can learn the inner springs of our state mechanism. Such people are required, not only for propaganda and agitation, but in a still larger measure for organization.

Is there a basis for activity among all classes of the population? Whoever doubts this lags in his consciousness behind the spontaneous awakening of the masses. The working-class movement has aroused and is continuing to arouse discontent in some, hopes of support for the opposition in others, and in still others the realization that the autocracy is unbearable and must inevitably fall. We would be 'politicians' and Social-Democrats in name only (as all too often happens in reality), if we failed to realize that our task is to utilize every manifestation of discontent, and to gather and turn to the best account every protest, however small. This is quite apart from the fact that the millions of the labouring peasantry, handicraftsmen, petty artisans, etc., would always listen eagerly to the speech of any Social-Democrat who is at all qualified. Indeed, is there a single social class in which there are no individuals, groups, or circles that are discontented with the lack of rights and with tyranny and, therefore, accessible to the propaganda of Social-Democrats as the spokesmen of the most pressing general democratic needs? To those who desire to have a clear idea of what the political agitation of a Social-Democrat among all classes and strata of the population should be like, we would point to political exposures in the broad sense of the word as the principal (but, of course, not the sole) form of this agitation.

'We must arouse in every section of the population that is at all politically conscious a passion for political exposure', I wrote in my article 'Where To Begin' [*Iskra*, May (No. 4), 1901], with which I shall deal in greater detail later. 'We must not be discouraged by the fact that the voice of political exposure is today so feeble, timid, and infrequent. This is not because of a wholesale submission to police despotism, but because those who are able and ready to make exposures have no tribune from which to speak, no eager and encouraging audience, they do not see anywhere among the people that force to which it would be worthwhile directing their complaint against the 'omnipotent' Russian Government. . . . We are now in a position to provide a tribune for the nation-wide exposure of the tsarist government, and it is our duty to do this. That tribune must be a Social-Democratic newspaper'.[21]

The ideal audience for political exposure is the working class, which is first and foremost in need of all-round and live political knowledge, and is most capable of converting this knowledge into active struggle, even when that struggle does not promise 'palpable results'. A tribune for nation-wide exposures can be only an all-Russia newspaper. 'Without a political organ, a political movement deserving that name is inconceivable in the Europe of today'; in this respect, Russia must undoubtedly be included in present-day Europe. The press long ago became a power in our country, otherwise the government would not spend tens of thousands of rubles to bribe it and to subsidize the Katkovs and Meshcherskys.[22] And it is no novelty in autocratic Russia for the underground press to break through the wall of censorship and compel the legal and conservative press to speak openly about it. This was the case in the seventies and even in the fifties. How much broader and deeper are now the sections of the people willing to read the illegal underground press, and to learn from it 'how to live and how to die', to use the expression of a worker who sent a letter

21 Lenin, 'Where to Begin', *Iskra*, no. 4, May 1901, *Collected Works*, vol. 5, pp. 21-22.

22 Mikhail Katkov (1818–1887) was a journalist with a curious combination of Russian nationalism and Westernization, driven in his periodicals *Russkii Vestnik* (Russian Messanger) and *Moskovkie Vedomosti* (Moscow News). Prince Vladimir Meschersky (1839-1914) was a journalist who contributed to Katkov's papers and edited *Grazhdanin* (The Citizen), which was the mouthpiece of the landed gentry. Leon Trotsky wrote of *Grazhdanin* that it was 'the sole paper which [Tsar] Nicholas read for years, and from which he derived his ideas'; the paper, Trotsky wrote, was 'published on state revenue by Prince Meshcersky, a vile, bribed journalist of the reactionary bureaucratic clique, despised even in his own circle' (*The History of the Russian Revolution*, 1930, Chapter 4).

to *Iskra* (no.7). Political exposures are as much a declaration of war against the government as economic exposures are a declaration of war against the factory owners. The moral significance of this declaration of war will be all the greater, the wider and more powerful the campaign of exposure will be and the more numerous and determined the social class that has declared war in order to begin the war. Hence, political exposures in themselves serve as a powerful instrument for disintegrating the system we oppose, as a means for diverting from the enemy his casual or temporary allies, and as a means for spreading hostility and distrust among the permanent partners of the autocracy.

In our time, only a party that will organize real nationwide exposure can become the vanguard of the revolutionary forces. The word 'nationwide' has a very profound meaning. The overwhelming majority of the non-working-class exposers (be it remembered that in order to become the vanguard, we must attract other classes) are sober politicians and level-headed men of affairs. They know perfectly well how dangerous it is to 'complain' even against a minor official, let alone against the 'omnipotent' Russian Government. And they will come to us with their complaints only when they see that these complaints can really have effect and that we represent a political force. In order to become such a force in the eyes of outsiders, much persistent and stubborn work is required to raise our own consciousness, initiative, and energy... To accomplish this, it is not enough to attach a 'vanguard' label to rearguard theory and practice.

But if we have to undertake the organization of a really nationwide exposure of the government, in what way will then the class character of our movement be expressed? — the overzealous advocate of 'close organic contact with the proletarian struggle' will ask us, as indeed he does. The reply is manifold, we Social-Democrats will organize these nationwide exposure; all questions raised by the agitation will he explained in a consistently Social-Democratic spirit, without any concessions to deliberate or undeliberate distortions of Marxism; the all-round political agitation will be conducted by a party which unites into one inseparable whole the assault on the government in the name of the entire people, the revolutionary training of the proletariat, and the safeguarding of its political independence, the guidance of the economic struggle of the working class, and the utilisation of all its spontaneous conflicts with its exploiters which rouse and bring into our camp increasing numbers of the proletariat.

But a most characteristic feature of Economism is its failure to understand this connection, more, this identity of the most pressing need of the proletariat (a comprehensive political education through the medium of political agitation and political exposures) with the need of the general democratic movement. This lack of understanding is expressed not only in 'Martynovite' phrases, but in the references to a supposedly class point of view identical in meaning with these phrases. Thus, the authors of the Economist letter in *Iskra*, No. 12, state:[23] 'This basic drawback of *Iskra* (overestimation of ideology) is also the cause of its inconsistency on the question of the attitude of Social-Democracy to the various social classes and tendencies. By theoretical reasoning (not by 'the growth of Party tasks, which grow together with the Party'), *Iskra* solved the problem of the immediate transition to the struggle against absolutism. In all probability, it senses the difficulty of such a task for the workers under the present state of affairs (not only senses, but knows full well that this task appears less difficult to the workers than to the Economist intellectuals with their nursemaid concern, for the workers are prepared to fight even for demands which, to use the language of the never-to-be-forgotten Martynov,

[23] Lenin — [Lack of space has prevented us from replying in detail, in *Iskra*, to this letter, which is highly characteristic of the Economists. We were very glad at its appearance, for the allegations that *Iskra* did not maintain a consistent class point of view had reached us long before that from various sources, and we were waiting for an appropriate occasion or for a formulated expression of this fashionable charge, to give our reply. Moreover, it is our habit to reply to attacks, not by defence, but by counter-attack].

do not 'promise palpable results') but lacking the patience to wait until the workers will have gathered sufficient forces for this struggle, *Iskra* begins to seek allies in the ranks of the liberals and intellectuals'. . . .

Yes, we have indeed lost all 'patience' 'waiting' for the blessed time, long promised us by diverse 'conciliators', when the Economists will have stopped charging the workers with their own backwardness and justifying their own lack of energy with allegations that the workers lack strength. We ask our Economists: What do they mean by 'the gathering of working-class strength for the struggle'? Is it not evident that this means the political training of the workers so that all the aspects of our vile autocracy are revealed to them? And is it not clear that precisely for this work, we need 'allies in the ranks of the liberals and intellectuals', who are prepared to join us in the exposure of the political attack on the Zemstvos, on the teachers, on the statisticians, on the students, etc.? Is this surprisingly 'intricate mechanism' really so difficult to understand? Has not P. B. Axelrod constantly repeated since 1897 that 'the task before the Russian Social-Democrats of acquiring adherents and direct and indirect allies among the non-proletarian classes will be solved principally and primarily by the character of the propagandist activities conducted among the proletariat itself'? But the Martynovs and the other Economists continue to imagine that 'by economic struggle against the employers and the government' the workers must first gather strength (for trade-unionist politics) and then 'go over' — we presume from trade-unionist 'training for activity' to Social-Democratic activity!

'In this quest', continue the Economists, '*Iskra* does not infrequently depart from the class point of view, obscures class antagonisms, and puts into the forefront the common nature of the discontent with the government, although the causes and the degree of the discontent vary considerably among the "allies". Such, for example, is *Iskra*'s attitude towards the Zemstvo'. *Iskra*, it is alleged, 'promises the nobles that are dissatisfied with the government's sops the assistance of the working class, but it does not say a word about the class antagonism that exists between these social strata'. If the reader will turn to the article 'The Autocracy and the Zemstvo' (*Iskra*, Nos. 2 and 4), to which, in all probability, the authors of the letter refer, he will find that they[24] deal with the attitude of the government towards the 'mild agitation of the bureaucratic Zemstvo, which is based on the social-estates', and towards the 'independent activity of even the propertied classes'. The article states that the workers cannot look on indifferently while the government is waging a struggle against the Zemstvo, and the Zemstvos are called upon to stop making mild speeches and to speak firmly and resolutely when revolutionary Social-Democracy confronts the government in all its strength. What the authors of the letter do not agree with here is not clear. Do they think that the workers will 'not understand' the phrases 'propertied classes' and 'bureaucratic Zemstvo based on the social-estates'? Do they think that urging the Zemstvo to abandon mild speeches and to speak firmly is 'overestimating ideology'? Do they imagine the workers can 'gather strength' for the struggle against the autocracy if they know nothing about the attitude of the autocracy towards the Zemstvo as well? All this too remains unknown. One thing alone is clear and that is that the authors of the letter have a very vague idea of what the political tasks of Social-Democracy are. This is revealed still more clearly by their remark: 'Such, too, is *Iskra*'s attitude towards the student movement' (i.e., it also 'obscures the class antagonisms'). Instead of calling on the workers to declare by means of public demonstrations that the real breeding place of unbridled violence, disorder, and outrage is not the university youth but the Russian Government (*Iskra*, No. 2 [19]) we ought

[24] Lenin — ['In the interval between these articles there was one (*Iskra*, No. 3), which dealt especially with class antagonisms in the countryside]. Lenin, 'The Workers Party and the Peasantry', *Iskra*, no. 2, February 1901, *Collected Works*, vol. 4, pp. 420-28.

probably to have inserted arguments in the spirit of *Rabochaya Mysl*! Such ideas were expressed by Social-Democrats in the autumn of 1901, after the events of February and March, on the eve of a fresh upsurge of the student movement, which reveals that even in this sphere, the 'spontaneous' protest against the autocracy is outstripping the conscious Social-Democratic leadership of the movement. The spontaneous striving of the workers to defend the students who are being assaulted by the police and the Cossacks surpasses the conscious activity of the Social-Democratic organisation!

'And yet, in other articles', continue the authors of the letter, '*Iskra* sharply condemns all compromise and defends, for instance, the intolerant conduct of the Guesdists'. We would advise those who are wont so conceitedly and frivolously to declare that the present disagreements among the Social-Democrats are unessential and do not justify a split, to ponder these words. Is it possible for people to work together in the same organization, when some among them contend that we have done extremely little to explain the hostility of the autocracy to the various classes and to inform the workers of the opposition displayed by the various social strata to the autocracy, while others among them see in this clarification a 'compromise' — evidently a compromise with the theory of 'economic struggle against the employers and the government'?

We urged the necessity of carrying the class struggle into the rural districts in connection with the fortieth anniversary of the emancipation of the peasantry (issue No. 2[25]) and spoke of the irreconcilability of the local government bodies and the autocracy in relation to Witte's secret Memorandum (No. 4). In connection with the new law, we attacked the feudal landlords and the government which serves them (No. 8[26]) and we welcomed the

25 Lenin, 'The Workers Party and the Peasantry', *Collected Works*, vol. 4, pp. 420–28.

26 Lenin, 'The Serf Owners at Work', *Iskra*, no. 8, September 1901, *Collected Works*, vol. 5, pp. 95–100.

illegal Zemstvo congress. We urged the Zemstvo to pass over from abject petitions (No. 8[27]) to struggle. We encouraged the students, who had begun to understand the need for the political struggle, and to undertake this struggle (No. 3), while, at the same time, we lashed out at the 'outrageous incomprehension' revealed by the adherents of the 'purely student' movement, who called upon the students to abstain from participating in the street demonstrations (No. 3, in connection with the manifesto issued by the Executive Committee of the Moscow students on 25 February). We exposed the 'senseless dreams' and the 'lying hypocrisy' of the cunning liberals of Rossiya (No. 5), while pointing to the violent fury with which the government-gaoler persecuted 'peaceful writers, aged professors, scientists, and well-known liberal Zemstvo members' (No. 5, 'Police Raid on Literature'). We exposed the real significance of the programme of 'state protection for the welfare of the workers' and welcomed the 'valuable admission' that 'it is better, by granting reforms from above, to forestall the demand for such reforms from below than to wait for those demands to be put forward' (No. 6[28]). We encouraged the protesting statisticians (No. 7) and censured the strike-breaking statisticians (No. 9). He who sees in these tactics an obscuring of the class-consciousness of the proletariat and a compromise with liberalism reveals his utter failure to understand the true significance of the programme of the Credo and carries out that programme de facto, however much he may repudiate it. For by such an approach, he drags Social-Democracy towards the 'economic struggle against the employers and the government' and yields to liberalism, abandons the task of actively intervening in every 'liberal' issue and of determining his own, Social-Democratic, attitude towards this question.

[27] Lenin, 'A Zemstvo Congress', *Iskra*, no. 8, September 1901, *Collected Works*, vol. 5, pp. 101–2.

[28] Lenin, 'A Valuable Addition', *Iskra*, no. 6, July 1901, *Collected Works*, vol. 5, pp. 87–88.

3.6. ONCE MORE 'SLANDERERS', ONCE MORE 'MYSTIFIERS'

These polite expressions, as the reader will recall, belong to *Rabocheye Dyelo*, which in this way answers our charge that it 'is indirectly preparing the ground for converting the working-class movement into an instrument of bourgeois democracy'. In its simplicity of heart, *Rabocheye Dyelo* decided that this accusation was nothing more than a polemical sally, these malicious doctrinaires are bent on saying all sorts of unpleasant things about us, and, what can be more unpleasant than being an instrument of bourgeois democracy? And so, they print in bold type a 'refutation', 'Nothing but downright slander', 'mystification', 'mummery' (*Two Conferences*, pp. 30, 31, 33). Like Jove, *Rabocheye Dyelo* (although bearing little resemblance to that deity) is wrathful because it is wrong, and proves by its hasty abuse that it is incapable of understanding its opponents' mode of reasoning. And yet, with only a little reflection it would have understood why *any* subservience to the spontaneity of the mass movement and *any* degrading of Social-Democratic politics to the level of trade-unionist politics mean preparing the ground for converting the working-class movement into an instrument of bourgeois democracy. The spontaneous working-class movement is by itself able to create (and inevitably does create) only trade-unionism, and working-class trade unionist politics is precisely working-class bourgeois politics. The fact that the working-class participates in the political struggle, and even in the political revolution, does not in itself make its politics Social-Democratic politics. Will *Rabocheye Dyelo* be bold enough to deny this? Will it, at long last, publicly, plainly, and without equivocation explain how it understands the urgent questions of international and Russian Social-Democracy? Hardly. It will never do anything of the kind, because it holds fast to the trick, which might be described as the 'not here' method — 'It's not me, it's not my horse, I'm not the driver. We are not Economists; *Rabochaya Mysl* does not stand for Economism; there is no Economism at all in Russia'.

This is a remarkably adroit and 'political' trick, which suffers from the slight defect, however, that the publications practising it are usually nicknamed, 'At your service, sir'.

Rabocheye Dyelo imagines that bourgeois democracy in Russia is, in general, merely a 'phantom' (Two Conferences, p. 32).[29] Happy people! Ostrich-like, they bury their heads in the sand and imagine that everything around has disappeared. Liberal publicists who month after month proclaim to the world their triumph over the collapse and even the disappearance of Marxism; liberal newspapers (S. Peterburgskiye Vedomosti, Russkiye Vedomosti, and many others) which encourage the liberals who bring to the workers the Brentano conception of the class struggle and the trade-unionist conception of politics; the galaxy of critics of Marxism, whose real tendencies were so very well disclosed by the Credo and whose literary products alone circulate in Russia without let or hindrance; the revival of revolutionary non-Social-Democratic tendencies, particularly after the February and March events — all these, apparently, are just phantoms![30] All these have nothing at all to do with bourgeois democracy!

[29] There follows a reference to the 'concrete Russian conditions which fatalistically impel the working-class movement onto the revolutionary path'. But these people refuse to understand that the revolutionary path of the working-class movement might not be a Social-Democratic path. When absolutism reigned, the entire West-European bourgeoisie 'impelled', deliberately impelled, the workers onto the path of revolution. We Social-Democrats, however, cannot be satisfied with that. And if we, by any means whatever, degrade Social-Democratic politics to the level of spontaneous trade-unionist politics, we thereby play into the hands of bourgeois democracy.

[30] *Rossiya* was a liberal newspaper published in St. Petersburg from 1899 to 1902. *St. Petersburgskiye Vedomosti* (*St. Petersburg Recorder*) was published by the Academy of Sciences (1728–1874) and by the Ministry of Education (1875–1917), having absorbed Russia's first newspaper — *Vedomosti* — formed in 1703. Lujo Brentano (1844–1931) was a German economist, an expert in British trade unions, and a social reformer. He got into a dispute with Marx over a quotation by William Gladstone. His view on class struggle was formed by his studies of the British trade union movement, namely through the idea of reconciliation of classes.

Rabocheye Dyelo and the authors of the Economist letter published in *Iskra*, No. 12, should 'ponder over the reason why the events of the spring brought about such a revival of revolutionary non-Social-Democratic tendencies instead of increasing the authority and the prestige of Social-Democracy'.

The reason lies in the fact that we failed to cope with our tasks. The masses of the workers proved to be more active than us. We lacked adequately trained revolutionary leaders and organizers possessed a thorough knowledge of the mood prevailing among all the opposition strata and able to head the movement, turn a spontaneous demonstration into a political one, broaden its political character, etc. Under such circumstances, our backwardness will inevitably be utilized by the more mobile and more energetic non-Social-Democratic revolutionaries, and the workers, however energetically and self-sacrificingly they may fight the police and the troops, however revolutionary their actions may be, will prove to be merely a force supporting those revolutionaries, the rearguard of bourgeois democracy, and not the Social-Democratic vanguard. Let us take, for example, the German Social-Democrats, whose weak aspects alone our Economists desire to emulate. Why is there not a single political event in Germany that does not add to the authority and prestige of Social-Democracy? Because Social-Democracy is always found to be in advance of all others in furnishing the most revolutionary appraisal of every given event and in championing every protest against tyranny. It does not lull itself with arguments that the economic struggle brings the workers to realize that they have no political rights and that the concrete conditions unavoidably impel the working-class movement onto the path of revolution. It intervenes in every sphere and in every question of social and political life; in the matter of Wilhelm's refusal to endorse a bourgeois progressist as city mayor (our Economists have not yet managed to educate. the Germans to the understanding that such an act is, in fact, a compromise with liberalism!); in the matter of the law against 'obscene' publications and pictures; in the matter of governmental influence on the election of professors, etc., etc. Everywhere, the Social-Democrats are found at the forefront, rousing political discontent among all classes, rousing the sluggards, stimulating the laggards, and providing a wealth of material for the development of the political consciousness and the political activity of the proletariat. As a result, even the avowed enemies of socialism are filled with respect for this advanced political fighter, and not infrequently an important document from bourgeois, and even from bureaucratic and Court circles, makes its way by some miraculous means into the editorial office of *Vorwarts*.

This, then, is the resolution of the seeming 'contradiction' that surpasses *Rabocheye Dyelo*'s powers of understanding to such an extent that it can only throw up its hands and cry, 'Mummery!'. Indeed, just think of it — we, *Rabocheye Dyelo*, regard the mass working-class movement as the corner-stone (and say so in bold type!); we warn all and sundry against belittling the significance of the element of spontaneity; we desire to lend the economic struggle itself — itself — a political character; we desire to maintain close and organic contact with the proletarian struggle. And yet, we are told that we are preparing the ground for the conversion of the working-class movement into an instrument of bourgeois democracy! And who are they that presume to say this? People who 'compromise' with liberalism by intervening in every 'liberal' issue (what a gross misunderstanding of 'organic contact with the proletarian struggle'!), by devoting so much attention to the students and even (oh horror!) to the Zemstvos! People who, in general, wish to devote a greater percentage (compared with the Economists) of their efforts to activity among non-proletarian classes of the population! What is this but 'mummery'?

Poor *Rabocheye Dyelo*! Will it ever find the solution to this perplexing puzzle?

Chapter 4

The Primitiveness of the Economists and the Organization of the Revolutionaries

Rabocheye Dyelo's assertions, which we have analyzed, that the economic struggle is the most widely applicable means of political agitation and that our task now is to lend the economic struggle itself a political character, etc., express a narrow view, not only of our political, but also of our organizational tasks. The 'economic struggle against the employers and the government' does not at all require an all-Russia centralized organization, and hence this struggle can never give rise to such an organization as will combine, in one general assault, all the manifestations of political opposition, protest, and indignation, an organization that will consist of professional revolutionaries and be led by the real political leaders of the entire people. This stands to reason. The character of any organization is naturally and inevitably determined by the content of its activity. Consequently, *Rabocheye Dyelo*, by the assertions analyzed above, sanctifies and legitimizes not only narrowness of political activity, but also of organizational work. In this case, *Rabocheye Dyelo*, as always, proves itself an organ whose consciousness yields to spontaneity. Yet subservience to spontaneously developing forms of organisation, failure to realize the narrowness and primitiveness of our organizational work, of our 'handicraft' methods in this most important sphere, failure to realize this, I say, is a veritable ailment from which our movement suffers. It is not an ailment that comes with decline, but one, of course, that comes with growth. It is however at the present time, when the wave of spontaneous indignation, as it were, is sweeping over us, leaders and organizers of the movement, that an irreconcilable struggle must be waged against all defence of backwardness, against any legitimation of narrowness in this matter. It is particularly necessary to arouse in all who participate in practical work, or are preparing to take up that work, discontent with the *amateurism* prevailing among us and an unshakable determination to rid ourselves of it.

4.1. WHAT IS PRIMITIVENESS?

We shall try to answer this question by giving a brief description of the activity of a typical Social-Democratic study circle of the period 1894–1901. We have noted that the entire student youth of the period was absorbed in Marxism. Of course, these students were not only, or even not so much, interested in Marxism as a theory; they were interested in it as an answer to the question, 'What is to be done?', as a call to take the field against the enemy. These new warriors marched to battle with astonishingly primitive equipment and training. In a vast number of cases, they had almost no equipment and absolutely no training. They marched to war like peasants from the plough, armed only with clubs. A students' circle establishes contacts with workers and sets to work, without any connection with the old members of the movement, without any connection with study circles in other districts, or even in other parts of the same city (or in other educational institutions), without any organization of the various divisions of revolutionary work, without any systematic plan of activity covering any length of time. The circle gradually expands its propaganda and agitation; by its activities, it wins the sympathies of fairly large sections of workers and of a certain section of the educated strata, which provide it with money and from among whom the 'committee' recruits new groups of young people. The attractive power of the committee (or League of Struggle) grows, its sphere of activity becomes wider, and the committee expands this activity quite spontaneously; the very people who a year or a few months previously spoke at the students' circle gatherings and discussed the question, 'Whither?', who established and maintained contacts with the workers and wrote and published leaflets, now, establish contacts with other groups of revolutionaries, procure literature, set to work to publish a local newspaper, begin to talk of organizing a demonstration, and finally turn to open warfare (which may, according to circumstances, take the form of issuing the first agitational leaflet or the first issue of a newspaper, or of organising the first demonstration). Usually, the initiation of such actions ends in an immediate and complete fiasco. Immediate and complete, because this open warfare was not the result of a systematic and carefully thought-out and gradually prepared plan for a prolonged and stubborn struggle, but simply the result of the spontaneous growth of traditional study circle work; because, naturally, the police, in almost every case, knew the principal leaders of the local movement, since they had already 'gained a reputation' for themselves in their student days, and the police waited only for the right moment to make their raid. They deliberately allowed the study circle sufficient time to develop its work so that they might obtain a palpable *corpus delicti*, and they always permitted several of the persons known to them to remain at liberty 'for breeding' (which, as far as I know, is the technical term used both by our people and by the gendarmes).[1] One cannot help comparing this kind of warfare with that conducted by a mass of peasants, armed with clubs, against modern troops. And one can only wonder at the vitality of the movement which expanded, grew, and scored victories despite the total lack of training on the part of the fighters. True, from the historical point of view, the primitiveness of equipment was not only inevitable at first, but *even legitimate* as one of the conditions for the wide recruiting of fighters, but as soon as serious war operations began (and they began in fact with the strikes in the summer of 1896), the defects in our fighting

[1] *Corpus Delicti* is a principle in European law that the crime must be proved to have occurred before anyone can be found guilty of it.

organisations made themselves felt to an ever-increasing degree. The government, at first thrown into confusion and committing a number of blunders (e.g., its appeal to the public describing the misdeeds of the socialists, or the banishment of workers from the capitals to provincial industrial centres), very soon adapted itself to the new conditions of the struggle and managed to deploy well its perfectly equipped detachments of *agents provocateurs*, spies, and gendarmes. Raids became so frequent, affected such a vast number of people, and cleared out the local study circles so thoroughly that the masses of workers lost literally all their leaders. The movement assumed an amazingly sporadic character, and it became utterly impossible to establish continuity and coherence in the work. The terrible dispersion of the local leaders; the fortuitous character of the study circle memberships; the lack of training in, and the narrow outlook on, theoretical, political, and organizational questions were all the inevitable result of the conditions described above. Things have reached such a pass that in several places the workers, because of our lack of self-restraint and the inability to maintain secrecy, begin to lose faith in the intellectuals and to avoid them; the intellectuals, they say, are much too careless and cause police raids!

Anyone who has the slightest knowledge of the movement is aware that all thinking Social-Democrats have at last begun to regard these amateurish methods as a disease. In order that the reader who is not acquainted with the movement may have no grounds for thinking that we are 'inventing' a special stage or special disease of the movement, we shall refer once again to the witness we have quoted. We trust we shall be forgiven for the length of the passage:

> 'While the gradual transition to more extensive practical activity', writes B-v in *Rabocheye Dyelo*, No. 6, 'a transition that is directly dependent on the general transitional period through which the Russian working-class movement is now

> passing, is a characteristic feature, . . . there is, however, another, no less interesting feature in the general mechanism of the Russian workers' revolution. *We refer to the general lack of revolutionary forces fit for action*, which is felt not only in St. Petersburg but throughout Russia. With the general revival of the working-class movement, with the general development of the working masses, with the growing frequency of strikes, with the increasingly open mass struggle of the workers and with the intensified government persecution, arrests, deportation, and exile, this *lack of highly skilled revolutionary forces is becoming more and more marked* and, without a doubt, *cannot but affect the depth and the general character of the movement.* Many strikes take place without any strong and direct influence upon them by the revolutionary organisations. . . . A shortage of agitational leaflets and illegal literature is felt. . . . The workers' study circles are left without agitators. . . . In addition, there is a constant dearth of funds. In a word, *the growth of the working-class movement is outstripping the growth and development of the revolutionary organizations.* The numerical strength of the active revolutionaries is too small to enable them to concentrate in their own hands the influence exercised upon the whole mass of discontented workers, or to give this discontent even a shadow of coherence and organization. . . . The separate study circles, the separate revolutionaries, scattered, uncombined, do not represent a single, strong, and disciplined organisation with proportionately developed parts.'

Admitting that the immediate organization of fresh study circles to replace those that have been broken up merely proves the vitality of the movement . . . but does not prove the existence of an adequate number of adequately prepared revolutionary workers, the author concludes:

> 'The lack of practical training among the St. Petersburg

revolutionaries is seen in the results of their work. The recent trials, especially that of the Self-Emancipation Group and the Labour-against-Capital group, clearly showed that the young agitator, lacking detailed knowledge of working class conditions and, consequently, of the conditions under which agitation can be carried on in a given factory, ignorant of the principles of secrecy, and understanding only the general principles of Social-Democracy [if he does], is able to carry on his work for perhaps four, five, or six months.[2] Then come arrests, which frequently lead to the break-up of the entire organisation, or at all events, of part of it. The question arises, therefore, can the group conduct successful activity if its existence is measured by months? . . . Obviously, the defects of the existing organizations cannot be wholly ascribed to the transitional period. . . . Obviously, the numerical, and above all the qualitative, make-up of the functioning organizations is no small factor, and the first task our Social-Democrats must undertake . . . is that of *effectively combining the organizations and making a strict selection of their membership*.'

4.2. PRIMITIVENESS AND ECONOMISM

We must now deal with a question that has undoubtedly come to the mind of every reader. Can a connection be established between primitiveness as growing pains that affect the whole movement, and Economism, which is one of the currents in Russian Social-Democracy? We think that it can. Lack of practical training, or the ability to carry on organizational work is certainly common to us all, including those who have, from the very outset, unswervingly stood for revolutionary Marxism. Of course, were it

[2] The Workers' Group for the Struggle Against Capital was formed in the spring of 1899, but lasted only a short time, during which the comrades produced one leaflet on their Economist views ('Our Programme'), which was never circulated due to the arrest of the entire group.

only a lack of practical training, no one could blame the practical workers. But the term 'primitiveness' embraces something more than lack of training; it denotes a narrow scope of revolutionary work generally, failure to understand that a good organization of revolutionaries cannot be built on the basis of such narrow activity, and lastly — and this is the main thing — attempts to justify this narrowness and to elevate it to a special 'theory', i.e., subservience to spontaneity on this question too. Once such attempts were revealed, it became clear that primitiveness is connected with Economism and that we shall never rid ourselves of this narrowness of our organizational activity until we rid ourselves of Economism generally (i.e., the narrow conception of Marxist theory, as well as of the role of Social-Democracy and of its political tasks). These attempts manifested themselves in a twofold direction. Some began to say that the working masses themselves have not yet advanced the broad and militant political tasks which the revolutionaries are attempting to 'impose' on them; that they must continue to struggle for immediate political demands, to conduct 'the economic struggle against the employers and the government'[3] (and, naturally, corresponding to this struggle which is 'accessible' to the mass movement there must be an organization that will be 'accessible' to the most untrained youth). Others, far removed from any theory of 'gradualness', said that it is possible and necessary to 'bring about a political revolution', but that this does not require building a strong organization of revolutionaries to train the proletariat in steadfast and stubborn struggle. All we need do is to snatch up our old friend, the 'accessible' cudgel. To drop metaphor, it means that we must organize a general strike,[4] or that we must stimulate the 'spiritless' progress of the working-

[3] Lenin — [*Rabochaya Mysl* and *Rabocheye Dyelo*, especially the *Reply* to Plekhanov].

[4] Lenin — [See 'Who Will Bring About the Political Revolution?', in the collection published in Russia, entitled *The Proletarian Struggle*. Re-issued by the Kiev Committee].

class movement by means of 'excitative terror'.[5] Both these trends, the opportunists and the 'revolutionists', bow to the prevailing amateurism; neither believes that it can be eliminated, neither understands our primary and imperative practical task to establish an organization of revolutionaries capable of lending energy, stability, and continuity to the political struggle.

We have quoted the words of B-v: 'The growth of the working-class movement is out-stripping the growth and development of the revolutionary organizations'. This 'valuable remark of a close observer' (*Rabocheye Dyelo*'s comment on B-v's article) has a twofold value for us. It shows that we were right in our opinion that the principal cause of the present crisis in Russian Social-Democracy is the lag of the leaders ('ideologists', revolutionaries, Social-Democrats) behind the spontaneous upsurge of the masses. It shows that all the arguments advanced by the authors of the Economist letter (in *Iskra*, No. 12), by Krichevsky and by Martynov, as to the danger of belittling the significance of the spontaneous element, of the drab everyday struggle, as to tactics-as-process, etc., are nothing more than a glorification and a defence of primitiveness. These people who cannot pronounce the word 'theoretician' without a sneer, who describe their genuflections to common lack of training and backwardness as a 'sense for the realities of life', reveal in practice a failure to understand our most imperative practical tasks. To laggards, they shout: Keep in step! Don't run ahead! To people suffering from a lack of energy and initiative in organizational work, from a lack of 'plans' for wide and bold activity, they prate about 'tactics-as-process'! The worst sin we commit is that we degrade our political and organisational tasks to the level of the immediate, 'palpable', 'concrete' interests of the everyday economic struggle; yet they keep singing to us the same refrain: Lend the economic struggle itself a political character! We repeat: this kind of thing displays as much 'sense

[5] Lenin — [*Regeneration of Revolutionism* and the journal *Svoboda*].

for the realities of life' as was displayed by the hero in the popular fable who cried out to a passing funeral procession, 'Many happy returns of the day!'.

Recall the matchless, truly 'Narcissus-like' superciliousness with which these wiseacres lectured Plekhanov on the 'workers' circles generally' (sic!) being 'unable to cope with political tasks in the real and practical sense of the word, i.e., in the sense of the expedient and successful practical struggle for political demands' (*Rabocheye Dyelo*'s Reply, p. 24). There are circles and circles, gentlemen! Circles of 'amateurs' are not, of course, capable of coping with political tasks so long as they have not become aware of their amateurism and do not abandon it. If, besides this, these amateurs are enamoured of their primitive methods, and insist on writing the word 'practical' in italics, and imagine that being practical demands that one's tasks be reduced to the level of understanding of the most backward strata of the masses, then they are hopeless amateurs and, of course, certainly cannot in general cope with any political tasks. But a circle of leaders, of the type of Alexeyev and Myshkin, of Khalturin and Zhelyabov, is capable of coping with political tasks in the genuine and most practical sense of the term, for the reason and to the extent that their impassioned propaganda meets with response among the spontaneously awakening masses, and their sparkling energy is answered and supported by the energy of the revolutionary class.[6] Plekhanov was profoundly

[6] Pyotr Alexeyevich Alexeyev (1849–1891) was one of the first factory workers to join the revolutionary underground, notably a *narodnik* circle led by Sophia Illarionovna Bardina (1853–1883). His trial speech in 1877 described the horrendous conditions of work and life in Russia. It was circulated widely. Ippolit Nikitich Myshkin (1848-1885) was a revolutionary worker, whose mission in life became the rescue of the socialist *narodnik* writer Nikolay Gavrilovich Chernyshenvsky (1828–1889) from Siberia. Myshkin's trial speech, like that of Alexeyev, was enormously popular. Andrei Ivanovich Zhelyabov (1851–1881) was a member of the executive committee of *Narodnaya Volya*, a clandestine organization formed in August 1879 in a split from the main Narodnik organization, *Zemlya Volya* (Land and Liberty). Stepan Nikolayevich Khalturin (1857–1882), a member of *Narodnaya Volya*, attempted to assassinate Tsar Alexander II in 1880. Of

right, not only in pointing to this revolutionary class and proving that its spontaneous awakening was inevitable, but in setting even the 'workers' circles' a great and lofty political task. But you refer to the mass movement that has sprung up since that time in order to degrade this task, to curtail the energy and scope of activity of the 'workers' circles'. If you are not amateurs enamoured of your primitive methods, what are you then? You boast that you are practical, but you fail to see what every Russian practical worker knows, namely, the miracles that the energy, not only of a circle, but even of an individual person, is able to perform in the revolutionary cause. Or do you think that our movement cannot produce leaders like those of the seventies? If so, why do you think so? Because we lack training? But we are training ourselves, we will go on training ourselves, and we will be trained! Unfortunately, it is true that the surface of the stagnant waters of the 'economic struggle against the employers and the government' is overgrown with fungus; people have appeared among us who kneel in prayer to spontaneity, gazing with awe (to take an expression from Plekhanov) upon the 'posterior' of the Russian proletariat. But we will get rid of this fungus. The time has come when Russian revolutionaries, guided by a genuinely revolutionary theory, relying upon the genuinely revolutionary and spontaneously awakening class, can at last — at long last! — rise to full stature in all their giant strength. All that is required is for the masses of our practical workers, and the still larger masses of those who dreamed of practical work when they were still at school, to pour scorn and ridicule upon any suggestion that may be made to degrade our political tasks and to restrict the scope of our organizational work. And we will achieve that, rest assured, gentlemen!

In the article 'Where To Begin', I wrote in opposition to

Narodnaya Volya, Lenin wrote, 'The *Narodovolsti* (members of the group) made a step forward in their transition to the political struggle, but they did not succeed in connecting it with socialism'. Lenin, 'Working-Class and Bourgeois Democracy', *Vperyod*, no. 3, January 1905, *Collected Works*, vol. 8, p. 72.

Rabocheye Dyelo: 'The tactics of agitation in relation to some special question, or the tactics with regard to some detail of party organization may be changed in twenty-four hours; but only people devoid of all principle are capable of changing, in twenty-four hours, or, for that matter, in twenty-four months, their view on the necessity — in general, constantly, and absolutely — of an organization of struggle and of political agitation among the masses'.[7] To this *Rabocheye Dyelo* replied: 'This, the only one of *Iskra*'s charges that makes a pretence of being based on facts, is totally without foundation. Readers of *Rabocheye Dyelo* know very well that from the outset we not only called for political agitation, without waiting for the appearance of *Iskra* . . . [saying at the same time that not only the workers' study circles, 'but also the mass working-class movement could not regard as its first political task the overthrow of absolutism', but only the struggle for immediate political demands, and that 'the masses begin to understand immediate political demands after one, or at all events, after several strikes'], . . . but that with our publications which we furnished from abroad for the comrades working in Russia, we provided the only Social-Democratic political and agitational material . . . [and in this sole material you not only based the widest political agitation exclusively on the economic struggle, but you even went to the extent of claiming that this restricted agitation was the 'most widely applicable'. And do you not observe, gentlemen, that your own argument — that this was the only material provided — proves the necessity for *Iskra*'s appearance, and its struggle against *Rabocheye Dyelo*?]. . . . On the other hand, our publishing activity actually prepared the ground for the tactical unity of the Party . . . [unity in the conviction that tactics is a process of growth of Party tasks that grow together with the Party? A precious unity indeed!] . . . and by that rendered possible the creation of a 'militant organization' for which the Union Abroad did all that an

[7] Lenin, 'Where to Begin', *Collected Works*, vol. 5, p. 18.

organization abroad could do' (*Rabocheye Dyelo*, No. 10, p. 15). A vain attempt at evasion! I would never dream of denying that you did all you possibly could. I have asserted and assert now that the limits of what is 'possible' for you to do are restricted by the narrowness of your outlook. It is ridiculous to talk of a 'militant organization' to fight for 'immediate political demands', or to 'conduct the economic struggle against the employers and the government'.

But, if the reader wishes to see the pearls of 'Economist' infatuation with amateurism, he must, of course, turn from the eclectic and vacillating *Rabocheye Dyelo* to the consistent and determined *Rabochaya Mysl*. In its Separate Supplement, p. 13, R. M. wrote: 'Now, two words about the so-called revolutionary intelligentsia proper. True, on more than one occasion it has proved itself prepared 'to enter into determined battle with tsarism'. The unfortunate thing, however, is that our revolutionary intelligentsia, ruthlessly persecuted by the political police, imagined the struggle against the political police to be the political struggle against the autocracy. That is why, to this day, it cannot understand where the 'forces for the struggle against the autocracy are to be obtained.'

Truly matchless is the lofty contempt for the struggle against the police displayed by this worshipper (in the worst sense of the word) of the spontaneous movement! He is prepared to justify our inability to organize secret activity by the argument that with the spontaneous mass movement, it is not at all important for us to struggle against the political police! Very few people indeed would subscribe to this appalling conclusion; to such an extent have our deficiencies in revolutionary organisations become a matter of acute importance. But if Martynov, for example, refuses to subscribe to this, it will only be because he is unable, or lacks the courage, to think out his ideas to their logical conclusion. Indeed, does the 'task' of advancing concrete demands by the masses, demands that promise palpable results, call for special efforts to create a stable, centralized, militant organization of revolutionaries? Cannot such a 'task' be carried out even by masses that do not 'struggle against the political police' at all? Could this task, moreover, be fulfilled if, in addition to the few leaders, it was not undertaken by such workers (the overwhelming majority) as are quite incapable of 'struggling against the political police'? Such workers, average people of the masses, are capable of displaying enormous energy and self-sacrifice in strikes and in the street, battles with the police and the troops, and are capable (in fact, are alone capable) of determining the outcome of our entire movement — but the struggle against the political police requires special qualities; it requires professional revolutionaries. And we must see to it, not only that the masses 'advance' concrete demands, but that the masses of the workers 'advance' an increasing number of such professional revolutionaries. Thus, we have reached the question of the relation between an organization of professional revolutionaries and the labour movement, pure and simple. Although this question has found little reflection in literature, it has greatly engaged us 'politicians' in conversations and polemics with comrades who gravitate more or less towards Economism. It is a question meriting special treatment. But before taking it up, let us offer one further quotation by way of illustrating our thesis on the connection between primitiveness and Economism.

In his Reply, Mr. N. N. wrote: 'The Emancipation of Labour group demands direct struggle against the government without first considering where the material forces for this struggle are to be obtained, and without indicating the path of the struggle'. Emphasizing the last words, the author adds the following footnote to the word 'path': 'This cannot be explained by purposes of secrecy, because the programme does not refer to a plot but to a mass movement. And the masses cannot proceed by secret paths. Can we conceive of a secret strike? Can we conceive of secret demonstrations and petitions?' (Vademecum, p. 59) Thus, the author comes quite close to the question of the 'material forces' (organizers of strikes and demonstrations) and to the 'paths' of the struggle, but, nevertheless, is still in a state of consternation, because he 'worships' the mass movement, i.e., he regards it as something that relieves us of the necessity of conducting the revolutionary activity and not as something that should encourage us and stimulate our revolutionary activity. It is impossible for a strike to remain a secret to those participating in it and to those immediately associated with it, but it may (and in the majority of cases does) remain a 'secret' to the masses of the Russian workers, because the government takes care to cut all communication with the strikers, to prevent all news of strikes from spreading. Here, indeed, is where a special 'struggle against the political police' is required, a struggle that can never be conducted actively by such large masses as take part in strikes. This struggle must be organized, according to 'all the rules of the art', by people who are professionally engaged in revolutionary activity. The fact that the masses are spontaneously being drawn into the movement does not make the organisation of this struggle less necessary. On the contrary, it makes it more necessary; for we socialists would be failing in our direct duty to the masses if we did not prevent the police from making a secret of every strike and every demonstration (and if we did not ourselves from time to time secretly prepare strikes and demonstrations). And we will succeed in doing this, because the spontaneously awakening masses will also produce increasing numbers of 'professional revolutionaries' from their own ranks (that is if we do not take it into our heads to advise the workers to keep on marking time).

4.3. ORGANIZATION OF WORKERS AND ORGANIZATION OF REVOLUTIONARIES

It is only natural to expect that for a Social-Democrat whose conception of the political struggle coincides with the conception of the 'economic struggle against the employers and the government', the 'organization of revolutionaries' will more or less coincide with the 'organization of workers'. This, in fact, is what actually happens; so that when we speak of organization, we literally speak in different tongues. I vividly recall, for example, a conversation I once had with a fairly consistent Economist, with whom I had not been previously acquainted. We were discussing the pamphlet, Who Will Bring About the Political Revolution? and were soon of the mind that its principal defect was its ignoring of the question of organization. We had begun to assume full agreement between us, but, as the conversation proceeded, it became evident that we were talking of different things. My interlocutor accused the author of ignoring strike funds, mutual benefit societies, etc., whereas I had in mind an organization of revolutionaries as an essential factor in 'bringing about' the political revolution. As soon as the disagreement became clear, there was hardly, as I remember, a single question of principle upon which I was in agreement with the Economist!

What was the source of our disagreement? It was the fact that on questions both of organization and of politics, the Economists are forever lapsing from Social-Democracy into trade-unionism. The political struggle of Social-Democracy is far more extensive and complex than the economic struggle of the workers against the employers and the government. Similarly (indeed for that reason), the organization of the revolutionary Social-Democratic Party must inevitably be of a kind different from the organization of the workers designed for this struggle. The workers' organization must, in the first place, be a trade union organization; secondly, it must be as broad as possible; and thirdly, it must be as public as conditions will allow (here, and further on, of course, I refer only to absolutist Russia). On the other hand, the organization of the revolutionaries must consist first and foremost of people who make revolutionary activity their profession (for which reason I speak of the organisation of revolutionaries, meaning revolutionary Social-Democrats). In view of this common characteristic of the members of such an organization, all distinctions between workers and intellectuals, not to speak of distinctions of trade and profession, in both categories, must be effaced. Such an organization must perforce not be very extensive and must be as secret as possible. Let us examine this threefold distinction.

In countries where political liberty exists, the distinction between a trade union and a political organization is clear enough, as is the distinction between trade unions and Social-Democracy. The relations between the latter and the former will naturally vary in each country according to historical, legal, and other conditions; they may be more or less close, complex, etc. (in our opinion they should be as close and as little complicated as possible); but there can be no question in free countries of the organization of trade unions coinciding with the organization of the Social-Democratic Party. In Russia, however, the yoke of the autocracy appears at first glance to obliterate all distinctions between the Social-Democratic organization and the workers' associations, since all workers' associations and all study circles are prohibited, and since the principal manifestation and weapon of the workers' economic struggle — the strike — is regarded as a criminal (and sometimes even as a political!) offence. Conditions in our country, therefore, on the one hand, strongly 'impel' the workers engaged in economic struggle to concern themselves with political questions, and, on the other, they 'impel' Social-Democrats to confound trade-unionism with Social-Democracy (and our Krichevskys, Martynoys, and Co., while diligently discussing the first kind of 'impulsion', fail to notice the second). Indeed, picture yourselves people who are immersed ninety-nine per cent in 'the economic struggle against the employers and the government'. Some of them will never, during the entire course of their activity (from four to six months), be impelled to think of the need for a more complex organization of revolutionaries. Others, perhaps, will come across the fairly widely distributed Bernsteinian literature, from which they will become convinced of the profound importance of the forward movement of 'the drab everyday struggle'. Still others will be carried away, perhaps, by the seductive idea of showing the world a new example of 'close and organic contact with the proletarian struggle' — contact between the trade union and the Social Democratic movements. Such people may argue that the later a country enters the arena of capitalism and, consequently, of the working-class movement, the more the socialists in that country may take part in, and support, the trade union movement, and the less the reason for the existence of non-Social-Democratic trade unions. So far, the argument is fully correct; unfortunately, however, some go beyond that and dream of a complete fusion of Social-Democracy with trade-unionism. We shall soon see, from the example of the Rules of the St. Petersburg League of Struggle, what a harmful effect such dreams have upon our plans of organization.

The workers' organizations for the economic struggle should be trade union organizations. Every Social-Democratic worker should, as far as possible, assist and actively work in these organizations. But, while this is true, it is certainly not in our interest to demand that only Social-Democrats should be eligible for membership in the 'trade' unions, since that would only narrow the scope of our influence upon the masses. Let every worker who understands the need to unite for the struggle against the employers and the government, join the trade unions. The very aim of the trade unions would be impossible of achievement, if they did not unite all who have attained at least this elementary degree of understanding, if they were not very broad organizations. The broader these organizations, the broader will be our influence over them — an influence due, not only to the 'spontaneous' development of the economic struggle, but to the direct and conscious effort of the socialist trade union members to influence their comrades. But a broad organization cannot apply methods of strict secrecy (since, this demands far greater training than is required for the economic struggle). How is the contradiction between the need for a large membership and the need for strictly secret methods to be reconciled? How are we to make the trade unions as public as possible? Generally speaking, there can be only two ways to this end: either the trade unions become legalized (in some countries this preceded the legalization of the socialist and political unions), or the organization is kept secret, but so 'free' and amorphous, lose [German 'loose' — Ed] as the Germans say, that the need for secret methods becomes almost negligible as far as the bulk of the members is concerned.

The legalization of non-socialist and non-political labour unions in Russia has begun, and there is no doubt that every advance made by our rapidly growing Social-Democratic working-class movement will multiply and encourage attempts at legalzation — attempts proceeding for the most part from supporters of the existing order, but partly also from the workers themselves and from liberal intellectuals. The banner of legality has already been hoisted by the Vasilyevs and the Zubatovs.[8] Support has been promised and rendered by the Ozerovs and the Wormses, and followers of the new tendency are now to be found among the workers. Henceforth, we cannot but reckon with this tendency. How we are to reckon with it, on this there can be no two opinions among Social-Democrats. We must steadfastly expose any part played in this movement by the Zubatovs and the Vasilyeys, the gendarmes and the priests, and explain their real intentions to the

[8] Lenin is referring to the state-authorized unions, notably those created by the police official Sergei Zubatov (1864–1917) and his associate Colonel N. V. Vasilyev. They called their view 'police socialism'. In 1902, Zubatov arrived in St. Petersburg to run the *osobyi otdel* (Special Section) of the police's Ministry of Internal Affairs. It was through this instrument that he — along with some workers — tried to form several unions, such as the Petersburg Mutual Aid Society of Workers in Machine Industries. It was widely known as a police-run organization and did not develop a mass base. Men such as Ivan Christoforovich Ozerov (1869–1942) provided Zubatov with intellectual ballast. The son of peasants, Ozerov became a professor of finance who gave lectures to workers in Zubatov's organizations and promoted the most tepid reforms, although he was a proponent of Russian industrialization. A. E. Worms, like Ozerov, was a professor at the Moscow University.

workers. We must also expose all the conciliatory, 'harmonious' notes that will be heard in the speeches of liberal politicians at legal meetings of the workers, irrespective of whether the speeches are motivated by an earnest conviction of the desirability of peaceful class collaboration, by a desire to curry favour with the powers that be, or whether they are simply the result of clumsiness. Lastly, we must warn the workers against the traps often set by the police, who at such open meetings and permitted societies spy out the 'fiery ones' and try to make use of legal organizations to plant their agents provocateurs in the illegal organizations.

Doing all this does not at all mean forgetting that in the long run the legalization of the working-class movement will be to our advantage and not to that of the Zubatovs. On the contrary, it is precisely our campaign of exposure that will help us to separate the tares from the wheat. What the tares are, we have already indicated. By the wheat, we mean attracting the attention of ever larger numbers, including the most backward sections, of the workers to social and political questions, and freeing ourselves, the revolutionaries, from functions that are essentially legal (the distribution of legal books, mutual aid, etc.), the development of which will inevitably provide us with an increasing quantity of material for agitation. In this sense, we may, and should, say to the Zubatovs and the Ozerovs: Keep at it, gentlemen, do your best! Whenever you place a trap in the path of the workers (either by way of direct provocation, or by the 'honest' demoralization of the workers with the aid of 'Struvism') we will see to it that you are exposed.[9] But, whenever you take a real step forward, though it be the most 'timid zigzag', we will say: Please continue! And the only step that can be a real step forward is a real, if small, extension of

[9] Lenin used the term Struvism to refer to a liberal-bourgeois view of Marxism. It was named after Pyotr Berngardovich Struve (1870-1944), a professor who was a Marxist, then became a liberal, and eventually an opponent of the October Revolution. Struve was the editor of several legal Marxist journals, such as *Novoye Slovo* (The New Word, 1897), *Nachalo* (The Beginning, 1899), and *Zhizn* (Life, 1899-1901).

the workers' field of action. Every such extension will be to our advantage and will help to hasten the advent of legal societies of the kind in which it will not be agents provocateurs who are detecting socialists, but socialists who are gaining adherents. In a word, our task is to fight the tares. It is not our business to grow wheat in flower-pots. By pulling up the tares, we clear the soil for the wheat. And while the Afanasy Ivanoviches and Pulkheria Ivanovnas are tending their flower-pot crops, we must prepare the reapers, not only to cut down the tares of today, but to reap the wheat of tomorrow.[10]

Thus, we cannot by means of legalization solve the problem of creating a trade union organization that will be as little secret and as extensive as possible (but we should be extremely glad if the Zubatovs and the Ozerovs disclosed to us even a partial opportunity for such a solution — to this end, however, we must strenuously combat them). There remains secret trade union organizations, and we must give all possible assistance to the workers who (as we definitely know) are adopting this course. Trade union organizations, not only can be of tremendous value in developing and consolidating the economic struggle, but can also become a very important auxiliary to political agitation and

[10] Lenin — [*Iskra*'s campaign against the tares evoked the following angry outburst from *Rabocheye Dyelo*: 'For *Iskra*, the signs of the times lie not so much in great events [of the spring], as in the miserable attempts of the agents of Zubatov to 'legalize' the working-class movement. It fails to see that these facts tell against it, for they testify that the working-class movement has assumed menacing proportions in the eyes of the government' (*Two Conferences*, p. 27). For all this, we have to blame the 'dogmatism' of the orthodox who 'turn a deaf ear to the imperative demands of life'. They obstinately refuse to see the yard-high wheat and are combating inch-high tares! Does this not reveal a 'distorted sense of perspective in regard to the Russian working-class movement' (*ibid.*, p. 27)?]

Afanasy Ivanovich Tovstogub and Pulkheriya Ivanovna Tovstogubikha are characters in Nikolai Gogol's 1835 story, 'The Old World Landowners'. They are simple people who love their cat, whose disappearance leads to the death of these two landowners. The landowner who follows lives far away and neglects the estate, which falls into ruin.

revolutionary organization. In order to achieve this purpose, and in order to guide the nascent trade union movement in the channels desired by Social-Democracy, we must first understand clearly the absurdity of the plan of organization the St. Petersburg Economists have been nursing for nearly five years. That plan is set forth in the 'Rules for a Workers' Mutual Benefit Fund' of July 1897 ('Listok' Rabotnika, No. 9–10, p. 46, taken from *Rabochaya Mysl*, No. 1), as well as in the 'Rules for a Trade Union Workers' Organization' of October 1900 (special leaflet printed in St. Petersburg and referred to in *Iskra*, no. 1). Both these sets of rules have one main shortcoming: they set up the broad workers' organization in a rigidly specified structure and confound it with the organization of revolutionaries. Let us take the last-mentioned set of rules since it is drawn up in greater detail. The body consists of fifty-two paragraphs. Twenty-three deal with the structure, the method of functioning, and the competence of the 'workers' circles', which are to be organized in every factory ('a maximum of ten persons') and which elect 'central (factory) groups'. 'The central group', says paragraph 2, 'observes all that goes on in its factory or workshop and keeps a record of events'. 'The central group presents to subscribers a monthly financial account' (par. 17), etc. Ten paragraphs are devoted to the 'district organization', and nineteen to the highly complex interconnection between the Committee of the Workers' Organization and the Committee of the St. Petersburg League of Struggle (elected representatives of each district and of the 'executive groups' — 'groups of propagandists, groups for maintaining contact with the provinces, and with the organization abroad, groups for managing stores; publications, and funds').

Social-Democracy = 'executive groups' in relation to the economic struggle of the workers! It would be difficult to show more glaringly how the Economists' ideas deviate from Social-Democracy to trade-unionism, and how alien to them is any idea that a Social-Democrat must concern himself first and foremost with an organization of revolutionaries capable of guiding the entire proletarian struggle for emancipation. To talk of 'the political emancipation of the working class' and of the struggle against 'tsarist despotism', and at the same time to draft rules like these means to have no idea whatsoever of the real political tasks of Social-Democracy. Not one of the fifty or so paragraphs reveal even a glimmer of understanding that it is necessary to conduct the widest possible political agitation among the masses, an agitation highlighting every aspect of Russian absolutism and the specific features of the various social classes in Russia. Rules like these are of no use even for the achievement of trade unions, let alone political aims, since trade unions are organized by trades, of which no mention is made.

But most characteristic, perhaps, is the amazing top-heaviness of the whole 'system', which attempts to bind each single factory and its 'committee' by a permanent string of uniform and ludicrously petty rules and a three-stage system of election. Hemmed in by the narrow outlook of Economism, the mind is lost in details that positively reek of red tape and bureaucracy. In practice, of course, three-fourths of the clauses are never applied; on the other hand, a 'secret' organization of this kind, with its central group in each factory, makes it very easy for the gendarmes to carry out raids on a vast scale. The Polish comrades have passed through a similar phase in their movement, with everybody enthusiastic about the extensive organization of workers' benefit funds; but they very quickly abandoned this idea when they saw that such organisations only provided rich harvests for the gendarmes. If we have in mind broad workers' organizations, and not widespread arrests, if we do not want to provide satisfaction to the gendarmes, we must see to it that these organizations remain without any rigid formal structure. But will they be able to function in that case?

Let us see what the functions are: '. . . 'To observe all that goes on in the factory and keep a record of events' (par. 2 of the Rules). Do we really require a formally established group for this purpose? Could not the purpose be better served by correspondence conducted in the illegal papers without the setting up of special groups? '. . .To lead the struggles of the workers for the improvement of their workshop conditions' (par. 3). This, too, requires no set organizational form. Any sensible agitator can, in the course of ordinary conversation, gather what the demands of the workers are and transmit them to a narrow — not a broad — organization of revolutionaries for expression in a leaflet. 'To organize a fund ... to which subscriptions of two kopeks per ruble [of wages earned] should be made' (par. 9) — and then to present to subscribers a monthly financial account (par. 17), to expel members who fail to pay their contributions (par. 10), and so forth. Why, this is a very paradise for the police; for nothing would be easier for them than to penetrate into such a secrecy of a 'central factory fund', confiscate the money, and arrest the best people. Would it not be simpler to issue one-kopek or two-kopek coupons bearing the official stamp of a well-known (very narrow and very secret) organization, or to make collections without coupons of any kind and to print reports in a certain agreed code in an illegal paper? The object would thereby be attained, but it would be a hundred times more difficult for the gendarmes to pick up clues.

I could go on analyzing the Rules, but I think that what has been said will suffice. A small, compact core of the most reliable, experienced, and hardened workers, with responsible representatives in the principal districts and connected by all the rules of strict secrecy with the organization of revolutionaries, can, with the widest support of the masses and without any formal organization, perform all the functions of a trade union organisation, in a manner, moreover, desirable to Social-Democracy. Only in this way can we secure the consolidation and development of a Social-Democratic trade union movement, despite all the gendarmes.

It may be objected that an organization that is so lose that it is not even definitely formed and which has not even an enrolled and registered membership cannot be called an organization at all. Perhaps so. Not the name is important. What is important is that this 'organization without members' shall do everything that is required, and from the very outset ensure a solid connection between our future trade unions and socialism. Only an incorrigible utopian would have a broad organization of workers, with elections, reports, universal suffrage, etc., under the autocracy.

The moral to be drawn from this is simple. If we begin with the solid foundation of a strong organization of revolutionaries, we can ensure the stability of the movement as a whole and carry out the aims both of Social-Democracy and of trade unions proper. If, however, we begin with a broad workers' organization, which is supposedly most 'accessible' to the masses (but which is actually most accessible to the gendarmes and makes revolutionaries most accessible to the police), we shall achieve neither the one aim nor the other; we shall not eliminate our rule-of-thumb methods, and, because we remain scattered and our forces are constantly broken up by the police, we shall only make trade unions of the Zubatov and Ozerov type the more accessible to the masses.

What, properly speaking, should be the functions of the organization of revolutionaries? We shall deal with this question in detail. First, however, let us examine a very typical argument advanced by our terrorist, who (sad fate!), in this matter, is also a next-door neighbour to the Economist. *Svoboda*, a journal published for workers, contains in its first issue an article entitled 'Organization', the author of which tries to defend his friends, the Economist workers of Ivanovo-Voznesensk. He writes:

> 'It is bad when the masses are mute and unenlightened when the movement does not come from the rank and file. For instance, the students of a university town leave for their homes during the summer and other holidays, and immediately the workers' movement comes to a standstill. Can a workers' movement, which has to be pushed on from outside, be a

> real force? No, indeed. . . . It has not yet learned to walk, it is still in leading-strings. So, it is in all matters. The students go off, and everything comes to a standstill. The most capable are seized; the cream is skimmed and the milk turns sour. If the 'committee' is arrested, everything comes to a standstill until a new one can be formed. And one never knows what sort of committee will be set up next — it may be nothing like the former. The first said one thing, the second may say the very opposite. Continuity between yesterday and tomorrow is broken, the experience of the past does not serve as a guide for the future. And all because no roots have been struck in depth, in the masses; the work is carried on not by a hundred fools, but by a dozen wise men. A dozen wise men can be wiped out at a snap, but when the organization embraces masses, everything proceeds from them, and nobody, however he tries, can wreck the cause (p. 63).'

The facts are described correctly. The picture of our amateurism is well drawn. But the conclusions are worthy of *Rabochaya Mysl*, both as regards their stupidity and their lack of political tact. They represent the height of stupidity, because the author confuses the philosophical and social-historical question of the 'depth' of the 'roots' of the movement with the technical and organizational question of the best method in combating the gendarmes. They represent the height of political tactlessness, because, instead of appealing from bad leaders to good leaders, the author appeals from the leaders in general to the 'masses'. This is as much an attempt to drag us back organizationally as the idea of substituting excitative terrorism for political agitation drags us back politically. Indeed, I am experiencing a veritable *embarras de richesses*, and hardly know where to begin to disentangle the jumble offered up by *Svoboda*. For clarity, let me begin by citing an example. Take the Germans. It will not be denied, I hope, that theirs is a mass organization, that in Germany, everything proceeds from the masses, that the working-class movement there has learned to walk. Yet, observe how these millions value their 'dozen' tried political leaders, and how firmly they cling to them. Members of the hostile parties in parliament have often taunted the socialists by exclaiming: 'Fine democrats you are indeed! Yours is a working-class movement only in name; in actual fact, the same clique of leaders is always in evidence, the same Bebel and the same Liebknecht, year in and year out, and that goes on for decades. Your supposedly elected workers' deputies are more permanent than the officials appointed by the Emperor!' But the Germans only smile with contempt at these demagogic attempts to set the 'masses' against the 'leaders', to arouse bad and ambitious instincts in the former, and to rob the movement of its solidity and stability by undermining the confidence of the masses in their 'dozen wise men'. Political thinking is sufficiently developed among the Germans, and they have accumulated sufficient political experience to understand that without the 'dozen' tried and talented leaders (and talented men are not born by the hundreds), professionally trained, schooled by long experience, and working in perfect harmony, no class in modern society can wage a determined struggle. The Germans too have had demagogues in their ranks who have flattered the 'hundred fools', exalted them above the 'dozen wise men', extolled the 'horny hand' of the masses, and (like Most and Hasselmann) have spurred them on to reckless 'revolutionary' action and sown distrust towards the firm and steadfast leaders. It was only by stubbornly and relentlessly combating all demagogic elements within the socialist movement that German socialism managed to grow and become as strong as it is. Our wiseacres, however, at a time when Russian Social-Democracy is passing through a crisis entirely due to the lack of sufficiently trained, developed, and experienced leaders to guide the spontaneously awakening masses, cry out, with the profundity of fools: 'It is a bad business when the movement does not proceed from the rank and file'.

'A committee of students is of no use; it is not stable.' Quite true. But the conclusion to be drawn from this is that we must have a committee of professional revolutionaries, and it is immaterial whether a student or a worker is capable of becoming a professional revolutionary. The conclusion you draw, however, is that the working-class movement must not be pushed on from the outside! In your political innocence, you fail to notice that you are playing into the hands of our Economists and fostering our amateurism. Wherein, may I ask, did our students 'push on' our workers? In the sense that the student brought to the worker the fragments of political knowledge he himself possesses, the crumbs of socialist ideas he has managed to acquire (for the principal intellectual diet of the present-day student, legal Marxism, could furnish only the rudiments, only scraps of knowledge). There has never been too much of such 'pushing on from outside'; on the contrary, there has so far been all too little of it in our movement, for we have been stewing too assiduously in our own juice; we have bowed far too slavishly to the elementary 'economic struggle of the workers against the employers and the government'. We, professional revolutionaries, must and will make it our business to engage in this kind of 'pushing on' a hundred times more forcibly than we have done hitherto. But the very fact that you select so hideous a phrase as 'pushing on from outside' — a phrase which cannot but rouse in the workers (at least in the workers who are as unenlightened as you yourselves) a sense of distrust towards all who bring them political knowledge and revolutionary experience from outside, which cannot but rouse in them an instinctive desire to resist all such people — proves you to be demagogues, and demagogues are the worst enemies of the working class.

And, please — don't hasten howling about my 'uncomradely methods' of debating. I have not the least desire to doubt the purity of your intentions. As I have said, one may become a demagogue out of sheer political innocence. But I have shown that you have descended to demagogy, and I will never tire of repeating that demagogues are the worst enemies of the working class. The worst enemies because they arouse base instincts in the masses, because the unenlightened worker is unable to recognize his enemies in men who represent themselves, and sometimes sincerely so, as his friends. The worst enemies, because in the period of disunity and vacillation, when our movement is just beginning to take shape, nothing is easier than to employ demagogic methods to mislead the masses, who can realize their error only later by bitter experience. That is why the slogan of the day for the Russian Social-Democrat must be — resolute struggle against *Svoboda* and *Rabocheye Dyelo*, both of which have sunk to the level of demagogy. We shall deal with this further in greater detail.[11]

'A dozen wise men can be more easily wiped out than a hundred fools.' This wonderful truth (for which a hundred fools will always applaud you) appears obvious only because in the very midst of the argument you have skipped from one question to another. You began by talking and continued to talk of the unearthing of a 'committee', of the unearthing of an 'organization', and now you skip to the question of unearthing the movement's 'roots' in their 'depths'. The fact is, of course, that our movement cannot be unearthed, for the very reason that it has countless thousands of roots deep down among the masses; but that is not the point at issue. As far as 'deep roots' are concerned, we cannot be 'unearthed' even now, despite all our amateurism, and yet we all complain, and cannot but complain, that the '*organizations*' are being unearthed and, as a result, it is impossible to maintain continuity in the movement. But since you raise the question of *organizations* being unearthed and persisting in your opinion, I assert that it is far more difficult to unearth a dozen wise men than a hundred fools. This position I will defend, no matter how much you instigate the masses against me

[11] Lenin — [For the moment, let us observe merely that our remarks on 'pushing on from outside' and *Svoboda*'s other disquisitions on organization apply in *their entirety to all* the Economists, including the adherents of *Rabocheye Dyelo*; for some of them have actively preached and defended such views on organization, while others among them have drifted into them].

for my 'anti-democratic' views, etc. As I have stated repeatedly, by 'wise men', in connection with the organization, I mean *professional revolutionaries*, irrespective of whether they have developed from among students or working men. I assert: (1) that no revolutionary movement can endure without a stable organization of leaders maintaining continuity; (2) that the broader the popular mass drawn spontaneously into the struggle, which forms the basis of the movement and participates in it, the more urgent the need for such an organization, and the more solid this organization must be (for it is much easier for all sorts of demagogues to side-track the more backward sections of the masses); (3) that such an organization must consist chiefly of people professionally engaged in revolutionary activity; (4) that in an autocratic state, the more we *confine* the membership of such an organization to people who are professionally engaged in revolutionary activity and who have been professionally trained in the art of combating the political police, the more difficult will it be to unearth the organisation; and (5) the *greater* will be the number of people from the working class and from the other social classes who will be able to join the movement and perform active work in it.

I invite our Economists, terrorists, and 'Economists-terrorists'[12] to confute these propositions. At the moment, I shall deal only with the last two points. The question as to whether it is easier to wipe out 'a dozen wisemen' or 'a hundred fools' reduces

[12] Lenin — [This term is perhaps more applicable to *Svoboda* than the former, for in an article entitled 'The Regeneration of Revolutionism' the publication defends terrorism, while in the article at present under review it defends Economism. One might say of *Svoboda* that 'it would if it could, but it can't'. Its wishes and intentions are of the very best — but the result is utter confusion; this is chiefly due to the fact that, while *Svoboda* advocates continuity of organization, it refuses to recognize continuity of revolutionary thought and Social-Democratic theory. It wants to revive the professional revolutionary ('The Regeneration of Revolutionism'), and to that end, proposes, firstly, excitative terrorism and, secondly, an organization of average workers' (*Svoboda*, No. 1, p. 66, et. seq.), as less likely to be 'pushed on from outside'. In other words, it proposes to pull the house down to use the timber for heating it].

itself to the question, above considered, whether it is possible to have a mass organisation when the maintenance of strict secrecy is essential. We can never give a mass organisation that degree of secrecy without which there can be no question of persistent and continuous struggle against the government. To concentrate all secret functions in the hands of as small a number of professional revolutionaries as possible does not mean that the latter will 'do the thinking for all' and that the rank and file will not take an active part in the movement. On the contrary, the membership will promote increasing numbers of the professional revolutionaries from its ranks; for it will know that it is not enough for a few students and for a few working men waging the economic struggle to gather in order to form a 'committee', but that it takes years to train oneself to be a professional revolutionary; and the rank and file will 'think', not only of amateurish methods, but of such training. Centralisation of the secret functions of the organisation by no means implies centralisation of all the functions of the movement. Active participation of the widest masses in the illegal press will not diminish because a 'dozen' professional revolutionaries centralize the secret functions connected with this work; on the contrary, it will increase tenfold. In this way, and in this way alone, shall we ensure that reading the illegal press, writing for it, and to some extent even distributing it, will almost cease to be secret work, for the police will soon come to realize the folly and impossibility of judicial and administrative red-tape procedure over every copy of a publication that is being distributed in the thousands. This holds not only for the press, but for every function of the movement, even for demonstrations. The active and widespread participation of the masses will not suffer; on the contrary, it will benefit by the fact that a 'dozen' experienced revolutionaries, trained professionally no less than the police, will centralize all the secret aspects of the work — the drawing up of leaflets, the working out of approximate plans; and the appointing of bodies of leaders for each urban district, for each institution, etc. (I know that exception will be taken to my 'undemocratic' views, but I shall reply below fully to this anything but intelligent objection.) Centralization of the most secret functions in an organization of revolutionaries will not diminish, but rather increase the extent and enhance the quality of the activity of a large number of other organizations that are intended for a broad public and are therefore as loose and non-secret as possible, such as workers' trade unions; workers' self-education circles and circles for reading illegal literature; and socialist, as well as democratic, circles among all other sections of the population; etc., etc. We must have such circles, trade unions, and organizations everywhere in as large a number as possible and with the widest variety of functions; but it would be absurd and harmful to confound them with the organization of revolutionaries, to efface the border-line between them, to make still more hazy the all too faint recognition of the fact that in order to 'serve' the mass movement, we must have people who will devote themselves exclusively to Social-Democratic activities, and that such people must train themselves patiently and steadfastly to be professional revolutionaries.

Yes, this recognition is incredibly dim. Our worst sin with regard to organization consists in the fact that by our primitiveness we have lowered the prestige of revolutionaries in Russia. A person who is flabby and shaky on questions of theory, who has a narrow outlook, who pleads the spontaneity of the masses as an excuse for his own sluggishness, who resembles a trade union secretary more than a spokesman of the people, who is unable to conceive of a broad and bold plan that would command the respect even of opponents, and who is inexperienced and clumsy in his own professional art — the art of combating the political police — such a man is not a revolutionary, but a wretched amateur!

Let no active worker take offence at these frank remarks, for as far as insufficient training is concerned, I apply them first and foremost to myself. I used to work in a study circle that set itself very broad, all-embracing tasks, and all of us, members of that circle, suffered painfully and acutely from the realization that we were acting as amateurs at a moment in history when we might have been able to say, varying a well-known statement: 'Give us an organization of revolutionaries, and we will overturn Russia'! The more I recall the burning sense of shame I then experienced, the bitterer become my feelings towards those pseudo-Social-Democrats whose preachings 'bring disgrace on the calling of a revolutionary', who fail to understand that our task is not to champion the degrading of the revolutionary to the level of an amateur, but to raise the amateurs to the level of revolutionaries.

4.4. THE SCOPE OF ORGANIZATIONAL WORK

We have heard B-v tell us about 'the lack of revolutionary forces fit for action which is felt not only in St. Petersburg, but throughout Russia'. Hardly anyone will dispute this fact. But the question is, how is it to be explained? B-v writes:

> 'We shall not go into an explanation of the historical causes of this phenomenon; we shall merely state that a society, demoralized by prolonged political reaction and split by past and present economic changes, promotes from its own ranks an *extremely small number of persons fit for revolutionary work*; that the working class does produce revolutionary workers who to some extent reinforce the ranks of the illegal organizations, but that the number of such revolutionaries is inadequate to meet the requirements of the times. This is all the more so because the worker who spends eleven and a half hours a day in the factory is in such a position that he can, in the main, perform only the functions of an agitator; but propaganda and organization, the delivery and reproduction of illegal literature, the issuance of leaflets, etc., are duties which must necessarily fall mainly upon the shoulders of an extremely small force of intellectuals (*Rabocheye Dyelo*, No. 6, pp. 38–39).'

On many points, we disagree with B-v, particularly with those we have emphasized, which most saliently reveal that, although weary of our amateurism (as is every thinking practical worker), B-v cannot find the way out of this intolerable situation because he is weighted down by Economism. The fact is that society produces very many persons fit for 'the cause', but we are unable to make use of them all. The critical, transitional state of our movement in this respect may be formulated as follows: There are no people — yet there is a mass of people. There is a mass of people, because the working class and increasingly varied social strata, year after year, produce from their ranks an increasing number of discontented people who desire to protest, who are ready to render all the assistance they can in the struggle against absolutism, the intolerableness of which, though not yet recognized by all, is more and more acutely sensed by increasing masses of the people. At the same time, we have no people, because we have no leaders, no political leaders, and no talented organizers capable of arranging extensive and, at the same time, uniform and harmonious work that would employ all forces, even the most inconsiderable. 'The growth and development of the revolutionary organizations' lag, not only behind the growth of the working-class movement, which even B-v admits, but behind that of the general democratic movement among all strata of the people. (In passing, probably B-v would now regard this as supplementing his conclusion.) The scope of revolutionary work is too narrow, compared to the breadth of the spontaneous basis of the movement. It is too hemmed in by the wretched theory of 'economic struggle against the employers and the government'. Yet, at the present time, not only Social-Democratic political agitators, but Social-Democratic organizers must 'go among all classes of the population'.[13] There is hardly a

[13] Lenin — [Thus, an undoubted revival of the democratic spirit has recently been observed among persons in military service, partly as a consequence of the more frequent street battles with 'enemies' like workers and students. As soon as our available forces permit, we must without fail devote the most serious attention to propaganda and agitation among soldiers and officers,

single practical worker who will doubt that the Social-Democrats could distribute the thousand and one minute functions of their organizational work among individual representatives of the most varied classes. Lack of specialization is one of the most serious defects of our technique, about which B-v justly and bitterly complains. The smaller each separate 'operation' in our common cause the more people we can find capable of carrying out such operations (people who, in the majority of cases, are completely incapable of becoming professional revolutionaries); the more difficult will it be for the police to 'net' all these 'detail workers', and the more difficult will it be for them to frame up, out of an arrest for some petty affair, a 'case' that would justify the government's expenditure on 'security'. As for the number of people ready to help us, we referred in the preceding chapter to the gigantic change that has taken place in this respect in the last five years or so. On the other hand, in order to unite all these tiny fractions into one whole, in order not to break up the movement while breaking up its functions, and in order to imbue the people who carry out the minute functions with the conviction that their work is necessary and important, without which conviction they will never do the work,[14] it is necessary to have a strong organization of

and to the creation of 'military organizations' affiliated to our Party].

[14] Lenin — [I recall that once a comrade told me of a factory inspector who wanted to help the Social-Democrats, and actually did, but complained bitterly that he did not know whether his 'information' reached the proper revolutionary centre, how much his help was really required, and what possibilities there were for utilizing his small and petty services. Every practical worker can, of course, cite many similar instances in which our primitiveness deprived us of allies. These services, each 'small' in itself but invaluable when taken in the mass, could and would be rendered to us by office employees and officials, not only in factories, but in the postal service, on the railways, in the Customs, among the nobility, among the clergy, and in *every* other walk of life, including even the police and the Court! Had we a real party, a real militant organization of revolutionaries, we would not make undue demands on every one of these 'aides', we would not hasten always and invariably to bring them right into the very heart of our 'illegality', but, on the contrary, we would husband them most carefully and would even train people especially, for such functions, bearing in mind that many students

tried revolutionaries. The more secret such an organization is, the stronger and more widespread will be the confidence in the Party. As we know, in times of war, it is not only of the utmost importance to imbue one's own army with confidence in its strength, but it is also important to convince the enemy and all neutral elements of this strength; friendly neutrality may sometimes decide the issue. If such an organization existed, one built upon a firm theoretical foundation and possessing a Social-Democratic organ, we should have no reason to fear that the movement might be diverted from its path by the numerous 'outside' elements that are attracted to it. (On the contrary, it is precisely at the present time, with amateurism prevalent, that we see many Social-Democrats leaning towards the Credo and only imagining that they are Social Democrats.) In a word, specialization necessarily presupposes centralization, and, in turn, imperatively calls for it.

But B-v himself, who has so excellently described the necessity for specialization, underestimates its importance, in our opinion, in the second part of the argument we have quoted. The number of working-class revolutionaries is inadequate, he says. This is perfectly true, and once again, we stress that the ' valuable communication of a close observer' fully confirms our view of the causes of the present crisis in Social-Democracy, and, consequently, of the means required to overcome it. Not only are revolutionaries, in general, lagging behind the spontaneous awakening of the masses, but even worker-revolutionaries are lagging behind the spontaneous awakening of the working-class masses. This *fact* confirms with clear evidence, from the 'practical' point of view, too, not only the absurdity but even the *politically reactionary nature* of the 'pedagogics' to which we are so often treated in the discussion of our duties to the workers. This fact

could be of much greater service to the Party as 'aides' holding some official post than as 'short-term' revolutionaries. But, I repeat, only an organization that is firmly established and has no lack of active forces would have the right to apply such tactics).

proves that our very first and most pressing duty is to help to train working-class revolutionaries who will be on the same level *in regard to Party activity* as the revolutionaries from amongst the intellectuals (we emphasize the words 'in regard to Party activity', for, although necessary, it is neither so easy nor so pressingly necessary to bring the workers up to the level of intellectuals in other respects). Attention, therefore, must be devoted *principally to raising* the workers to the level of revolutionaries; it is not at all our task *to descend* to the level of the 'working masses' as the Economists wish to do, or to the level of the 'average worker' as *Svoboda* desires to do (and by this, ascends to the second grade of Economist 'pedagogics'). I am far from denying the necessity for popular literature for the workers, and especially popular (of course, not vulgar) literature for the especially backward workers. But what annoys me is this constant confusion of pedagogics with questions of politics and organization. You, gentlemen, who are so much concerned about the 'average worker', as a matter of fact, rather insult the workers by your desire *to talk down* to them when discussing working-class politics and working-class organization. Talk about serious things in a serious manner; leave pedagogics to the pedagogues, and not to politicians and organizers! Are there not advanced people, 'average people', and 'masses' among the intelligentsia too? Does not everyone recognize that popular literature is also required for the intelligentsia, and is not such literature written? Imagine someone, in an article on organizing college or high-school students, repeating over and over again, as if he had made a new discovery, that first of all we must have an organisation of 'average students'. The author of such an article would be ridiculed, and rightly so. Give us your ideas on organization, if you have any, he would be told, and we ourselves will decide who is 'average', who above average, and who below average. But if you have no organizational ideas *of your own*, then all your exertions on behalf of the 'masses' and 'average people' will be simply boring. You must realize that these questions of 'politics' and 'organization' are so serious in themselves that they cannot be dealt with in any other but a serious way. We can and must *educate* workers (and university and Gymnasium students) so that we *may be able to discuss* these questions with them. But once you do bring up these questions, you must give real replies to them; do not fall back on the 'average', or on the 'masses'; do not try to dispose of the matter with facetious remarks and mere phrases.[15]

To be fully prepared for his task, the worker-revolutionary must likewise become a professional revolutionary. Hence, B-v is wrong in saying that since the worker spends eleven and a half hours in the factory, the brunt of all other revolutionary functions (apart from agitation) '*must necessarily* fall mainly upon the shoulders of an extremely small force of intellectuals'. But this condition does not obtain out of sheer 'necessity'. It obtains because we are backwards because we do not recognize our duty to assist every capable worker to become a *professional* agitator, organizer, propagandist, literature distributor, etc., etc. In this respect, we waste our strength in a positively shameful manner; we lack the ability to husband that which should be tended and reared with special care. Look at the Germans: their forces are a hundredfold greater than ours. But they understand perfectly well that really capable agitators, etc., are not often promoted from the ranks of the 'average'. For this reason, they immediately try to place every capable working man in conditions that will enable him to develop and apply his abilities to the fullest: he is made a professional agitator, he is encouraged to widen the field of his activity, to spread it from one factory to the whole of the industry, from a single locality to the whole country. He acquires

[15] Lenin — [*Svoboda*, No. 1, p. 66, in the article 'Organization': 'The heavy tread of the army of workers will reinforce all the demands that will be advanced on behalf of Russian Labour' — Labour with a capital L, of course. And the author exclaims, 'I am not in the least hostile towards the intelligentsia, but (but — the word that Shchedrin translated as meaning: The ears never grow higher than the forehead!) I always get frightfully annoyed when a man comes to me uttering beautiful and charming words and demands that they be accepted for their (his?) beauty and other virtues' (p. 62). Yes, I always get 'frightfully annoyed', too].

experience and dexterity in his profession; he broadens his outlook and increases his knowledge; he observes at close quarters the prominent political leaders from other localities and of other parties; and he strives to rise to their level and combine in himself the knowledge of the working-class environment and the freshness of socialist convictions with professional skill, without which the proletariat *cannot* wage a stubborn struggle against its excellently trained enemies. In this way alone do the working masses produce men of the stamp of Bebel and Auer. But what is to a great extent, automatic in a politically free country must, in Russia, be done deliberately and systematically by our organizations. A worker-agitator who is at all gifted and 'promising' *must not be left* to work eleven hours a day in a factory. We must arrange that he be maintained by the Party; that he may go underground in good time; that he changes the place of his activity, if he is to enlarge his experience, widen his outlook, and be able to hold out for at least a few years in the struggle against the gendarmes. As the spontaneous rise of their movement becomes broader and deeper, the working-class masses promote from their ranks not only an increasing number of talented agitators, but also talented organizers, propagandists, and 'practical workers' in the best sense of the term (of whom there are so few among our intellectuals who, for the most part, in the Russian manner, are somewhat careless and sluggish in their habits). When we have forces of specially trained worker-revolutionaries who have gone through extensive preparation (and, of course, revolutionaries 'of all arms of the service'), no political police in the world will then be able to contend with them, for these forces, boundlessly devoted to the revolution, will enjoy the boundless confidence of the widest masses of the workers. We are directly to *blame* for doing too little to 'stimulate' the workers to take this path, common to them and to the 'intellectuals', of professional revolutionary training, and for all too often dragging them back by our silly speeches about what is 'accessible' to the masses of the workers, to the 'average workers', etc.

In this, as in other respects, the narrow scope of our organizational work is without a doubt due directly to the fact (although the overwhelming majority of the 'Economists' and the novices in practical work do not perceive it) that we restrict our theories and our political tasks to a narrow field. Subservience to spontaneity seems to inspire a fear of taking even one step away from what is 'accessible' to the masses, a fear of rising too high above mere attendance on the immediate and direct requirements of the masses. Have no fear, gentlemen! Remember that we stand so low on the plane of organization that the very idea that we could rise *too* high is absurd!

4.5. 'CONSPIRATORIAL' ORGANIZATION AND 'DEMOCRATISM'

Yet, there are many people among us who are so sensitive to the 'voice of life' that they fear it more than anything in the world and charge the adherents of the views here expounded with following a Narodnaya Volya line, with failing to understand 'democratism', etc. These accusations, which, of course, have been echoed by *Rabocheye Dyelo*, need to be dealt with.

The writer of these lines knows very well that the St. Petersburg Economists levelled the charge of Narodnaya Volya tendencies also against *Rabochaya Gazeta* (which is quite understandable when one compares it with *Rabochaya Mysl*). We were not in the least surprised, therefore, when, soon after the appearance of *Iskra,* a comrade informed us that the Social-Democrats in the town of X describe *Iskra* as a Narodnaya Volya organ. We, of course, were flattered by this accusation; for what decent Social-Democrat has not been accused by the Economists of being a Narodnaya Volya sympathizer?

These accusations are the result of a two-fold misunderstanding. First, the history of the revolutionary movement is so little known among us that the name 'Narodnaya Volya' is used to denote any idea of a militant centralized organization which declares determined war upon tsarism. But the magnificent organization that the revolutionaries had in the seventies, and that should serve us as a model, was not established by the Narodnaya Volya, but by the Zemlya i Volya, which split up into the Chorny Peredel and the Narodnaya Volya.[16] Consequently, to regard a militant revolutionary organization as something specifically Narodnaya Volya in character is absurd both historically and logically; for *no* revolutionary trend, if it seriously thinks of struggle, can dispense with such an organization. The mistake the Narodnaya Volya committed was not in striving to enlist all the discontented in the organization and to direct this organization to a resolute struggle against the autocracy; on the contrary, that was its great historical merit. The mistake was in relying on a theory that, in substance, was not a revolutionary theory at all, and the Narodnaya Volya members either did not know how or were unable to link their movement inseparably with the class struggle in the developing capitalist society. Only a gross failure to understand Marxism (or an 'understanding' of it in the spirit of 'Struveism') could prompt the opinion that the rise of a mass, spontaneous working-class movement *relieves* us of the duty of creating as good an organization of revolutionaries as the Zemlya i Volya had, or, indeed, an incomparably better one. On the contrary, this movement *imposes* the duty upon us; for the spontaneous struggle of the proletariat will not become its genuine 'class struggle' until this struggle is led by a strong organization of revolutionaries.

Secondly, many people, including apparently B. Krichevsky

[16] Zemlya i Volya, or Land and Liberty, worked clandestinely from 1861 to 1864 and then became a political party from 1876 to 1879. It was inspired by the writers Alexander Herzen (1812–1870) and Nikolay Chrnyshevsky (1828–1889) and sought to build momentum towards a peasant revolution in Russia. Plekhanov was a member of its political party in the second phase. The organization broke up around a debate over strategy, whether to operate as a political front or to develop into a terrorist outfit. The terrorist wing became Narodnaya Volya (People's Will), which lasted from 1879 to 1887, and the political front became Chorny Peredel (Black Repartition), which lasted from 1879 to 1881.

(*Rabocheye Dyelo*, No. 10, p. 18), misunderstand the polemics that Social-Democrats have always waged against the 'conspiratorial' view of the political struggle. We have always protested, and will, of course, continue to protest against *confining* the political struggle to conspiracy.[17] But this does not, of course, mean that we deny the need for a strong revolutionary organization. Thus, in the pamphlet mentioned in the preceding footnote, after the polemics against reducing the political struggle to a conspiracy, a description is given (as a Social-Democratic ideal) of an organization so strong as to be able to 'resort to . . . rebellion' and to every 'other form of attack, in order to 'deliver a smashing blow against absolutism'.[18] In *form,* such a strong revolutionary organization in an autocratic country may also be described as a 'conspiratorial' organization, because the French word 'conspiration' is the equivalent of the Russian word '*zagovar*' (conspiracy), and such an organization must have the utmost secrecy. Secrecy is such a necessary condition for this kind of organization that all the other conditions (number and selection of members, functions, etc.) must be made to conform to it. It would be extremely naive indeed, therefore, to fear the charge that we Social-Democrats desire to create a conspiratorial organization. Such a charge should be as flattering

[17] Lenin — [Cf. *The Tasks of the Russian Social-Democrats*, p. 21, polemics against P. L. Lavrov]. The Lenin quote is from 'The Task of Russian Social Democrats', *Collected Works*, vol. 2, pp. 340–41.

[18] Lenin — [*The Tasks of the Russian Social-Democrats*, p. 23. Apropos, we shall give another illustration of the fact that *Rabocheye Dyelo* either does not understand what it is talking about or changes its views 'with the wind'. In No. 1 of *Rabocheye Dyelo*, we find the following passage in italics: 'The substance set forth in the pamphlet accords entirely with the editorial programme of '*Rabocheye Dyelo*' (p. 142). Really? Does the view that the overthrow of the autocracy must not be set as the first task of the mass movement accord with the views expressed in *The Tasks of the Russian Social-Democrats?* Do the theory of 'the economic struggle against the employers and the government' and the stages theory accord with the views expressed in that pamphlet? We leave it to the reader to judge whether a periodical that understands the meaning of 'accordance in opinion' in this peculiar manner can have firm principles]. The Lenin quote is from 'The Task of Russian Social Democrats', *Collected Works*, vol. 2, p. 342.

to every opponent of Economism as the charge of following a Narodnaya Volya line.

The objection may be raised that such a powerful and strictly secret organization, which concentrates in its hands all the threads of secret activities, an organization which of necessity is centralized, may too easily rush into a premature attack, may thoughtlessly intensify the movement before the growth of political discontent, the intensity of the ferment and anger of the working class, etc., have made such an attack possible and necessary. Our reply to this is: Speaking abstractly, it cannot be denied, of course, that a militant organization may thoughtlessly engage in battle, which *may* end in a defeat entirely avoidable under other conditions. But we cannot confine ourselves to abstract reasoning on such a question, because every battle bears within itself the abstract possibility of defeat, and there is no way of *reducing* this possibility except by organized preparation for battle. If, however, we proceed from the concrete conditions at present obtaining in Russia, we must come to the positive conclusion that a strong revolutionary organization is absolutely necessary precisely for the purpose of giving stability to the movement and of *safeguarding* it against the possibility of making thoughtless attacks. Precisely at the present time, when no such organization yet exists, and when the revolutionary movement is rapidly and spontaneously growing, we *already observe* two opposite extremes (which, as is to be expected, 'meet'). These are: the utterly unsound Economism and the preaching of moderation, and the equally unsound 'excitative terror', which strives 'artificially to call forth symptoms of the end of the movement, which is developing and strengthening itself, when this movement is as yet nearer to the start than to the end' (V. Zasulich, in *Zarya*, No. 2–3, p. 353). And the instance of *Rabocheye Dyelo* shows that *there* exist Social-Democrats who give way to both these extremes. This is not surprising, for, apart from other reasons, the 'economic struggle against the employers and the government' can *never* satisfy revolutionaries, and opposite extremes will therefore always appear here and there. Only a centralized, militant organization that consistently carries out a Social-Democratic policy, that satisfies, so to speak, all revolutionary instincts and strivings, can safeguard the movement against making thoughtless attacks and prepare attacks that hold out the promise of success.

A further objection may be raised, that the views on organization here expounded contradict the 'democratic principle'. Now, while the earlier accusation was specifically Russian in origin, this one *is specifically foreign* in character. And, only an organization abroad (the Union of Russian Social-Democrats Abroad) was capable of giving its Editorial Board instructions like the following:

> '*Organizational Principle.* In order to secure the successful development and unification of Social-Democracy, the broad democratic principle of Party organization must be emphasized, developed, and fought for; this is particularly necessary in view of the anti-democratic tendencies that have revealed themselves in the ranks of our Party' (*Two Conferences,* p. 18).

We shall see in the next chapter how *Rabocheye Dyelo* combats *Iskra*'s 'anti-democratic tendencies'. For the present, we shall examine more closely the 'principle' that the Economists advance. Everyone will probably agree that 'the broad democratic principle' presupposes the two following conditions: firstly, full publicity, and secondly, election to all offices. It would be absurd to speak of democracy without publicity, moreover, without a publicity that is not limited to the membership of the organization. We call the German Socialist Party a democratic organization because all its activities are carried out publicly; even its party congresses are held in public. But no one would call an organization democratic that is hidden from everyone but its members by a veil of secrecy. What is the use, then, of advancing 'the *broad* democratic principle' when the fundamental condition for this principle *cannot be fulfilled* by a secret organization? 'The broad principle' proves itself simply to be a resounding but hollow phrase. Moreover, it reveals a total lack of understanding of the urgent tasks of the moment in regard to organization. Everyone knows how great the lack of secrecy is among the 'broad' masses of our revolutionaries. We have heard the bitter complaints of B-v on this score and his absolutely just demand for a 'strict selection of members' (*Rabocheye Dyelo*, no. 6, p. 42). Yet, persons who boast a keen 'sense of realities' *urge,* in a situation like this, not the strictest secrecy and the strictest (consequently, more restricted) selection, of members, but '*the broad* democratic principle'! This is what you call being wide of the mark.

Nor is the situation any better with regard to the second attribute of democracy, the principle of election. In politically free countries, this condition is taken for granted. 'They are members of the Party who accept the principles of the Party programme and render the Party all possible support', reads Clause 1 of the Rules of the German Social-Democratic Party. Since the entire political arena is as open to the public view as is a theatre stage to the audience, this acceptance or non-acceptance, support or opposition, is known to all from the press and from public meetings. Everyone knows that a certain political figure began in such and such a way, passed through such and such an evolution, behaved in a trying moment in such and such a manner, and possesses such and such qualities; consequently, *all* party members, knowing all the facts, can elect or refuse to elect this person to a particular party office. The general control (in the literal sense of the term) exercised over every act of a party man in the political field brings into existence an automatically operating mechanism which produces what in biology is called the 'survival of the fittest'. 'Natural selection' by full publicity, election, and general control provides the assurance that, in the last analysis, every political figure will be 'in his proper place', do the work for which lie is best fitted by his powers and abilities, feel the effects of his mistakes on himself, and prove before all the world his ability to recognize mistakes and to avoid them.

Try to fit this picture into the frame of our autocracy! Is it conceivable in Russia for all who accept the principles of the Party programme and render the Party all possible support to control every action of the revolutionary working in secret? Is it possible for all to elect one of these revolutionaries to any particular office, when, in the very interests of the work, the revolutionary must conceal his identity from nine out of ten of these 'all'?

Reflect somewhat over the real meaning of the high-sounding phrases to which *Rabocheye Dyelo* gives utterance, and you will realize that 'broad democracy' in Party organization, amidst the gloom of the autocracy and the domination of gendarmerie, is nothing more than a *useless and harmful* toy. It is a useless toy because, in point of fact, no revolutionary organization has ever practiced, or could practice, *broad* democracy, however much it may have desired to do so. It is a harmful toy because any attempt to practise 'the broad democratic principle' will simply facilitate the work of the police in carrying out large-scale raids, will perpetuate the prevailing primitiveness, and will divert the thoughts of the practical workers from the serious and pressing task of training themselves to become professional revolutionaries to that of drawing up detailed 'paper' rules for election systems. Only abroad, where very often people with no opportunity for conducting really active work gather, could this 'playing at democracy' develop here and there, especially in small groups.

To show the unseemliness of *Rabocheye Dyelo*'s favourite trick of advancing the plausible 'principle' of democracy in revolutionary affairs, we shall again summon a witness. This witness, Y. Serebryakov, editor of the London magazine, *Nakanune,* has a soft spot for *Rabocheye Dyelo* and is filled with a great hatred for Plekhanov and the 'Plekhanovites'. In its articles on the split in the Union of Russian Social-Democrats Abroad, *Nakanune* definitely sided with *Rabocheye Dyelo* and poured a stream of petty abuse upon Plekhanov. All the more valuable, therefore, is this witness in the question at issue. In *Nakanune*, for July (No. 7) 1899, an article entitled 'Concerning the Manifesto of the Self-Emancipation of the Workers Group', Serebryakov[19] argued that it was 'indecent' to talk about such things as 'self-deception, leadership, and the so-called Areopagus in a serious revolutionary movement' and, *inter alia,* wrote:

> 'Myshkin, Rogachov, Zhelyabov, Mikhailov, Perovskaya, Figner, and others never regarded themselves as leaders, and no one ever elected or appointed them as such, although in actuality, they were leaders, because, in the propaganda period, as well as in the period of the struggle against the government, they took the brunt of the work upon themselves, they went into the most dangerous places, and their activities were the most fruitful. They became leaders, not because they wished it, but because the comrades surrounding them had confidence in their wisdom, in their energy, in their loyalty. To be afraid of some kind of Areopagus (if it is not feared, why write about it?) that would arbitrarily govern the movement is far too naive. Who would pay heed to it?'

We ask the reader, in what way does the 'Areopagus' differ from 'anti-democratic tendencies'? And is it not evident that *Rabocheye Dyelo*'s 'plausible' organizational principle is equally naive and indecent; naive, because no one would pay heed to the 'Areopagus', or people with 'anti- democratic tendencies', if 'the comrades surrounding them had' no 'confidence in their wisdom, energy, and loyalty'; indecent, because it is a demagogic sally calculated to play on the conceit of some, on the ignorance of others regarding

[19] Esper Aleksandrovich Serebriakov (1854–1921), a member of Narodnaya volya, and a close friend of George Bernard Shaw when he was in London at the turn of the century, was the chief editor of *Nakanune*.

the actual state of our movement, and on the lack of training and the ignorance of the history of the revolutionary movement on the part of still others. The only serious organisational principle for the active workers of our movement should be the strictest secrecy, the strictest selection of members, and the training of professional revolutionaries. Given these qualities, something even more than 'democratism' would be guaranteed to us, namely, complete, comradely, mutual confidence among revolutionaries. This is absolutely essential for us, because there can be no question of replacing it by general democratic control in Russia. It would be a great mistake to believe that the impossibility of establishing real 'democratic' control renders the members of the revolutionary organization beyond control altogether. They have not the time to think about toy forms of democratism (democratism within a close and compact body of comrades in which complete, mutual confidence prevails), but they have a lively sense of their *responsibility,* knowing as they do from experience that an organization of real revolutionaries will stop at nothing to rid itself of an unworthy member. Moreover, there is a fairly well-developed public opinion in Russian (and international) revolutionary circles which has a long history behind it, and which sternly and ruthlessly punishes every departure from the duties of comradeship (and 'democratism', real and not toy democratism, certainly forms a component part of the conception of comradeship). Take all this into consideration and you will realize that this talk and these resolutions about 'anti-democratic tendencies' have the musty odour of the playing at generals which is indulged in abroad.

It must be observed also that the other source of this talk, viz., naivete is likewise fostered by the confusion of ideas concerning the meaning of democracy. In Mr. and Mrs. Webb's book on the English trade unions there is an interesting chapter entitled 'Primitive Democracy'.[20] In it the authors relate how the English

[20] Sidney and Beatrice Webb, *Industrial Democracy*, Longman, Green and Company, London, 1897. It was translated by Lenin into Russian and

workers, in the first period of existence of their unions, considered it an indispensable sign of democracy for all the members to do all the work of managing the unions; not only were all questions decided by the vote of all the members, but all official duties were fulfilled by all the members in turn. A long period of historical experience was required for workers to realize the absurdity of such a conception of democracy and to make them understand the necessity for representative institutions, on the one hand, and for full-time officials, on the other. Only after a number of cases of financial bankruptcy of trade union treasuries had occurred did the workers realize that the rates of contributions and benefits cannot be decided merely by a democratic vote, but that this requires also the advice of insurance experts. Let us take also Kautsky's book on parliamentarism and legislation by the people.[21] There we find that the conclusions drawn by the Marxist theoretician coincide with the lessons learned from many years of practical experience by the workers who organized 'spontaneously'. Kautsky strongly protests against Rittinghausen's primitive conception of democracy[22]; he ridicules those who in the name of democracy demand that 'popular newspapers shall be edited directly by the people'; he shows the need for *professional* journalists, parliamentarians, etc., for the Social-Democratic leadership of the proletarian class struggle; he attacks the socialism of anarchists and *litterateurs* who in their 'striving for effect' extol direct legislation by the whole people, completely failing to understand that this idea can be applied only relatively in modern society.

published as *Teoriya I praktika anglijskago tréd-yunionizma*, St. Petersburg: O. N. Popovoj, 1900–1901.

21 Karl Kautsky, *Der Parlamentarismus, die Volksgesetzgebung und die Sozialdemokratie*, J. H. W. Dietz, Stuttgart, 1893.

22 Moritz Rittinghausen (1814–1890) was one of the founders of the Social Democratic Workers Party in Germany in 1869. He was a proponent of direct democracy in society and in trade unions. He was the German delegate to the First International meetings at Basel (1869) and The Hague (1872). He knew Marx from the Democratic Society in Köln in the 1840s and, like Marx, was a contributor to *Neue Rheinische Zeitung*.

Those who have performed practical work in our movement know how widespread the 'primitive' conception of democracy is among the masses of the students and workers. It is not surprising that this conception penetrates also into rules of organizations and into literature. The Economists of the Bernsteinian persuasion included in their rules the following: '§10. All affairs affecting the interests of the whole of the union organization shall be decided by a majority vote of all its members'. The Economists of the terrorist persuasion repeat after them. 'The decisions of the committee shall become effective only after they have been referred to all the circles' *(Svoboda,* No. 1, p. 67). Observe that this proposal for a widely applied referendum is advanced *in addition* to the demand that *the whole of* the organization be built on an elective basis! We would not, of course, on this account condemn practical workers who have had too few opportunities for studying the theory and practice of real democratic organizations. But when *Rabocheye Dyelo*, which lays claim to leadership, confines itself, under such conditions, to a resolution on broad democratic principles, can this be described as anything but a mere 'striving for effect'?

4.6. LOCAL AND ALL-RUSSIA WORK

The objections raised against the plan of organisation here outlined on the grounds that it is undemocratic and conspiratorial are totally unsound. Nevertheless, there remains a question which is frequently put and which deserves detailed examination. This is the question of the relations between local work and all-Russia work. Fears are expressed that the formation of a centralized organization may shift the centre of gravity from the former to the latter, damage the movement through weakening our contacts with the working masses and the continuity of local agitation generally. To these fears, we reply that our movement in the past few years has suffered precisely from the fact that local workers have been too absorbed in local work; therefore, it is absolutely necessary to shift the centre of gravity somewhat to national work; and that, far from weakening this would strengthen our ties and the continuity of our local agitation. Let us take the question of central and local newspapers. I would ask the reader not to forget that we cite the publication of newspapers only as *an example* illustrating an immeasurably broader and more varied revolutionary activity in general.

In the first period of the mass movement (1896–98), an attempt was made by local revolutionary workers to publish an all-Russia paper — *Rabochaya Gazeta.* In the next period (1898–1900), the movement made an enormous stride forward, but the attention of the leaders was wholly absorbed by local publications. If we compute the total number of local papers that were published, we shall find that, on average, one issue per month was published.[23] Does this not clearly illustrate our amateurism? Does this not clearly show that our revolutionary organization lags behind the spontaneous growth of the movement? If *the same number* of issues had been published, not by scattered local groups, but by a single organization, we would not only have saved an enormous amount of effort, but we would have secured immeasurably greater stability and continuity in our work. This simple point is frequently lost sight of by those practical workers who work *actively* and almost exclusively on local publications (unfortunately, this is true even now in the overwhelming majority of cases), as well as by the publicists who display an astonishing quixotism on this question. The practical workers usually rest content with the argument that 'it is difficult'[24] for local workers to engage in the organization of an all-Russia newspaper, and that local newspapers are better than

[23] Lenin — [See *Report to the Paris Congress*, p. 14. From that time (1897) to the spring of 1900, thirty issues of various papers were published in various places. . . . 'On an average, over one issue per month was published'].

[24] Lenin — [This difficulty is more apparent than real. In fact, *there is not* a single local study circle that lacks the opportunity of taking up some function or other in connection with all-Russia work. 'Don't say, I can't; say, I won't'].

no newspapers at all. This argument is, of course, perfectly just, and we, no less than any practical worker, appreciate the enormous importance and usefulness of local newspapers *in general.* But not this is the point. The point is, can we not overcome the fragmentation and primitiveness that are so glaringly expressed in the thirty issues of local newspapers that have been published throughout Russia in the course of two and a half years? Do not restrict yourselves to the indisputable, but too general, statement about the usefulness of local newspapers generally; have the courage frankly to admit their negative aspects revealed by the experience of two and a half years. This experience has shown that under the conditions in which we work, these local newspapers prove, in the majority of cases, to be unstable in their principles, devoid of political significance, extremely costly in regard to expenditure of revolutionary forces, and totally unsatisfactory from a technical point of view (I have in mind, of course, not the technique of printing, but the frequency and regularity of publication). These defects are not accidental; they are the inevitable outcome of the fragmentation, which, on the one hand, explains the predominance of local newspapers in the period under review, and, on the other, is *fostered by* this predominance. It is positively beyond the strength of a separate local organization to raise its newspaper to the level of a political organ maintaining the stability of principles; it is *beyond its strength* to collect and utilize sufficient material to shed light on the whole of our political life. The argument usually advanced to support the need for numerous local newspapers in free countries that the cost of printing by local workers is low and that the people can be kept more fully and quickly informed — this argument as experience has shown, speaks *against* local newspapers in Russia. They turn out to be excessively costly in regard to the expenditure of revolutionary forces, and appear very rarely, for the simple reason that the publication of an *illegal* newspaper, however small its size, requires an extensive secret apparatus, such as is possible with large-scale factory production; for this apparatus cannot be created in a small, handicraft workshop. Very frequently, the primitiveness of the secret apparatus (every practical worker can cite numerous cases) enables the police to take advantage of the publication and distribution of one or two issues to make *mass* arrests, which result in such a clean sweep that it becomes necessary to start all over again. A well-organized secret apparatus requires professionally well-trained revolutionaries and a division of labour applied with the greatest consistency, but both these requirements are beyond the strength of a separate local organisation, however strong it may be at any given moment. Not only the general interests of our movement as a whole (training of the workers in consistent socialist and political principles) but also specifically local interests are *better served by non-local newspapers*. This may seem paradoxical at first sight, but it has been proved to the hilt by the two-and-a-half years of experience referred to. Everyone will agree that had all the local forces that were engaged in the publication of the thirty issues of newspapers worked on a single newspaper, sixty, if not a hundred, issues could easily have been published, with a fuller expression, in consequence, of all the specifically local features of the movement. True, it is no easy matter to attain such a degree of organisation, but we must realize the need for it. Every local study circle must think about it and *work actively* to achieve it, without waiting for an impetus from outside, without being tempted by the popularity and closer proximity of a local newspaper, which, as our revolutionary experience has shown, proves to a large extent to be illusory.

And, it is a bad service indeed, those publicists render to the practical work who, thinking themselves particularly close to the practical workers, fail to see this illusoriness, and make shift with the astoundingly hollow and cheap argument that we must have local newspapers, we must have district newspapers, and we must have all-Russia newspapers. Generally speaking, of course, all these are necessary, but once the solution of a concrete organisational problem is undertaken, surely time and circumstances must be taken into consideration. Is it not quixotic for *Svoboda* (No. 1, p. 68) to write in a special article 'dealing with *the question of a newspaper*': 'It seems to us that every locality, with any appreciable number of workers, should have its own workers' newspaper; not a newspaper imported from somewhere, but its very own'. If the publicist who wrote these words refuses to think of their meaning, then at least the reader may do it for him. How many scores, if not hundreds, of 'localities' with any appreciable number of workers there are in Russia, and what a perpetuation of our amateurish methods this would mean if, indeed, every local organization set about publishing its own newspaper! How this diffusion would facilitate the gendarmerie's task of netting — and without 'any appreciable' effort — the local revolutionary workers at the very outset of their activity and of preventing them from developing into real revolutionaries. A reader of an all-Russia newspaper, continues the author, would find little interest in the descriptions of the malpractices of the factory owners and the 'details of factory life in various towns not his own'. But 'an inhabitant of Orel would not find Orel affairs dull reading. In every issue, he would learn who had been "picked for a lambasting" and who had been "flayed", and he would be in high spirits' (p. 69). Certainly, the Orel reader is in high spirits, but our publicist's flights of imagination are also high — too high. He should have asked himself whether such concern with trivialities is tactically in order. We are second to none in appreciating the importance and necessity of factory exposures, but it must be borne in mind that we have reached a stage when St. Petersburg folk find it dull reading the St. Petersburg correspondence of the St. Petersburg *Rabochaya Mysl*. Leaflets are the medium through which local factory exposure have always been *and must continue* to be made, but we must raise the level of the *newspaper*, not lower it to the level of a factory leaflet. What we ask of a newspaper is not so much 'petty' exposures, as exposures of the major, typical evils of factory life, exposures based on especially striking facts and capable, therefore, of arousing the interest of all workers and all leaders of the movement, of really enriching their knowledge, broadening their outlook, and serving as a starting-point for awakening new districts and workers from ever-newer trade areas.

'Moreover, in a local newspaper, all the malpractices of the factory administration and other authorities may be denounced then and there. In the case of a general distant newspaper, however, by the time the news reaches it, the facts will have been forgotten in the source localities. The reader, on getting the paper, will exclaim: 'When was that — who remembers it?' (*ibid.*). Precisely — who remembers it! From the same source, we learn that the 30 issues of newspapers which appeared in the course of two-and-a-half years were published in six cities. This averages *one issue per city per half-year*! And, even if our frivolous publicist *trebled* his estimate of the productivity of local work (which would be wrong in the case of an average town, since it is impossible to increase productivity to any considerable extent by our rule-of-thumb methods), we would still get only one issue every two months, i.e., nothing at all like 'denouncing then and there'. It would suffice, however, for ten local organizations to combine and send their delegates to take an active part in organizing a general newspaper, to enable us every fortnight to 'denounce', over the *whole of Russia*, not petty, but really outstanding and typical evils. No one who knows the state of affairs in our organizations can have the slightest doubt on that score. As for catching the enemy red-handed — if we mean it seriously and not merely as a pretty phrase — that is quite beyond the ability of an illegal paper generally. It can be done only by a leaflet, because the time limit for exposures of that nature can be a day or two at the most (e.g., the usual brief strikes, violent factory clashes, demonstrations, etc.).

'The workers live not only at the factory, but also in the city', continues our author, rising from the particular to the general, with a strict consistency that would have done honour to Boris Krichevsky himself; and he refers to matters like municipal councils, municipal hospitals, municipal schools, and demands that workers' newspapers should not ignore municipal affairs in general.

This demand — excellent in itself — serves as a particularly vivid illustration of the empty abstraction to which discussions of local newspapers are all too frequently limited. In the first place, if indeed newspapers appeared 'in every locality with any appreciable number of workers' with such detailed information on municipal affairs as *Svoboda* desires, this would, under our Russian conditions, inevitably degenerate into actual concern with trivialities, lead to a weakening of the consciousness of the importance of an all-Russia revolutionary assault upon the tsarist autocracy, and strengthen the extremely virile shoots not uprooted but rather hidden or temporarily suppressed — of the tendency that has become noted as a result of the famous remark about revolutionaries who talk a great deal about non-existent parliaments and too little about existent municipal councils. We say 'inevitably', in order to emphasize that *Svoboda* obviously does not desire this, but the contrary, to come about. But good intentions are not enough. For municipal affairs to be dealt with in their proper perspective, in relation to our entire work, this perspective must *first* be clearly conceived, firmly established, not only by argument, but by numerous examples, so that it may acquire the stability of a *tradition*. This is still far from being the case with us. Yet this must be done *first*, before we can allow ourselves to think and talk about an extensive local press.

Secondly, to write really well and interestingly about municipal affairs, one must have first-hand knowledge, not bookish knowledge, of the issues. But there are hardly any Social-Democrats *anywhere in Russia* who possess such knowledge. To be able to write in newspapers (not in popular pamphlets) about municipal and state affairs, one must have fresh and varied material gathered and written up by able people. And, in order to be able to gather and write up such material, we must have something more than the 'primitive democracy' of a primitive circle, in which everybody does everything, and all entertain themselves by playing at referendums. It is necessary to have a staff of expert writers and correspondents, an army of Social-Democratic reporters who establish contacts far and wide, who are able to fathom all sorts of 'state secrets' (the knowledge of which makes the Russian government official so puffed up, but the blabbing of which is such an easy matter to him), who are able to penetrate 'behind the scenes' — an army of' people who must, as their 'official duty', be ubiquitous and omniscient. And we, the Party that fights against all economic, political, social, and national oppression, can and must find, gather, train, mobilize, and set into motion such an army of omniscient people — all of which requires still to be done. Not only has not a single step in this direction been taken in the overwhelming majority of localities, but even the recognition of its necessity is very often lacking. One will search in vain in our Social-Democratic press for lively and interesting articles, correspondence, and exposures dealing with our big and little affairs — diplomatic, military, ecclesiastical, municipal, financial, etc. There is *almost nothing*, or very little, about these matters.[25] That is why 'it always annoys me frightfully when a man comes to me, utters beautiful and charming words' about the need for newspapers in 'every locality with any appreciable number of workers' that will expose factory, municipal, and government evils.

[25] Lenin — [That is why even examples of exceptionally good local newspapers fully confirm our point of view. For example, *Yuzhny Rabochy* is an excellent newspaper, entirely free of instability of principle. But it has been unable to provide what it desired for the local movement, owing to the infrequency of its publication and to extensive police raids. Principled presentation of the fundamental questions of the movement and wide political agitation, which our Party most urgently requires at the present time, has proved too big a job for the local newspaper. The material of particular value it has published, like the articles on the mine owners' convention and on unemployment, was not strictly local material, *it was required for the whole of Russia*, not for the South alone. No such articles have appeared in any of our Social-Democratic newspapers].

The predominance of the local papers over a central press may be a sign of either poverty or luxury. Of poverty, when the movement has not yet developed the forces for large-scale production, continues to flounder in amateurism, and is all but swamped with 'the petty details of factory life'. Of luxury, when the movement *has fully mastered* the task of comprehensive exposure and comprehensive agitation, and it becomes necessary to publish numerous local newspapers in addition to the central organ. Let each decide for himself what the predominance of local newspapers implies in present-day Russia. I shall limit myself to a precise formulation of my own conclusion, to leave no grounds for misunderstanding. Hitherto, the majority of our local organizations have thought almost exclusively in terms of local newspapers, and have devoted almost all their activities to this work. This is abnormal; the very opposite should have been the case. The majority of the local organizations should think principally of the publication of an all-Russia newspaper and devote their activities chiefly to it. Until this is done, we shall not be able to establish a *single* newspaper capable, to any degree, of serving the movement with *comprehensive* press agitation. When this is done, however, normal relations between the necessary central newspaper and the necessary local newspapers will be established automatically.

It would seem at first glance that the conclusion on the necessity for shifting the centre of gravity from local to all-Russia work does not apply to the sphere of the specifically economic struggle. In this struggle, the immediate enemies of the workers are the individual employers or groups of employers, who are not bound by any organization having even the remotest resemblance to the purely military, strictly centralized organization of the Russian Government — our immediate enemy in the political struggle — which is led in all its minutest details by a single will.

But that is not the case. As we have repeatedly pointed out, the economic struggle is a trade struggle, and for that reason, it requires that the workers be organized according to trades, not only according to place of employment. Organization by trade becomes all the more urgently necessary, the more rapidly our employers organize in all sorts of companies and syndicates. Our fragmentation and our amateurism are an outright hindrance to this work of organization, which requires the existence of a single, all-Russia body of revolutionaries capable of giving leadership to the all-Russia trade unions. We have described above the type of organization that is needed for this purpose; we shall now add but a few words on the question of our press in this connection.

Hardly anyone will doubt the necessity for every Social-Democratic newspaper to have a *special department* devoted to the trade union (economic) struggle. But the growth of the trade union movement compels us to think about the creation of a trade union press. It seems to us, however, that with rare exceptions, there can be no question of trade union newspapers in Russia at the present time; they would be a luxury, and many a time we lack even our daily bread. The form of trade union press that would suit the conditions of our illegal work and is already required at the present time is *trade union pamphlets.* In these pamphlets, *legal*[26]

[26] Lenin — [Legal material is particularly important in this connection, and we are particularly behind in our ability to gather and utilizes it systematically. It would not be an exaggeration to say that one could somehow compile a trade union pamphlet on the basis solely of legal material, but it could not be done on the basis of illegal material alone. In gathering illegal material from workers, all questions like those dealt with in the publications of *Rabochaya Mysl*, we waste a great deal of the efforts of revolutionaries (whose place in this work could very easily be taken by legal workers), and yet we never obtain good material. The reason is that a worker who very often knows only a single department of a large factory and almost always the economic results, but not the general conditions and standards of his work, cannot acquire the knowledge which is possessed by the office staff of a factory, by inspectors, doctors, etc., and which is scattered in petty newspaper reports and in special industrial, medical, Zemstvo, and other publications. I vividly recall my 'first experiment', which I would never like to repeat. I spent many weeks 'examining' a worker, who would often visit me, regarding every aspect of the conditions prevailing in the enormous factory at which he was employed. True, after great effort, I managed to obtain material for a description (of the one single factory!), but at the end of the interview the worker would wipe the sweat from his brow, and say to me

and illegal material should be gathered and grouped systematically, on the working conditions in a given trade, on the differences in this respect in the various parts of, Russia; on the main demands advanced by the workers in the given trade; on the inadequacies of legislation affecting that trade; on outstanding instances of economic struggle by the workers in the trade; on the beginnings, the present state, and the requirements of their trade union organisation, etc. Such pamphlets would, in the first place, relieve our Social-Democratic press of a mass of trade details that are of interest only to workers in the given trade. Secondly, they would record the results of our experience in the trade union struggle, they would preserve the gathered material, which now literally gets lost in a mass of leaflets and fragmentary correspondence; and they would summarize this material. Thirdly, they could serve as guides for agitators, because working conditions change relatively slowly, and the main demands of the workers in a given trade are extremely stable (cf., for example, the demands advanced by the weavers in the Moscow district in 1885 and in the St. Petersburg district in 1896). A compilation of such demands and needs might serve for years as an excellent handbook for agitators on economic questions in backward localities or among the backward strata of the workers. Examples of successful strikes in a given region, information on higher living standards, on improved working conditions in one locality would encourage the workers in other localities to take up the fight again and again. Fourthly, having made a start in generalizing the trade union struggle and, in this way, strengthening the link between the Russian trade union movement and socialism, the Social-Democrats would at the same time see to it that our trade union work occupied neither too small nor too large a place in our Social-Democratic work as

smilingly: 'I find it easier to work overtime than to answer your questions'. The more energetically we carry on our revolutionary struggle, the more the government will be compelled to legalize part of the 'trade union' work, thereby relieving us of part of our burden].

a whole. A local organization that is cut off from organizations in other towns finds it very difficult, sometimes almost impossible, to maintain a correct sense of proportion (the example of *Rabochaya Mysl* shows what a monstrous exaggeration can be made in the direction of trade unionism). But an all-Russia organization of revolutionaries that stands undeviatingly on the basis of Marxism, that leads the entire political struggle and possesses a staff of professional agitators, will never find it difficult to determine the proper proportion.

Chapter 5

The 'Plan' for an All-Russia Political Newspaper

'The most serious blunder *Iskra* committed in this connection', writes B. Krichevsky (*Rabocheye Dyelo,* No. 10, p. 30), charging us with a tendency to 'convert theory into a lifeless doctrine by isolating it from practice', 'was its plan' for a general party organization' (viz., the article entitled 'Where To Begin'[1]). Martynov echoes this idea in declaring that '*Iskra*'s tendency to belittle the significance of the forward march of the drab everyday struggle in comparison with the propaganda of brilliant and completed ideas . . .was crowned with the plan for the organisation of a party which it sets forth in the article entitled 'Where To Begin' in issue No. 4' (ibid., p. 61). Finally, L. Nadezhdin has of late joined in the chorus of indignation against this 'plan' (the quotation marks were meant to express sarcasm).[2] In his pamphlet, which we have just received, entitled *The Eve of the Revolution* (published by the 'Revolutionary-Socialist Group' *Svoboda*, whose acquaintance we have made), he declares (p. 126): 'To speak now of an organization held together by an all-Russia newspaper means propagating armchair ideas and armchair work' and represents a manifestation of 'bookishness', etc.

That our terrorist turns out to be in agreement with the

[1] Lenin, 'Where To Begin', *Collected Works*, vol. 5, pp. 13-24.

[2] L. Nadezhdin or E. O. Zelensky (died, in 1905) published the magazine *Svoboda* (Freedom) from Switzerland in two numbers in 1901 and 1902. Lenin considered the group that published this magazine to be 'rootless', which had 'neither settled serious views, programmes, tactics, and organizations, nor roots in the masses'. Lenin, 'Adventurism', *Rabochy*, no. 7, 1914, *Collected Works*, vol. 20, pp. 356–357.

champions of the 'forward march of the drab everyday struggle' is not surprising, since we have traced the roots of this intimacy between them in the chapters on politics and organization. But must draw attention here to the fact that Nadezhdin is the only one who has conscientiously tried to grasp the train of thought in an article he disliked and has made an attempt to reply to the point, whereas *Rabocheye Dyelo*, has said nothing that is material to the subject, but has tried merely to confuse the question by a series of unseemly, demagogic sallies. Unpleasant though the task maybe, we must first spend some time in cleansing this Augean stable.

5.1. WHO WAS OFFENDED BY THE ARTICLE 'WHERE TO BEGIN'

Let us present a small selection of the expletives and exclamations that *Rabocheye Dyelo* hurled at us. 'It is not a newspaper that can create a party organization, but vice versa . . .. A newspaper, standing above the party, outside of its control, and independent of it, thanks to its having its own staff of agents. By what miracle has *Iskra* forgotten about the actually existing Social-Democratic organisations of the party to which it belongs?'. 'Those who possess firm principles and a corresponding plan are the supreme regulators of the real struggle of the party and dictate to it their plan'. 'The plan drives our active and virile organizations into the kingdom of shadows and desires to call into being a fantastic network of agents. 'Were *Iskra's* plan carried into effect, every trace of the Russian Social-Democratic Labour Party, which is taking shape, would be obliterated'. 'A propagandist organ becomes an uncontrolled autocratic law-maker for the entire practical revolutionary struggle'. 'How should our Party react to the suggestion that it be *completely* subordinated to an autonomous editorial board?', etc., etc.

As the reader can see from the contents and the tone of these above quotations, *Rabocheye Dyelo has taken offence.* Offence, not for its own sake, but for the sake of the organizations and committees of our Party, which it alleges *Iskra* desires to drive into the kingdom of shadows and whose very traces it would obliterate. How terrible! But a curious thing should be noted. The article 'Where To Begin' appeared in May 1901. The articles in *Rabocheye Dyelo* appeared in September 1901. Now we are in mid-January 1902. During these five months (prior to and after September), *not a single* committee and *not a single* organization of the Party protested formally against this monster that seeks to drive them into the kingdom of shadows; and yet scores and hundreds of communications from all parts of Russia have appeared during this period in *Iskra,* as well as in numerous local and non-local publications. How could it happen that those who would be driven into the realm of shadows are not aware of it and have not taken offence, though a third party has?

The explanation is that the committees and other organizations are engaged in real work and are not playing at 'democracy'. The committees read the article 'Where To Begin', and saw that it represented an attempt 'to elaborate a definite plan for an organization, so *that its formation may be undertaken from all aspects*'; and since they knew and saw very well that *not one* of these 'sides' would dream of 'setting about to build it' until it was convinced of its necessity, and of the correctness of the architectural plan, it has naturally never occurred to them to take offence at the boldness of the people who said in *Iskra:* 'In view of the pressing importance of the question we, on our part, take the liberty of submitting to the comrades a skeleton plan to be developed in greater detail in a pamphlet now in preparation for the print'. With a conscientious approach to the work, was it possible to view things otherwise than that if the comrades *accepted* the plan submitted to them, they would carry it out, not because they are 'subordinate', but because they would be convinced of its necessity for our common cause, and that if they *did not accept it,* then the 'skeleton' (a pretentious word, is it not?) would remain merely a skeleton? Is it, not demagogy to fight against the skeleton of a plan, not only by 'picking it to pieces' and advising comrades to reject it, but by *inciting* people inexperienced in revolutionary matters against its authors *merely on the grounds* that they *dare* to 'legislate' and come out as the 'supreme regulators', i.e., because they dare *to propose* an outline of a plan? Can our Party develop and make progress if an attempt *to raise* local functionaries to broader views, tasks, plans, etc., is objected to, not only with the claim that these views are erroneous, but on the grounds that the very 'desire' *to 'raise'* us gives 'offence'? Nadezhdin, too, 'picked' our plan 'to pieces', but he did not sink to such demagogy as cannot be explained solely by naivete or by the primitiveness of political views. From the outset, he emphatically rejected the charge that we intended to establish an 'inspectorship over the Party'. That is why Nadezhdin's criticism of the plan can and should be answered on its merits, while *Rabocheye Dyelo* deserves only to be treated with contempt.

But contempt for a writer who sinks so low as to shout about autocracy and 'subordination' does not relieve us of the duty of disentangling the confusion that such people create in the minds of their readers. Here we can clearly demonstrate to the world the nature of catchwords like 'broad democracy'. We are accused of forgetting the committees, of desiring or attempting to drive them into the kingdom of shadows, etc. How can we reply to these charges when, out of considerations of secrecy, we can give the reader *almost no facts* regarding our real relationships with the committees? Persons hurling vehement accusations calculated to provoke the crowd proved to be ahead of us because of their brazenness and their disregard for the duty of a revolutionary to conceal carefully from the eyes of the world the relationships and contacts which he maintains, which he is establishing or trying to establish. Naturally, we refuse once and for all to compete with such people in the field of 'democratism'. As to the reader, who is not initiated in all Party affairs, the only way in which we can discharge our duty to him is to acquaint him, not with what is and what is *Im Werden* [in process] but with *a particle* of what has taken place and what may be told as a thing of the past.

The Bund hints that we are 'impostors'[3]; the Union Abroad accuses us of attempting to obliterate all traces of the Party. Gentlemen, you will get complete satisfaction when we relate to the public *four facts* concerning the past.

First fact.[4] The members of one of the Leagues of Struggle, who took a direct part in founding our Party and in sending a delegate to the Inaugural Party Congress, reached an agreement with a member of the *Iskra* group regarding the publication of a series of books for workers that were to serve the entire movement. The attempt to publish the series failed and the pamphlets written for it, *The Tasks of the Russian Social-Democrats* and *The New Factory Law*, by a circuitous course and through the medium of third parties, found their way abroad, where they were published.[5]

Second fact. Members of the Central Committee of the Bund approached a member of the *Iskra* group with the proposal to organize what the Bund then described as a 'literary laboratory'. In making the proposal, they stated that unless this was done, the movement would greatly retrogress. The result of these negotiations was the appearance of the pamphlet *The Working-Class Cause in Russia*.[6]

[3] Lenin — [*Iskra*, No. 8. The reply of the Central Committee of the General Jewish Union of Russia and Poland to our article on the national question].

[4] Lenin — [We deliberately refrain from relating these facts in the sequence of their occurrence].

[5] Lenin, 'The Task of Russian Social Democrats', *Collected Works*, vol. 2, pp. 323–347; Lenin, 'To the Workers and Socialists of St. Petersburg from the League of Struggle', *Collected Works*, vol. 2, pp. 348–351; Lenin, 'The New Factory Law' (1899), *Collected Works*, vol. 2, pp. 267–315.

[6] Lenin — [The author requests me to state that, like his previous pamphlets, this one was sent to the Union Abroad on the assumption that its publications were edited by the Emancipation of Labour group (owing to certain circumstances, he could not then — February 1899 — know of the change in editorship). The pamphlet will be republished by the League at an early date].

Third fact. The Central Committee of the Bund, via a provincial town, approached a member of the *Iskra* group with the proposal that he undertake the editing of the revived *Rabochaya Gazeta* and, of course, obtained his consent. The offer was later modified: the comrade in question was invited to act as a contributor, in view of a new plan for the composition of the Editorial Board. Also, this proposal, of course, obtained his consent. Articles were sent (which we managed to preserve). 'Our Programme' which was a direct protest against Bernsteinism, against the change in the line of the legal literature and of *Rabochaya Mysl*; 'Our Immediate Task' ('to publish a Party organ that shall appear regularly and ha close contacts with all the local groups', the drawbacks of the prevailing 'amateurism'), 'An Urgent Question' (an examination of the objection that it is necessary *first* to develop the activities of local groups before undertaking the publication of a common organ; an insistence on the paramount importance of a 'revolutionary organization' and on the necessity of 'developing organization, discipline, and the technique of secrecy to the highest degree of perfection').[7] The proposal to resume publication of *Rabochaya Gazeta was* not carried out, and the articles were not published.

Fourth fact. A member of the committee that was organizing the second regular congress of our Party communicated to a member of the *Iskra* group the programme of the congress and proposed that group as editorial board of the revived *Rabochaya Gazeta*. This preliminary step, as it were, was later sanctioned by the committee to which this member belonged, and by the Central Committee of the Bund. The *Iskra* group was notified of the place and time of the congress and (uncertain of being able, for certain reasons, to send a delegate) drew up a written report for the congress. In the report, the idea was suggested that the mere election of a Central Committee would not only fail to solve the question of

[7] Lenin, 'Our Programme', *Collected Works*, vol. 4, pp. 210–214; 'Our Immediate Task', *Collected Works*, vol. 4, pp. 215-220; 'An Urgent Question', *Collected Works*, vol. 4, pp. 221–226.

unification at a time of such complete disorder as the present, but would even compromise the grand idea of establishing a party, in the event of an early, swift, and thorough police round-up, which was more than likely in view of the prevailing lack of secrecy; that therefore, a beginning should be made by inviting all committees and all other organisations to support the revived common organ, which would establish *real* contacts between all the committees and *really* train a group of leaders for the entire movement; and that the committees and the Party would very easily be able to transform such a group into a Central Committee as soon as the group had grown and become strong. In consequence of a number of police raids and arrests, however, the congress could not take place. For security reasons, the report was destroyed, having been read only by a few comrades, including the representatives of one committee.

Let the reader now judge for himself the character of the methods employed by the Bund in hinting that we were impostors, or by *Rabocheye Dyelo,* which accuses us of trying to relegate the committees to the kingdom of shadows and to 'substitute' for the organisation of a party an organisation disseminating the ideas advocated by a single newspaper. It was to the committees, *on their repeated invitation*, that we reported on the necessity for adopting a definite plan of concerted activities. It was precisely for the Party organisation that we elaborated this plan in articles sent to *Rabochaya Gazeta* and in the report to the Party congress, again on the invitation of those who held such an influential position in the Party that they took the initiative in its (actual) restoration. Only after the *twice* repeated attempts of the Party organization, *in conjunction with ourselves, officially* to revive the central organ of the Party had failed, did we consider it our bounden duty to publish an *unofficial* organ, in order that with the *third* attempt the comrades might have before them the results of *experience* and not merely conjectural proposals. Now certain results of this experience are present for all to see, and all comrades may now judge whether we properly understood our duties and what should be thought of people who strive to mislead those unacquainted with the immediate past, simply because they are piqued at our having pointed out to some their inconsistency on the 'national' question, and to others, the inadmissibility of their vacillation in matters of principle.

5.2. CAN A NEWSPAPER BE A COLLECTIVE ORGANIZER?

The quintessence of the article 'Where To Begin' consists in the fact that it discusses *precisely* this question and gives an affirmative reply to it. As far as we know, the only attempt to examine this question on its merits and to prove that it must be answered in the negative was made by L. Nadezhdin, whose argument we reproduce in full:

> 'It pleased us greatly to see *Iskra* (no. 4) present the question of the need for an all-Russia newspaper, but we cannot agree that this presentation bears relevance to the title 'Where to Begin'. Undoubtedly, this is an extremely important matter, but neither a newspaper, nor a series of popular leaflets, nor a mountain of manifestoes, can serve as the basis for a militant organization in revolutionary times. We must set to work to build strong political organizations in the localities. We lack such organizations; we have been carrying on our work mainly among enlightened workers while the masses have been engaged almost exclusively in the economic struggle. If strong political organizations are not trained locally, what significance will even an excellently organized all-Russia newspaper have? It will be a burning bush, burning without being consumed, but firing no one! *Iskra* thinks that around it and in the activities on its behalf, people will gather and organize. But they will find it far easier to gather and organize around activities that are more concrete. This

> something more concrete must and should be the extensive organization of local newspapers, the immediate preparation of the workers' forces for demonstrations, the constant activity of local organizations among the unemployed (indefatigable distribution of pamphlets and leaflets, convening of meetings, appeals to actions of protest against the government, etc.). We must begin live political work in the localities, and when the time comes to unite on this real basis, it will not be an artificial, paper unity; not by means of newspapers can such a unification of local work into an all-Russia cause be achieved!' (The Eve of the Revolution, p. 54.)'

We have emphasized the passages in this eloquent tirade that most clearly show the author's incorrect judgement of our plan, as well as the incorrectness of his point of view in general, which is here contraposed to that of *Iskra.* Unless we train strong political organizations in the localities, even an excellently organized all-Russia newspaper will be of no avail. This is incontrovertible. But the whole point is that *there is no other way* of *training* strong political organizations except through the medium of an all-Russia newspaper. The author missed the most important statement *Iskra* made *before it proceeded* to set forth its 'plan'— that it was necessary 'to call for the formation of a revolutionary organization, capable of uniting all forces and guiding the movement in actual practice and *not in name alone,* that is, *an organization ready at any time to support every protest and every outbreak* and use it to build up and consolidate the fighting forces suitable for the decisive struggle'. But now, after the February and March events, everyone will agree with this, in principle, continues *Iskra.* Yet what we need is not a solution to the question in principle, but its *practical solution;* we must immediately advance a definite constructive plan through which all may immediately set to work to build *from every side.* Now we are again being dragged away from the practical solution towards something which in principle is correct, indisputable, and great, but which is entirely inadequate and incomprehensible to the broad masses of workers, namely, 'to rear strong political organizations'! This is not the point at issue, the most worthy author. The point is how to go about the rearing and how to accomplish it.

It is not true to say that 'we have been carrying on our work mainly among enlightened workers, while the masses have been engaged almost exclusively in the economic struggle'. Presented in such a form, the thesis reduces itself to *Svoboda's* usual but fundamentally false contraposition of the enlightened workers to the 'masses'. In recent years, even the enlightened workers have been 'engaged almost exclusively in the economic struggle'. That is the first point. On the other hand, the masses will never learn to conduct the political struggle until we help *to train* leaders for this struggle, both from among the enlightened workers and from among the intellectuals. Such leaders can acquire training *solely* by systematically evaluating *all* the everyday aspects of our political life, *all attempts* at protest and struggle on the part of the various classes and on various grounds. Therefore, to talk of 'rearing political organizations' and at the same time *to contrast* the 'paperwork' of a political newspaper to 'live political work in the localities' is plainly ridiculous. *Iskra* has adapted its 'plan' for a newspaper to the 'plan' for creating a 'militant preparedness' to support the unemployed movement, peasant revolts, discontent among the Zemstvo people, 'popular indignation against some tsarist bashi-bazouk on the rampage', etc. Anyone who is acquainted at all with the movement knows full well that the vast majority of local organizations have *never even dreamed* of these things; that many of the prospects of 'live political work' here indicated *have never* been realized by a single organization; that the attempt, for example, to call attention to the growth of discontent and protest among the Zemstvo intelligentsia rouses feelings of consternation and perplexity in Nadezhdin ('Good Lord, is this newspaper intended for Zemstvo people? — *The Eve*,

p. 129), among the Economists (Letter to *Iskra,* No. 12), and among many practical workers. Under these circumstances, it is possible to 'begin' *only* by inducing people *to think* about all these things, to summarize and generalize all the diverse signs of ferment and active struggle. In our time, when Social-Democratic tasks are being degraded, *the only way* 'live political work' can be *begun is* with live political agitation, which is impossible unless we have an all-Russia newspaper, frequently issued and regularly distributed.

Those who regard the *Iskra* 'plan' as a manifestation of 'bookishness' have totally failed to understand its substance and take for the goal that which is suggested as the most suitable means for the present time. These people have not taken the trouble to study the two comparisons that were drawn to present a clear illustration of the plan. *Iskra* wrote: The publication of an all-Russia political newspaper must be *the main line* by which we may unswervingly develop, deepen, and expand the organization (viz., the revolutionary organization that is ever ready to support every protest and every outbreak). Pray, tell me, when bricklayers lay bricks in_various parts of an enormous, unprecedentedly large structure, is it 'paper' work to use a line to help them find the correct place for the bricklaying; to indicate to them the ultimate goal of the common work; to enable them to use, not only every brick, but even every piece of brick which, cemented to the bricks laid before and after it, forms a finished, continuous line? And, are we not now passing through precisely such a period in our Party life when we have bricks and bricklayers, but lack the guideline for all to see and follow? Let them shout that in stretching out the line, we want to command. Had we desired to command, gentlemen, we would have written on the title page, not '*Iskra*, No. 1', but '*Rabochaya Gazeta*, No. 3', as we were invited to do by certain comrades, and *as we would have had a perfect right to do* after the events described above. But we did not do that. We wished to have our hands free to wage an irreconcilable struggle against all pseudo-Social- Democrats; we wanted our line, if properly laid, to be respected because it was correct and not because it had been laid by an official organ.

'The question of uniting local activity in central bodies runs in a vicious circle', Nadezhdin lectures us; 'unification requires homogeneity of the elements, and homogeneity can be created only by something that unites; but the unifying element may be the product of strong local organizations which at the present time are by no means distinguished for their homogeneity'. This truth is as revered and as irrefutable as that we must train strong political organizations. And it is equally barren. *Every* question 'runs in a vicious circle' because political life as a whole is an endless chain consisting of an infinite number of links. The whole art of politics lies in finding and taking as firm a grip as we can of the link that is least likely to be struck from our hands, the one that is most important at the given moment, the one that most of all guarantees its possessor the possession of the whole chain.[8] If we had a crew of experienced bricklayers who had learned to work so well together that they could lay their bricks exactly as required without a guideline (which, speaking abstractly, is by no means impossible), then perhaps we might take hold of some other link. But it is unfortunate that as yet we have no experienced bricklayers trained for teamwork, that bricks are often laid where they are not needed at all, that they are not laid according to the general line, but are so scattered that the enemy can shatter the structure as if it were made of sand and not of bricks.

Another comparison: 'A newspaper is not only a collective propagandist and a collective agitator, it is also a collective organizer. In this respect, *it may be compared to the scaffolding* erected round a building under construction; it marks the contours of the structure and facilitates communication between

[8] Lenin — [Comrade Krichevsky and Comrade Martynov! I call your attention to this outrageous manifestation of 'autocracy', 'uncontrolled authority', 'supreme regulating', etc. Just think of it, a desire to *possess* the whole chain!! Send in a complaint at once. Here you have a ready-made topic for two leading articles for no. 12 of *Rabocheye Dyelo*!].

the builders, permitting them to distribute the work and to view the common results achieved by their organized labour'.[9] Does this sound anything like the attempt of an armchair author to exaggerate his role? The scaffolding is not required at all for the dwelling; it is made of cheaper material, is put up only temporarily, and is scrapped for firewood as soon as the shell of the structure is completed. As for the building of revolutionary organizations, experience shows that sometimes they may be built without scaffolding, as the seventies showed. But at the present time, we cannot even imagine the possibility of erecting the building we require without scaffolding.

Nadezhdin disagrees with this, saying: '*Iskra* thinks that around it and in the activities in its behalf people will gather and organize. *But they will find it far easier* to gather and organize around *activities that are more concrete*!'. Indeed, 'far easier around activities that are more concrete'. A Russian proverb holds: 'Don't spit into a well, you may want to drink from it'. But there are people who do not object to drinking from a well that has been spat into. What despicable things our magnificent, legal 'Critics of Marxism' and illegal admirers of *Rabochaya Mysl* have said in the name of this something more concrete! How restricted our movement is by our own narrowness, lack of initiative, and hesitation, which are justified by the traditional argument about finding it 'far easier to gather around something more concrete'! And Nadezhdin — who regards himself as possessing a particularly keen sense of the 'realities of life', who so severely condemns 'armchair' authors and (with pretensions to wit) accuses *Iskra* of a weakness for seeing Economism everywhere, and who sees himself standing far above the division between the orthodox and the Critics — fails to see that with his arguments he contributes to the narrowness that

[9] Lenin — [Martynov, in quoting the first sentence of this passage in *Rabocheye Dyelo* (No. 10, p. 62), omitted the second, as if desiring to emphasize either his unwillingness to discuss the essentials of the question or his inability to understand them].

arouses his indignation and that he is drinking from the most spat-in well! The sincerest indignation against narrowness, the most passionate desire to raise its worshippers from their knees, will not suffice if the indignant one is swept along without sail or rudder and, as 'spontaneously' as the revolutionaries of the seventies, clutches at such things as 'excitative terror', 'agrarian terror', 'sounding the tocsin', etc. Let us take a glance at these 'more concrete' activities around which he thinks it will be 'far easier' to gather and organize: (1) local newspapers; (2) preparations for demonstrations; and (3) work among the unemployed. It is immediately apparent that all these things have been seized upon at random as a pretext for saying something; for, however we may regard them, it would be absurd to see in them anything especially suitable for 'gathering and organizing'. The self-same Nadezhdin says in a few pages further: 'It is time we simply stated the fact that activity of a very pitiable kind is being carried on in the localities, the committees are not doing a tenth of what they could do… the coordinating centres we have at present are the purest fiction, representing a sort of revolutionary bureaucracy, whose members mutually grant generalships to one another; and so, it will continue until strong local organizations grow up'. These remarks, though exaggerating the position somewhat, no doubt contain many a bitter truth; but can it be said that Nadezhdin does not perceive the connection between the pitiable activity in the localities and the narrow mental outlook of the functionaries, the narrow scope of their activities, inevitable in the circumstances of the lack of training of Party workers confined to local organizations? Has he, like the author of the article on organization published in *Svoboda*, forgotten how the transition to a broad local press (from 1898) was accompanied by a strong intensification of Economism and 'primitiveness'? Even if a 'broad local press' could be established at all satisfactorily (and we have shown this to be impossible, save in very, exceptional cases) — even then the local organs could not 'gather and organise' *all* the revolutionary forces for a *general* attack upon the autocracy and for leadership of the *united* struggle. Let us not forget that we are here discussing *only* the 'rallying', organizing significance of the newspaper, and we could put to Nadezhdin, who defends fragmentation, the question he himself has ironically put: 'Have we been left a legacy of 200,000 revolutionary organizers?'. Furthermore, 'preparations for demonstrations' cannot be *contraposed* to *Iskra's* plan, for the very reason that this plan includes the organisation of the broadest possible demonstrations *as one of its aims;* the point under discussion is the selection of the practical *means.* On this point also, Nadezhdin is confused, for he has lost sight of the fact that only forces that are 'gathered and organized' can 'prepare for' demonstrations (which hitherto, in the overwhelming majority of cases, have taken place spontaneously) and that we *lack* precisely *the ability* to rally and organize. 'Work among the unemployed.' Again, the same confusion; for this too represents one of the field operations of the mobilized forces and not a plan for mobilizing the forces. The extent to which Nadezhdin here too underestimates the harm caused by our fragmentation, by our lack of '200,000 organizers', can be seen from the fact that: many people (including Nadezhdin) have reproached *Iskra* for the paucity of the news it gives on unemployment and for the casual nature of the correspondence it publishes about the most common affairs of rural life. The reproach is justified; but *Iskra is* 'guilty without sin'. We strive 'to stretch a line' through the countryside too, where there are hardly any bricklayers anywhere, and we are *obliged* to encourage *everyone* who informs us even as regards the most common facts, in the hope that this will increase the number of our contributors in the given field and will ultimately *train us all* to select facts that are really the most outstanding. But the material on which we can train is so scanty that, unless we generalize it for the whole of Russia, we shall have very little to train on at all. No doubt, one with at least as much ability as an agitator and as much knowledge of the life of the vagrant as Nadezhdin manifests could render priceless service to the movement by carrying on agitation among the unemployed; but such a person would be simply hiding his light under a bushel if he failed to inform all comrades in Russia as regards every step he took in his work, so that others, who, in the mass, still lack the ability to undertake new kinds of work, might learn from his example.

All without exception now talk of the importance of unity, of the necessity for 'gathering and organzsing'; but in the majority of cases, what is lacking is a definite idea of where to begin and how to bring about this unity. Probably all will agree that if we 'unite', say, the district circles in a given town, it will be necessary to have for this purpose common institutions, i.e., not merely the common title of 'League', but genuinely common work, exchange of material, experience, and forces, distribution of functions, not only by districts but through specialization on a town-wide scale. All will agree that a big secret apparatus will not pay its way (to use a commercial expression) 'with the resources' (in both money and manpower, of course) of a single district, and that this narrow field will not provide sufficient scope for a specialist to develop his talents. But the same thing applies to the coordination of activities of a number of towns, since even a specific locality will be and, in the history of our Social-Democratic movement, has proved to be, far too narrow a field; we have demonstrated this above in detail with regard to political agitation and organisational work. What we require foremost and imperatively is to broaden the field, establish real contacts between the towns on the basis of regular, and common work; for fragmentation weighs down on the people and they are 'stuck in a hole' (to use the expression employed by a correspondent to *Iskra*), not knowing what is happening in the world, from whom to learn, or how to acquire experience and satisfy their desire to engage in broad activities. I continue to insist that we can start establishing real contacts only with the aid of a common newspaper, as the only regular, all-Russia enterprise, one which will summarize the results of the most diverse forms of activity and thereby stimulate people to march forward untiringly along all the innumerable paths leading to revolution, in the same way as all roads lead to Rome. If we do not want unity in name only, we must arrange for all local study circles immediately to assign, say, a fourth of their forces to active work for the common cause, and the newspaper will immediately convey to them[10] the general design, scope, and character of the cause; it will give them a precise indication of the most keenly felt shortcomings in the all-Russia activity, where agitation is lacking and contacts are weak, and it will point out which little wheels in the vast general mechanism a given study circle might repair or replace with better ones. A study circle that has not yet begun to work, but which is only just seeking activity, could then start, not like a craftsman in an isolated little workshop unaware of the earlier development in 'industry' or of the general level of production methods prevailing in industry, but as a participant in an extensive enterprise that reflects the whole general revolutionary attack on the autocracy. The more perfect the finish of each little wheel and the larger the number of detail workers engaged in the common cause, the closer will our network become and the less will be the disorder in the ranks consequent on inevitable police, raids.

The mere function of distributing a newspaper would help to establish actual contacts (if it is a newspaper worthy of the name, i.e., if it is issued regularly, not once a month like a magazine, but at least four times a month). At the present time, communication between towns on revolutionary business is an extreme rarity, and, at all events, is the exception rather than the rule. If we had a newspaper, however, such communication would become the rule and would secure, not only the distribution of the newspaper, of

[10] Lenin — [*A reservation*: that is, if a given study circle sympathizes with the policy of the newspaper and considers it useful to become a collaborator, meaning by that, not only for literary collaboration, but for revolutionary collaboration generally. *Note for Rabocheye Dyelo*: Among revolutionaries who attach value to the cause and not to playing at democracy, who do not separate 'sympathy' from the most active and lively participation, this reservation is taken for granted].

course, but (what is more important) an exchange of experience, of material, of forces, and of resources. Organizational work would immediately acquire much greater scope, and the success of one locality would serve as a standing encouragement to further perfection; it would arouse the desire to utilize the experience gained by comrades working in other parts of the country. Local work would become far richer and more varied than it is at present. Political and economic exposures gathered from all over Russia would provide mental food for workers of all trades and *all stages* of *development;* they would provide material and occasion for talks and readings on the most diverse subjects, which would, in addition, be suggested by hints in the legal press, by talk among the people, and by 'shamefaced' government statements. Every outbreak, every demonstration, would be weighed and, discussed in its every aspect in all parts of Russia and would thus stimulate a desire to keep up with, and even surpass, the others (we socialists do not by any means flatly reject all emulation or all 'competition'!) and consciously prepare that which at first, as it were, sprang up spontaneously, a desire to take advantage of the favourable conditions in a given district or at a given moment for modifying the plan of attack, etc. At the same time, this revival of local work would obviate that desperate, 'convulsive' exertion of all efforts and risking of *all* forces which every single demonstration or the publication of every single issue of a local newspaper now frequently entails. On the one hand, the police would find it much more difficult to get at the 'roots', if they did not know in what district to dig down for them. On the other hand, regular common work would train our people to adjust the force of a *given* attack to the strength of the given contingent of the common army (at the present time, hardly anyone ever thinks of doing that, because in nine cases out of ten these attacks occur spontaneously); such regular common work would facilitate the 'transportation' from one place to another, not only of literature, but also of revolutionary forces.

In a great many cases, these forces are now being bled white on restricted local work, but under the circumstances we are discussing, it would be possible to transfer a capable agitator or organizer from one end of the country to the other, and the occasion for doing this would constantly arise. Beginning with short journeys on Party business at the Party's expense, the comrades would become accustomed to being maintained by the Party, to becoming professional revolutionaries, and to training themselves as real political leaders.

And if indeed we succeeded in reaching the point when all, or at least a considerable majority, of the local committees' local groups, and study circles took up active work for the common cause, we could, in the not distant future, establish a weekly newspaper for regular distribution in tens of thousands of copies throughout Russia. This newspaper would become part of an enormous pair of smith's bellows that would fan every spark of the class struggle and of popular indignation into a general conflagration. Around what is in itself still a very innocuous and very small, but regular and *common,* effort, in the full sense of the word, a regular army of tried fighters would systematically gather and receive their training. On the ladders and scaffolding of this general organizational structure, there would soon develop and come to the fore Social-Democratic Zhelyabovs from among our revolutionaries and Russian Bebels from among our workers, who would take their place at the head of the mobilized army and rouse the whole people to settle accounts with the shame and the curse of Russia.

That is what we should dream of! 'We should dream!'. I wrote these words and became alarmed. I imagined myself sitting at a 'unity conference' and opposite me were the *Rabocheye Dyelo* editors and contributors. Comrade Martynov rises and, turning to me, says sternly: 'Permit me to ask you, has an autonomous editorial board the right to dream without first soliciting the opinion of the Party committees?'. He is followed by Comrade

Krichevsky; who (philosophically deepening Comrade Martynov, who long ago rendered Comrade Plekhanov more profound) continues even more sternly: 'I go further. I ask, has a Marxist any right at all to dream, knowing that according to Marx, mankind always sets itself the tasks it can solve and that tactic is a process of the growth of Party tasks which grow together with the Party?'.

The very thought of these stern questions sends a cold shiver down my spine and makes me wish for nothing but a place to hide in. I shall try to hide behind the back of Pisarev.[11]

'There are rifts and rifts,' wrote Pisarev of the rift between dreams and reality. 'My dream may run ahead of the natural march of events or may fly off at a tangent in a direction in which no natural march of events will ever proceed. In the first case, my dream will not cause any harm; it may even support and augment the energy of the working men. . . . There is nothing in such dreams that would distort or paralyze labour-power. On the contrary, if man were completely deprived of the ability to dream in this way, if he could not from time to time run ahead and mentally conceive, in an entire and completed picture, the product to which his hands are only just beginning to lend shape, then I cannot at all imagine what stimulus there would be to induce man to undertake and complete extensive and strenuous work in the sphere of art, science, and practical endeavour. . . . The rift between dreams and reality causes no harm if only the person dreaming believes seriously in his dream, if he attentively observes life, compares his observations with his castles in the air, and if, generally speaking, he works conscientiously for the achievement of his fantasies. If there is some connection between dreams and life then all is well.'

[11] Dmitry Ivanovich Pisarev (1840–1868) was Russia's leading nihilist philosopher who rejected all traditional morality. While in prison, where he was condemned after his graduation, he wrote, 'What can be smashed must be smashed. Whatever withstands the blow is fit to survive; what flies into pieces is rubbish. In any case, strike out right and left, no harm can come of it'. Nadezhda Krupskaya noted that 'Lenin was of the generation that grew up under the influence of Pisa.

Of this kind of dreaming, there is unfortunately too little in our movement. And the people most responsible for this are those who boast of their sober views, their 'closeness' to the 'concrete', the representatives of legal criticism and of illegal 'tail-ism'.

5.3. WHAT TYPE OF ORGANIZATION DO WE REQUIRE?

From what has been said, the reader will see that our 'tactics-as-a-plan' consists in rejecting an immediate *call* for assault; in demanding 'to lay effective siege to the enemy fortress'; or, in other words, in demanding that all efforts be directed towards gathering, organizing, and *mobilizing* a permanent army. When we ridiculed *Rabocheye Dyelo* for its leap from Economism to shouting for an assault (for which it clamoured in *April 1901*, in *'Listok' Rabochego Dyela*, 157 No. 6), it of course came down on us with accusations of being 'doctrinaire', of failing to understand our revolutionary duty, of calling for caution, etc. Of course, we were not in the least surprised to hear these accusations from those who totally lack principles and who evade all arguments by references to a profound 'tactics-as-process', any more than we were surprised by the fact that these charges were repeated by Nadezhdin, who in general has a supreme contempt for durable programmes and the fundamentals of tactics.

It is said that history does not repeat itself. But Nadezhdin exerts every effort to cause it to repeat itself and he zealously imitates Tkachev in strongly condemning 'revolutionary culturism', in shouting about 'sounding the tocsin' and about a special 'eve-of-the- revolution point of view', etc.[12] Apparently, he has forgotten the well-known maxim that while an original historical event represents a tragedy, its replica is merely a farce. The attempt to

[12] Pyotr Nikitich Tkachev (1844–1886) was a revolutionary theorist who advocated for the creation of a revolutionary vanguard and for a revolutionary dictatorship to steer Russia on the path to socialism. Tkachev underestimated the role of the masses in this struggle. Nevertheless, Lenin frequently said that he learned a great deal from Tkachev.

seize power, which was prepared by the preaching of Tkachev and carried out by means of the 'terrifying' terror that did really terrify, had grandeur, but the 'excitative' terror of a Tkachev the Little is simply ludicrous, particularly so when it is supplemented with the idea of an organization of average people.

'If *Iskra* would only emerge from its sphere of bookishness', wrote Nadezhdin, 'it would realize that these (instances like the worker's letter to *Iskra, No. 7,* etc.) are symptoms of the fact that soon, very soon, the "assault" will begin, and to speak now [sic!] of an organization linked with an all-Russia newspaper means to propagate armchair ideas and armchair activity'. What an unimaginable muddle — on the one hand, excitative terror and an 'organization of average people', along with the opinion that it is far 'easier' to gather around something 'more concrete', like a local newspaper, and, on the other, the view that to talk 'now' about an all-Russia organization means to propagate armchair thoughts, or, bluntly put, 'now' it is already too late! But what of the 'extensive organization of local newspapers' — is it not too late for that, my dear L. Nadezhdin? And compare with this *Iskra's* point of view and tactical line: excitative terror is nonsense; to talk of an organization of average people and of the *extensive* publication of local newspapers means to fling the door wide open to Economism. We must speak of a single all-Russia organization of revolutionaries, and it will never be too late to talk of that until the real, not a paper, assault begins.

> 'Yes, as far as organization is concerned the situation is anything but brilliant', continues Nadezhdin. 'Yes, *Iskra is* entirely right in saying that the mass of our fighting forces consists of volunteers and insurgents...You do well to give such a sober picture of the state of our forces. But why, at the same time, do you forget that *the masses are not ours at all,* and consequently, will *not ask us* when to begin military operations; they will simply go and 'rebel'.... When the crowd itself breaks out

> with its elemental destructive force it *may* overwhelm and sweep aside the 'regular troops' among whom we prepared all the time to introduce extremely systematic organization, but never *managed* to do so.' [Our italics.]

Astounding logic! *For the very reason* that the 'masses are not ours' it is stupid and unseemly to shout about an immediate 'assault', for assault means attack by regular troops and not a spontaneous mass upsurge. For the very reason that the masses *may* overwhelm and sweep aside the regular troops we must without fail 'manage to keep up' with the spontaneous upsurge by our work of 'introducing extremely systematic organization' in the regular troops, for the more we 'manage' to introduce such organization, the more probably will the regular troops not be overwhelmed by the masses, but will take their place at their head. Nadezhdin is confused because he imagines that troops in the course of systematic organization are engaged in something that isolates them from the masses, when in actuality they are engaged exclusively in all-sided and all-embracing political. agitation, i.e., precisely in work that *brings closer and merges into a single whole* the elemental destructive force of the masses and the conscious destructive force of the organization of revolutionaries. You, gentlemen, wish to lay the blame where it does not belong. For it is precisely the *Svoboda* group that, by including terror *in its programme,* calls for an organization of terrorists, and such an organization would indeed prevent our troops from establishing closer contacts with the masses, which, unfortunately, are still not ours, and which, unfortunately, do not yet ask us, or rarely ask us, when and how to launch their military operations.

'We shall miss the revolution itself', continues Nadezhdin in his attempt to scare *Iskra,* 'in the same way as we missed . . .the recent events, which came upon us like a bolt from the blue'. This sentence, taken in connection with what has been quoted above, clearly demonstrates the absurdity of the 'eve-of-the-revolution point of view' invented by *Svoboda*.[13] Plainly put, this special 'point of view' boils down to this that it is too late 'now' to discuss and prepare. If that is the case, most worthy opponent of 'bookishness', what was the use of writing a pamphlet of 132 pages on 'questions of theory and tactics'?[14] Don't you think it would have been more becoming for the 'eve-of- the-revolution point of view' to have issued 132,000 leaflets containing the summary call, 'Bang them — knock'em down!'?

Those who make nation-wide political agitation the cornerstone of their programme, *their tactics, and their organizational work*, as *Iskra* does, stand the least risk of missing the revolution. The people who are now engaged throughout Russia in weaving the network of connections that spread from the all-Russia newspaper not only did not miss the spring events, but, on the contrary, gave us an opportunity to foretell them. Nor did they miss the demonstrations that were described in *Iskra*, Nos. 13 and 14; on the contrary, they took part in them, clearly realizing that it was their duty to come to the aid of the spontaneously rising masses and, at the same time, through the medium of the newspaper, help all the comrades in Russia to inform themselves of the demonstrations and to make use of their gathered experience. And if they live,

13 Lenin — [*The Eve of the Revolution*, p. 62].

14 Lenin — [In his *Review of Questions of Theory*, Nadezhdin, by the way, made almost no contribution whatever to the discussion of questions of theory, apart, perhaps, from the following passage, a most peculiar one from the 'eve-of-the-revolution point of view': 'Bernsteinism, on the whole, is losing its acuteness for us at the present moment, as is the question whether Mr. Adamovich will prove that Mr. Struve has already earned a lacing, or, on the contrary, whether Mr. Struve will refute Mr. Adamovich and will refuse to resign — it really makes no difference, because the hour of revolution has struck' (p. 110). One can hardly imagine a more glaring illustration of Nadezhdin's infinite disregard for theory. We have proclaimed 'the eve of the revolution', *therefore* 'it really makes no difference' whether or not the orthodox will succeed in finally driving the Critics from their positions! Our wiseacre fails to see that it is precisely during the revolution that we shall stand in need of the results of our theoretical battles with the Critics in order to be able resolutely to combat their *practical* positions!].

they *will* not miss the revolution, which, first and foremost, will demand of us experience in agitation, ability to support (in a Social-Democratic manner) every protest, as well as direct the spontaneous movement, while safeguarding it from the mistakes of friends and the traps of enemies.

We have thus come to the last reason that compels us so strongly to insist on the plan of an organization centred round an all-Russia newspaper, through the common work for the common newspaper. Only such organization will ensure the *flexibility* required of a militant Social-Democratic organization, viz., the ability to adapt itself immediately to the most diverse and rapidly changing conditions of struggle, the ability, 'on the one hand, to avoid an open battle against an overwhelming enemy, when the enemy has concentrated all his forces at one spot and yet, on the other, to take advantage of his unwieldiness and to attack him when and where he least expects it'.[15] It would be a grievous error indeed to build the Party organization in anticipation only of outbreaks and street fighting, or only upon the 'forward march of the drab everyday struggle'. We must *always* conduct our everyday work and always be prepared for every situation, because very frequently it is almost impossible to foresee when a period of outbreak will give way to a period of calm. In the instances, however, when it is possible to do so, we could not turn this foresight to account for the purpose of reconstructing our organization; for in an

[15] Lenin — [*Iskra*, No. 4, 'Where To Begin'. 'Revolutionary culturists, who do not accept the eve-of-the-revolution point of view, are not in the least perturbed by the prospect of working for a long period of time,' writes Nadezhdin (p. 62). This brings us to observe: Unless we are able to devise political tactics and an organizational plan for *work over a very long period* while ensuring, in *the very process of this work*, our Party's readiness to be at its post and fulfil its duty in every contingency whenever the march of events is accelerated — unless we succeed in doing this, we shall prove to him but miserable political adventurers. Only Nadezhdin, who began but yesterday to describe himself as a Social-Democrat, can forget that the aim of Social-Democracy is to transform radically the conditions of life of the whole of mankind and that, for this reason, it is not permissible for a Social-Democrat to be 'perturbed' by the question of the duration of the work].

autocratic country, these changes take place with astonishing rapidity, being sometimes connected with a single night raid by the tsarist janizaries. And the revolution itself must not by any means be regarded as a single act (as the Nadezhdins apparently imagine), but as a series of more or less powerful outbreaks rapidly alternating with periods of more or less complete calm. For that reason, the principal content of the activity of our Party organization, the focus of this activity, should be work that is both possible and essential in the period of a most powerful outbreak as well as in the period of complete calm, namely, work of political agitation, connected throughout Russia, illuminating all aspects of life, and conducted among the broadest possible strata of the masses. But this work *is unthinkable* in present-day Russia without an all-Russia newspaper, issued very frequently. The organization, which will form round this newspaper, the organization of its *collaborators* (in the broad sense of the word, i.e., all those working for it), will be ready *for everything,* from upholding the honour, the prestige, and the continuity of the Party in periods of acute revolutionary 'depression' to preparing for, appointing the time for, and carrying out the *nation-wide armed uprising.*

Indeed, picture to yourselves a very ordinary occurrence in Russia-the total round-up of our comrades in one or several localities. In the absence of a *single,* common, regular activity that combines all the local organizations, such round-ups frequently result in the interruption of the work for many months. if, however, all the local organizations had one common activity, then, even in the event of a very serious round-up, two or three energetic persons could in the course of a few weeks establish contact between the common centre and new youth circles, which, as we know, spring up very quickly even now. And when the common activity, hampered by the arrests, is apparent to all, new circles will be able to come into being and make connections with the centre even more rapidly.

On the other hand, picture to yourselves a popular uprising.

Probably everyone will now agree that we must think of this and prepare for it. But how? Surely the Central Committee cannot appoint agents to all localities for the purpose of preparing the uprising. Even if we had a Central Committee, it could achieve absolutely nothing by such appointments under present-day Russian conditions. But a network of agents[16] that would form in the course of establishing and distributing the common newspaper would not have to 'sit about and wait' for the call for an uprising, but could carry on the regular activity that would guarantee the highest probability of success in the event of an uprising. Such activity would strengthen our contacts with the broadest strata of the working masses and with all social strata that are discontented with the autocracy, which is of such importance for an uprising. Precisely, such activity would serve to cultivate the ability to estimate correctly the general political situation and, consequently, the ability to select the proper moment for an uprising. Precisely, such activity would train all local organizations to respond simultaneously to the same political questions, incidents, and events that agitate the whole of Russia and to react to such 'incidents' in the most vigorous, uniform, and expedient manner possible; for an uprising is in essence the most vigorous, most uniform, and most expedient 'answer' of the entire people to the government. Lastly, it is precisely such activity that would train all revolutionary organizations throughout Russia to maintain the

[16] Lenin — [Alas, alas! Again, I have let slip that awful word 'agents', which jars so much on the democratic cars of the Martynovs! I wonder why this word did not offend the heroes of the seventies and yet off ends the amateurs of the nineties? I like the word, because it clearly and trenchantly indicates *the common cause* to which all the agents bend their thoughts and actions, and if I had to replace this word with another, the only word I might select would be the word 'collaborator', if it did not suggest a certain bookishness and vagueness. The thing we need is a military organization of agents. However, the numerous Martynovs (particularly abroad), whose favourite pastime is 'mutual grants of generalships to one another', may, instead of saying 'passport agent', prefer to say, 'Chief of the Special Department for Supplying Revolutionaries with Passports'. etc.]

most continuous, and at the same time the most secret, contacts with one another, thus creating *real* Party unity; for without such contacts, it will be impossible collectively to discuss the plan for the uprising and to take the necessary preparatory measures on the eve, measures that must be kept in the strictest secrecy.

In a word, the 'plan for an all-Russia political newspaper', far from representing the fruits of the labour of armchair workers, infected with dogmatism and bookishness (as it seemed to those who gave but little thought to it), is the most practical plan for immediate and all-round preparation of the uprising, with, at the same time, no loss of sight for a moment of the pressing day-to-day work.